CHOROLOGY

Studies in Continental Thought

John Sallis, GENERAL EDITOR

CHOROLOGY

On Beginning in Plato's *Timaeus*

JOHN SALLIS

Indiana University Press

BLOOMINGTON AND INDIANAPOLIS

This book is a publication of
Indiana University Press
601 North Morton Street
Bloomington, Indiana 47404-3797 USA

www.indiana.edu/~iupress

Telephone orders 800-842-6796
Fax orders 812-855-7931
Orders by e-mail iuporder@indiana.edu

Library of Congress Cataloging-in-Publication Data

Sallis, John, date
Chorology : on beginning in Plato's Timaeus / John Sallis.
  p.   cm. — (Studies in Continental Thought)
Includes bibliographical references and index.
ISBN 0-253-33568-X (cloth : alk. paper) —
ISBN 0-253-21308-8 (pbk. : alk paper)
1. Plato. Timaeus. 2. Chōra (The Greek word) 3. Beginning.   I. Title.   II. Series
B387.S24 1999
113—dc21   99-24065

1 2 3 4 5   04 03 02 01 00 99

For Anneke Chappelle and Emily Claire

. . . εἰ μέλλομεν ἄρξεσθαι κατὰ τρόπον.

Timaeus 54a

CONTENTS

ACKNOWLEDGMENTS

My work on this project goes back to a series of lectures that I presented at Villanova University in 1989 at the invitation of Walter Brogan. Subsequently I had opportunities to present additional series of lectures in which various issues arising from Plato's *Timaeus* could be explored: at St. John's College (Annapolis) in 1994, at the University of Helsinki in 1995, at the University of Warwick in 1997, and at DePaul University in 1999. Some results of my research were also presented at Boston University in 1994 in a lecture sponsored by The Boston Area Colloquium in Ancient Philosophy and subsequently published in the Colloquium Proceedings (1995); and at several of the annual meetings on hermeneutics organized at the Universität Heidelberg by James Risser and Lawrence Schmidt.

I am especially grateful to three friends who in various ways have been decisive for my work on the *Timaeus:* to Hans-Georg Gadamer for encouragement and unlimited dialogue; to Jacques Derrida for the intense discussion of questions concerning the χώρα that we have pursued for more than a decade; and to Walter Brogan for the initial invitation and for continuing encouragement and dialogue.

Thanks also to John Ellis, Robert Metcalf, and Nancy Fedrow.

Boalsburg
May 1999

CHOROLOGY

Prologue

Chorology.

    One finds it, first of all, in a single text signed by Plato. Even though within an extended narrative for which Plato forged the signature of Timaeus.

    Hence, this chorology—and there is perhaps no other—bears two signatures. As does every other discourse in this text and in all those that, at the risk of reduction, one calls Platonic dialogues. For the double signature is irreducible: what is said in these texts, what is said to be said, is always signed by—that is, said to be said by—someone other than Plato. The double signature thus marks the reserve of the writer, the practice of a certain graphic ventriloquy.

    In the doubling Plato's signature is yoked to a manifold of others. This manifold, too, is irreducible, primarily (though not solely) because of the irreducibility of the double signature as such: because no one voice in a dialogue can be identified with Plato's own, no one voice can be accorded absolute authority so as then to be essentially separable from the others and assimilable to Plato's own. Not only is nothing said to be said by Plato himself, but also nothing is said to be said in his name, by one who would be his dialogical surrogate. The voices remain multiple, at best echoing one another, generating a play of echoes through which the dialogue, in the end, makes something manifest, yet without producing simple univocity. In their multiplicity the voices are interactive, peculiarly performative, producing speeches that are also deeds on the part of those who (are said to) voice them. This is why, most directly, one must always be attentive to the dramatic character of a dialogue. In its polyphony a dialogue deploys discourses, stories, and deeds (λόγοι, μῦθοι, ἔργα), which in their multiplicity release a mirror-play illuminating that which the dialogue as a whole would render manifest. One will always need to read a dialogue in such a way as to let its distinctive manifestation occur, listening as its manifold voices resound, hovering within the space of their resonance. Even if, as in the *Timaeus,* the dialogue undergoes a transmutation into monologue. Even if, as in the *Timaeus,* that which a certain discourse would say proves to withdraw from discourse, to retreat by its very nature, as the very nature of nature. Even if, as in the *Timaeus,* a manifold silence prevails—first of all, that of Socrates himself, who shortly after the opening of the dialogue falls into silence and from that point on listens silently to Timaeus' long monologue on the cosmos.

In any case one cannot but approach the *Timaeus* with a certain reticence. Of all the dialogues it is the one that has been most continuously and directly effective. Ever since the early Academy it has been the subject of commentary and debate. Aristotle's extensive discussions and critiques of the *Timaeus* are well-known, and through Plutarch some indications remain concerning the debate over it that took place in the early Academy between Xenocrates and his pupil Crantor. Indeed, up through the fifth century A.D. there was a continuous tradition of commentary on the *Timaeus,* a tradition that included, in addition to Plutarch, also Plotinus, Proclus, and Chalcidius. Through Chalcidius' Latin translation, the dialogue was transmitted to the Middle Ages, and as such it served as one of the chief sources of medieval Platonism, indeed as the primary genuinely Platonic source. Its influence showed little decline with the advent of the Renaissance (Ficino wrote a commentary on it) and of modernity (Kepler greatly admired it for its mathematical approach to nature). The dialogue gained enormous significance during the era of German Idealism, especially for Schelling, who wrote a recently discovered commentary on the *Timaeus;* indeed it can be shown by reference to this commentary, composed at the very outset of Schelling's career, that the *Timaeus* was to remain decisive even in Schelling's great work on the essence of human freedom. If it can be said that, following the era of German Idealism, the *Timaeus* underwent a certain eclipse, attention focusing instead on the more explicitly ontological and dialectical dialogues, it appears that the very strangeness that set this dialogue apart from those others has recently come to provoke a renewed engagement with it.

Yet it is not only because of this history that one is compelled to approach the *Timaeus* with reticence, not only because of the extent and depth of the commentary it has received from ancients and moderns alike. But also because the dialogue itself calls for reticence, provided one is attentive to the texture of its discourses, noting, for instance, the appropriateness with which the introduction to one of those discourses is marked by repeated occurrences of the word χαλεπόν: severe, difficult, troublesome, even dangerous. To say nothing yet about the way in which the dialogue turns upon and withdraws its own discourse. Nor about the utter strangeness of what that discourse would say, the elusiveness with which it would remain foreign even to discourse itself.

It is, then, a dialogue of strangeness; even saying that it is utterly singular does not go far enough, or rather, does not convey a sense of the strange movement of this dialogue, which is anything but mere progression. In its directionality and texture, the dialogue has the form of a story. Yet it is a story that, by almost any standards, seems badly told: for it is a story in which there are interruptions and regressions, discontinuities and abrupt new beginnings. The discontinuity is indeed marked as such at the point where Timaeus breaks off his account of the god's fabrication of the cosmos and then, having interrupted that account, makes a new, second start, producing a second discourse that is not continuous with the discourse interrupted. It is this second discourse that is strangest of all: for what it introduces (that which Timaeus finally names χώρα) not only refuses to be integrated into the fundamental schema governing the discourse up to that point (the very schema of fundament, one could call it) but also proves elusive to discourse as such, "most difficult to catch," as Timaeus will say (51a–b).[1]

The peculiar texture of this dialogue, its discontinuities, its repetitions, its indecisiveness, has not gone unnoticed in the incomparably vast and complex history of interpretation and appropriation of the dialogue.[2] Yet, more often than not, the reinscriptions produced by interpretation as well as by philosophical appropriation have tended to efface or at least compensate for the apparently faulty texture of the dialogue. It is the chorology itself that has been most consistently submitted to effacement and compensation, indeed, an effacement and compensation designed to render it readable within a certain restricted economy. Oriented in advance to this economy—I shall call it an economy of meaning, an eidetic economy—the readings in effect enforced the demand that

1. Translations of Platonic texts are my own, though I have consulted, for the *Timaeus,* the translation by F. M. Cornford (in *Plato's Cosmology* [New York: The Liberal Arts Press, 1957]), that by R. G. Bury (in the Loeb edition), and occasionally that by Thomas Taylor (*The Timaeus and the Critias or Atlanticus* [1810; reprint, New York: Pantheon Books, 1944]). For the *Republic* I have consulted the translation by Allan Bloom (*The Republic of Plato* [New York: Basic Books, 1968]). Citations from Thucydides are adapted from the Crawley translation (*The Peloponnesian War* [New York: Modern Library, 1982]).

2. Gadamer's formulation is incisive. He characterizes the *Timaeus* as "a kind of story which, in fairy tale fashion, is peculiarly loose, incoherent, and allusive." He explains: "The incoherence is especially obvious in the way the natural sequence in which a narrative would usually unfold is interrupted by regressions, corrections, repetitions, and abrupt new beginnings." Gadamer notes, in particular, that the discourse delivered by Timaeus after he has interrupted himself and launched another beginning "cannot be inserted straightaway and unobtrusively into the story being told . . . [but] *has a completely new look to it*" (Hans-Georg Gadamer, "Idea and Reality in Plato's *Timaeus,*" in *Dialogue and Dialectic: Eight Hermeneutical Studies on Plato,* trans. P. Christopher Smith [New Haven: Yale University Press, 1980], 160, 170).

everything exposed in the reading be situated within that economy, appropriated to it. By insisting on a reading of the chorology in which the meaning of the χώρα would come to be determined, the resulting interpretations produced a reduction of the χώρα, situating it within a horizon of sense that it would otherwise both limit and escape, effacing its distinctiveness in the very gesture of interpretation, in the very demand that the chorology make sense, in the refusal to read in it, instead, a limiting both of making and of sense.

To interrupt the orientation to an economy of meaning is to expose the discourse to unspeakable insecurity. It is also to risk, in interpreting the dialogue, doubling its discourse with another that could hardly be expected to be any more secure.

An element of insecurity is inevitable even at the beginning, even in beginning to read and interpret the dialogue. Where is one to begin? Presumably at the beginning—at least if one is to follow the injunction given in the *Timaeus* itself, though not at the beginning, not even quite at the beginning of the particular discourse in which Timaeus advances it: "With regard to everything it is most important to begin at the natural beginning" (29b).[3] In responding to this injunction, one will not be able to evade entirely the series of questions that it unleashes. What is the natural beginning? Where, if anywhere, is the natural beginning—in what kind of where? When was it? Across what interval of time must it be recalled in order that one begin with it? Is it a beginning *in* time or a beginning *of* time? Or even a beginning that—in some other, unsaid order—would precede the beginning of time? Is this beginning—this origin (ἀρχή)—with which one is to begin sufficiently manifest at the beginning that one can begin straightaway with it? Or is it perhaps the case that what is manifest in the beginning is precisely not the natural beginning, so that, instead of *beginning* with the natural beginning, one could only *arrive* at it by way of a discourse capable of bringing it to light?

Such questions would become especially pertinent if the natural beginning were indeed the χώρα. In the *Timaeus* there is much to warrant considering it the natural beginning, at least in the sense of its being the beginning, the origin, of nature, even a kind of nature before nature, the mother, as Timaeus calls it, of all natural things. Then it would become decisive that the χώρα in fact becomes manifest—if it can be said at all to become manifest in the *Timaeus*—not at the beginning of the dialogue but near the middle. In this case the Timaeus would prove not to have begun at

---

3. μέγιστον δὴ παντὸς ἄρξασθαι κατὰ φύσιν ἀρχήν. Two constructions are possible, depending on whether παντός is taken together with μέγιστον δή or as depending on ἄρξασθαι. Both constructions have been proposed since antiquity. The other would read: "What is most important of all is to begin at the natural beginning." See A. E. Taylor, *A Commentary on Plato's Timaeus* (Oxford: Oxford University Press, 1928), 73f.

the natural beginning; it would seem, then, to be a badly told story, one that violates the very injunction it issues about how to begin.

One could imagine rewriting the dialogue from the natural beginning, rewriting in the sense of an interpretive reinscription. One could imagine cutting into the dialogue at just the right juncture, making the initial incision right at what proves to be (what would already have to have proven to be) the beginning. One could imagine reinscribing the entire dialogue from the beginning, setting out from the chorology (or at least from the initial portion of Timaeus' second discourse, which issues in the chorology) and then reordering everything from the beginning, circling back to and resituating all that Timaeus' first discourse, constantly ahead of itself, introduced out of order. One could dream for a long time about such a reinscription. And even though one would eventually discover that the effect of thus beginning at the beginning would be to dismember the dialogue to the point of utter incoherence, a certain persistence in the dream will not by any means have been in vain. If one cannot even begin to reinscribe the *Timaeus* as it appears in the dream, one can—as in the reinscription ventured here—orient the reinscription to the chorology, ordering the discourse from that bastardly center, so that it will always be either ahead of itself as it races on toward the chorology or behind itself as it continues to linger there even while moving on.

But outside the dream's spell, even if along with it, one will need to consider an inevitable consequence of venturing to interpret the dialogue, to begin interpreting it, by following the injunction it issues about beginning. Precisely through following the injunction, one would have violated it; for one would have begun, not at the beginning, but with the injunction, which does not occur at the beginning of the dialogue and which does not even make manifest the beginning with which one is told to begin. This entanglement, this impossibility, is an index of just how complex the question of beginning is and of just how readily it can lead one onto an errant path or into the thickest of thickets. One thing can be said with assurance, even if only in anticipation, without having properly begun, thus already in violation of the injunction: in the *Timaeus* nothing is more vigorously interrogated than the question of beginning.

After the extended introduction linked to Socrates' discourse of the previous day, at a point where Socrates and the other two are about to withdraw completely into the silence that will not be broken until after the end, Timaeus begins the long discourse—or rather, series of discourses—that occupies most of the dialogue and that includes the chorology. Almost at the beginning, or rather, as he is about to begin, as he is invoking the gods just before going on to draw the distinction with which philosophy itself begins, he inserts a declaration of intention: "we who are intending to produce a discourse concerning the universe . . . [ἡμᾶς δὲ τοὺς περὶ τοῦ παντὸς λόγους ποιεῖσθαί πῃ μέλλοντας . . .]" (27c). The word is the same as in the conditional that will be inserted just after the chorology: ". . . if we intend to make a suitable beginning [εἰ μέλλομεν ἄρξεσθαι κατὰ τρόπον]" (54a). The duplicity of the word (μέλλω) opens the interval: to intend to begin, to be about to begin, is also to delay, to defer the very beginning that one is about to make. It is also to hover at the limit—assuming that limit (πέρας) is understood, not simply as the end of something, but as that from which something begins.

But if, on the other hand, one would just read the dialogue, is there need to delay? Need one defer the beginning and open instead an interval of reflection on beginning? For, when one comes to read the dialogue, surely—one will say—it is a question only of the beginning *of the text:* one ought to begin reading at the beginning of the text, at its natural beginning. But can one ever be certain where a text begins? Can one ever establish with assurance its *natural* beginning, bringing the concept of nature to bear upon discourse, to which one usually opposes it, as the Greeks opposed φύσις to λόγος? Is there anything natural about discourse, about a text? Is even its linearity something that would allow one to establish its natural beginning? Can one be certain that the beginning of the text does not require a retrospective activation by what comes later in the linear order of the text? Are there not texts that begin only after having already begun, that always require therefore double reading? Is the *Timaeus* perhaps such a text? Is it perhaps only in doubling back to the beginning that one can then read with understanding those opening words by Socrates, words that, at least since Proclus, have seldom ceased to provoke Plato's interpreters?

1

Remembrance of the City

RECEPTION

One, two, three—

One takes this as the beginning, these three words, the words *one, two, three*. Reading them from the point where the inscription begins, reading them at the beginning of its first line, one takes them as the beginning, sets them down as the beginning, takes them to be set down as the beginning in the manner of a hypothesis (in the Greek sense), vowing to remember in all that follows the need to circle back upon them.

Proclus marked their appropriateness, marked it with a word that could be taken to signal from afar the very heart of the matter to be put in question in the dialogue: "Suitably [εἰκότως], therefore, the discourse at its beginning proceeds through numbers and uses numbers as things numbered."[1] Suitably, fittingly, as an image (εἰκών) is suited or fitted to image its original, its paradigm.

The first three words of the *Timaeus* bespeak the dialogue as a whole. These three words, the words *one, two, three,* enact an operation that will be repeated at several decisive junctures and in several basic articulations in and of the dialogue. For with these words Socrates is counting; he is counting off the persons who, as he counts, are receiving him as their guest. Hence, these opening words do not just express the first three positive integers but also enact a counting. Indeed, as Jacob Klein has shown,[2] the Greek understanding of number is intrinsically as well as lin-

1. Proclus, *In Platonis Timaeum Commentaria,* ed. E. Diehl (Amsterdam: Verlag Adolf M. Hakkert, 1965), 1:16.
2. Jacob Klein, *Greek Mathematical Thought and the Origin of Algebra,* trans. Eva Brann (Cambridge: MIT Press, 1968), 46–60.

guistically linked to counting. The link is posed by the linguistic connection. The verb ἀριθμέω means primarily: to count out, to count off, a number of things. The word that is uttered last in counting off a number of things is the number (the counting number: ἀριθμός) of these things. Number signifies, therefore, a definite number of definite things. Thus, the intentionality is quite different from that which would set numbers over against things and submit such detached numbers to operations carried out quite apart from things and the link to things. For the Greeks the intentionality is rather one by which a number intends things insofar as they are present in this number. A sentence from Aristotle is explicit: "And a number, whatever it may be, is always of something, for example, of parts of fire, or of parts of earth, or of units" (*Mtp.* N 1092b19-21). Thus it is that *one* is not regarded as a number: only what can be counted, a number of things, is a number, the smallest of which is therefore *two.* On the other hand, this basic intentionality does not preclude a transition— the very transition ventured in the Platonic dialogues—to a level at which the things counted would no longer be sensibly presented things, the level of theoretical arithmetic where number becomes a number of pure units, a number of ones—still, however, a number *of something.*[3]

Thus counting, *one, two, three,* Socrates marks a beginning by setting forth, in the strict sense, not three numbers but only one, the (counting) number *three.* It is this number and the counting numbered by it that will be decisively repeated throughout the *Timaeus.*

Socrates is being received by three persons, Timaeus, Critias, and Hermocrates. Since Hermocrates presents no speech but only a single remark enjoining Critias to speak, there are in fact three speakers in the dialogue. Counting them off by name in the order in which they present their speeches, *Socrates, Critias, Timaeus,* one notices that it is the third that is the major speaker, at least assuming that what is actually presented has precedence over a brief remembrance of an earlier speech and a mere anticipation of a speech promised for later. Timaeus' speech, which is several times the length of the other speeches, is itself divided into three distinct speeches, the transitions marked by explicit interruptions in the discourse (at 47e and 69a).

This counting, *one, two, three,* will be repeated many times in the course of the *Timaeus,* and each time it will be imperative to circumscribe precisely what is being counted. In a sense everything will hinge on the third: for instance, when in the first of his three discourses Timaeus tells of the

---

3. The basic intentionality linking numbers to things and the modification of this intentionality are graphically presented in a passage in Book 7 of the *Republic.* Socrates has spoken of employing the study of calculation (λογιστική) for the sake of turning the soul itself toward truth and being. When Glaucon asks about such use of this study, about the way in which it could accomplish such an end, Socrates replies: "It leads the soul powerfully upward and compels it to discuss numbers themselves. It will not at all permit anyone to propose for discussion numbers that are attached to visible or tangible bodies" (*Rep.* 525d).

ingredients put into the soul of the cosmos, counting off (1) being, (2) that which is generated, and (3) that which is blended from the first two, blended midway between them and then, in a further blending, blended with them. Such counting of kinds becomes both more decisive and more aporetic in Timaeus' second discourse, at the point where he sets about introducing that which, as the discourse proceeds, he comes finally to call the χώρα. In this counting, three is again the counting-number, and it is precisely as a third kind (τρίτον γένος) that the χώρα is introduced. Here the counting is explicitly *of kinds,* not of persons or things present before him and capable of being counted off by way of the appropriate arithmetic gestures. Yet what complicates matters is not simply that one would now count something not sensibly present; rather, the complications, announced by the word χαλεπόν, stem from the fact that the counting is *of kinds.* When one counts a number of things, the one requirement, the precondition for the counting, is that the things to be counted either be of the same kind or at least be such as can be considered of the same kind. One cannot count apples and oranges except insofar as they are considered fruit, that is, are gathered, in advance of the counting, under a single kind. What, then, about a counting of kinds themselves? Would there not have to be a more inclusive kind in reference to which the kinds to be counted could be considered all of the same kind, the same kind of kinds? What if for certain kinds such as those three that Timaeus counts there should prove to be no such inclusive kind? What if they could in no respect be considered all of the same kind? Would not the counting then also prove difficult, troublesome, even perhaps dangerous—in a word, χαλεπόν?

Difficulties of this kind will prove to haunt that most decisive counting ventured in Timaeus' second discourse. Indeed, as I shall undertake to show, these difficulties will become so extraordinarily troublesome as to threaten the very discourse in which the counting would be elaborated. It will not be surprising, then, that this counting will itself be pluralized, repeated many times in different forms, with various permutations.

Yet at the beginning, in marking a beginning, Socrates is counting off the three who are receiving him: "One, two, three—but where, my dear Timaeus, is the fourth of our guests of yesterday, our hosts of today?" (17a). Counting off those present, Socrates counts only to *three.* After three words, after the word *three,* he interrupts the counting, abruptly breaking it off in order to inquire about a fourth person who is not present. Marking the difference by his use of the ordinal number (τέταρ-τος), he asks about the whereabouts of the absent one, the absent fourth. The opening question of the *Timaeus* is thus a question of where (ποῦ), a question of place. It is a question of the place of someone who is absent from the scene of the dialogue, absent from the place where it takes place, where its words are uttered and its deeds enacted. The opening words themselves enact a deed, turning the dialogue toward the chorology from the moment its inscription begins. For the χώρα has at least enough to do with place that it could come to be translated—or mistranslated—as *locus* by Chalcidius[4] and as *place* by Thomas Taylor.[5] It has enough to do with place that in, for instance, the confusion of a dream it might even appear as a kind of place. In any case, the question that opens the *Timaeus* orients it from its beginning toward the question of the χώρα, toward the chorology.

The fourth person counted—or rather, not really counted, counted only in the interruption of counting—is not only absent himself. His name also is absent: it is not mentioned in the opening exchange nor anywhere else in the dialogue. Hence, the absence of the absent fourth is a double absence. What about this one who is not there either in person or in name? In asking about him, in asking who the absent fourth is, one resumes the speculation that, from the ancient commentators on, has again and again been ventured about the identity of the one who is—and is said to be—absent. Already by the time of Proclus the debate about his identity was an old one. Proclus reviews some of the alternatives that had been proposed. Among them was Theaetetus, whom Aristocles identified as the absent fourth on the grounds that Theaetetus, like the unnamed fourth, was said (though elsewhere) to be ill. Proclus mentions also the Platonic Ptolemy, who took the absent one to be Cleitophon, since in the dialogue bearing his name Cleitophon is thought not to deserve an answer from Socrates. Inevitably, perhaps, the absent one had been taken to be Plato himself: Proclus mentions such a proposal by Dercylidas, put forth on the grounds that Plato was absent, because of illness, from the scene of Socrates' death. Detailing the inconclusiveness of all these proposals, Proclus himself declares that none of them are reliable. He also mentions, without explicit criticism, the connection proposed by Iamblicus between the absent fourth and the orientation of the *Timaeus* to the sensible, natural cosmos: the fourth would be one fitted to discussion of the intelligible, one who is thus absent from the Timaean discussion of φύσις, his absence marking that shift from intelligible to sensible.[6] Though modern commentators are for the most part more cautious than those whose particular identifications are mentioned and criticized by Proclus, they have added other proposals to those put forth by the ancients. For example, while cautioning that "it is not very profitable to speculate on the identity of the unnamed person," A. E. Taylor is "sure that he is meant to be a representative of the type of doctrine current in Sicily and Italy, since Timaeus agrees to take his place." Taylor ventures support for the particular identification proposed by Burnet, namely, Philolaus, on the

4. *Timaeus: A Calcidio Translatus Commentarioque Instructus* (London: The Warburg Institute, 1962), 50. This translation is generally believed to date from the early fifth century A.D.

5. Plato, *The Timaeus and the Critias*, 171 (page citation is to the reprint edition).

6. Proclus, *In Platonis Timaeum Commentaria*, 1: 19–20.

grounds that, like Timaeus, Philolaus combined Pythagoreanism with medical theories based on Empedocles. Taylor even suggests that Empedocles himself would be a good candidate, were it not that his death preceded the supposed dramatic date of the dialogue.[7] Cornford, on the other hand, ventures no such speculations, declaring rather that "there is no ground for any conjecture as to the identity of the fourth person, who is absent."[8] Certainly this is the case at the moment one reads—and as long as one reads only—the opening passage in which Socrates counts off the three and inquires about the whereabouts of the fourth. It remains to be seen whether the reiterations of this counting will provide a basis for returning to the question of the absent fourth, especially when the counting becomes what might be called, if improperly, a counting of being. As in the chorology.

Both time and illness figure in the absence of the fourth. Socrates describes him as "the fourth of our guests of yesterday, our hosts of today" (17a). One is to understand that the fourth, who is absent now (νῦν), was present yesterday (χθές) as one of Socrates' guests along with the other three, and that all four were to have hosted Socrates today and would indeed have done so had the fourth not, as Timaeus explains, fallen ill. His absence results from a certain compulsion, from necessity: for Timaeus assures Socrates that the fourth would "not willingly have stayed away" (17a). The absence of the fourth thus portends in deed the turn to necessity (ἀνάγκη) that Timaeus himself will be compelled to make, the turn by which the second of his three discourses is launched—to say nothing of the turn to illness and disease in Timaeus' third discourse. The fourth's absence on account of illness interrupts the continuity otherwise posed between yesterday and today, posed as the prescription that, as Socrates entertained the four yesterday, they in turn are to entertain him today.

They will indeed entertain him, at least the three who are not incapacitated. He will be their invited guest (δαιτυμών). They will be his hosts (ἑστιάτωρ), receiving him hospitably, as one hospitably receives (ἑστιάω) guests into one's home, welcoming them (perhaps even with feasting) to one's very hearth (ἑστία). The Greeks call the goddess who guards the hearth and home by the same name: Ἑστία. It will turn out that the discourse about to be recalled by Socrates, the discourse with which yesterday he offered a feast to his four guests, will have been one that threatens hearth and home. There will be need, then, to call on the protectress. Since Ἑστία was always the first of the immortals to be invoked at festivals and since it will turn out that the today of the dialogue is a festival day, one might well suspect that Ἑστία has been covertly invoked right here at the start. As guardian of hearth and home, of household and family.

---

7. Taylor, *Commentary on Plato's Timaeus,* 25.
8. Cornford, *Plato's Cosmology,* 3.

The three who are present are to host Socrates, to receive him hospitably (ἑστιάω). There is another word to designate a hospitable reception, one that will come to have unprecedented weight in Timaeus' second discourse: ὑποδοχή. In the sense primarily of receptacle, this will be one of the names for that which will also be called χώρα. The connection could hardly be more sharply delineated: in being set as the scene of a reception, the *Timaeus* dramatically enacts precisely that on which its discourse will come to focus at the center of the dialogue: the very reception of being, one could call it. Or simply the receptacle. Or the χώρα.

Socrates proposes that it is up to those present to fill the part of the one who is absent. Timaeus agrees that to the extent of their capability (κατὰ δύναμιν) they will not fall short of doing so. No indication is given as to the part that the absent fourth would have played. But whatever that part might be, Socrates and Timaeus have from this point agreed that what Timaeus and the others are to say and do will serve—or will be intended to serve—to fill that part, to compensate for the absence of the fourth.

Timaeus concludes the opening exchange by putting in force again the continuity between yesterday and today, between the two receptions: those who were hosted by Socrates yesterday are today to be his hosts, at least those who are left, three of the four. But now, as he reaffirms this continuity disturbed only by the absence of the fourth, Timaeus' words refer to the hospitality due to strangers (ξενίοις); the effect is to shift the focus from the hearth and home where a guest is received to the guest who may be a stranger, even a foreigner. It is noteworthy, too, how Timaeus presents the connection between today's reception and yesterday's: if they failed now to receive Socrates hospitably, it would not be just (οὐδὲ δίκαιον). It will turn out that the discourse with which Socrates entertained his four guests yesterday was precisely a discourse on justice.

THE EIDETIC CITY

Socrates asks about the discourse of yesterday. It is a question of memory: Does Timaeus remember the topic and the extent of that discourse? In response Timaeus proposes that Socrates go back over it briefly from the beginning (ἐξ ἀρχῆς) in order to fill out their partial remembrance of what Socrates said on the previous day. Or rather, Timaeus asks that Socrates go back over it "if it is not somewhat troublesome for you" (17b). His request puts into play for the first time a word that will serve as an indispensable marker later in the dialogue, a word that could indeed serve to mark the character of the *Timaeus* as a whole—the word χαλεπόν: severe, difficult, troublesome, even dangerous. Socrates does not respond directly to the conditional. To Timaeus' proposal he answers simply: "This shall be" (17c). He does not say whether it will be difficult for him to go back over the discourse briefly from the beginning, nor whether it is troublesome to have to do so. But as he recalls the discourse of yesterday, he will remark that certain points in that discourse are easy to remember and thereby will set these points in relief.

The first venture of the dialogue will be, then, an exercise in remembrance. There will be numerous other remembrances of various kinds in the course of the *Timaeus*, and indeed it would not be entirely out of the question to regard the entire dialogue as a complex of remembrances. But what is remembrance? What is it to remember? To remember is to bring something back to mind, to bring back before one's inner vision something remote, something past, something removed from the present, from presence. It is to bring back to a certain presence something that nonetheless, in its pastness, is—and remains—absent.

In the exercise in remembrance that Socrates is about to undertake, he will remind the others of yesterday's discourse by briefly going back over it, by repeating it. Thus, the remembrance is not only a remembrance *of* a discourse but also a remembrance linked to retelling, to going back over again, that is, to repetition in discourse. In this remembrance the relation to repetition is manifold. Remembrance makes discursive repetition possible: Socrates can repeat yesterday's discourse only if he remembers it. But discursive repetition is in deed a remembering: as Socrates speaks, he is in deed remembering. And, in turn, discursive repetition makes remembering possible: Socrates repeats the discourse as an aid to the others' remembering, that they might be enabled to remember whatever they might have forgotten of yesterday's discourse.

In this first venture of the dialogue there is something peculiar, a certain retraction of the beginning. Rather than simply beginning, Socrates refers back to a previous discourse, draws the beginning of the *Timaeus* back to another beginning that will have preceded it. Rather than simply beginning, Socrates makes yesterday's discourse the beginning of today's. Such an operation will recur frequently and decisively in the *Timaeus:* a beginning retracted by being referred back to a prior beginning. This palintropic operation will determine the movement by which the *Timaeus* will carry out its vigilant interrogation of beginnings, a movement of return to beginnings.

Socrates speaks. He begins what will be his only speech in the *Timaeus,* the first in a series of speeches that will largely constitute the dialogue. Throughout his speech, in distinction from the others, there will be intermittent responses, each indicating simply and briefly that the remembrance to which Timaeus is being led by what Socrates says corresponds in content to what Socrates is saying in his present discourse.

From the beginning Socrates speaks of the speech he gave yesterday: "The chief part [τὸ κεφάλαιον] of the discourse I delivered yesterday was about the constitution [πολιτεία], what sort seemed to me best and from what sort of men it came" (17c). The word τὸ κεφάλαιον can of course mean the chief part, the main part, the capital points as one might present them in a summary. But such a meaning presupposes a metonymical operation based on another meaning: derived from ἡ κεφαλή, the head, τὸ κεφάλαιον means, first of all, that which belongs to the head. Socrates is speaking, then, of the head of the discourse,[9] the head of the discourse he delivered yesterday. The head of that discourse concerned the πολιτεία, the constitution of the city,[10] how the city could be best constituted and from what sort of men it should be constituted in order to be the best of cities. Suspicion cannot but arise immediately that Socrates' discourse of yesterday either belongs to that of the *Republic* or at least resembles it. One recalls from the *Republic* that when Socrates went down to (the) Piraeus and engaged in the long conversation in Polemarchus' house, the first interlocutor he encountered was named Cephalos (Κέφαλος). If one recalls that the character thus named turned out to be all head, an old man who had lost all the desires of the body, then one cannot but wonder about a discourse such as the one that Socrates is now about to present, a discourse that is *merely head.* Are there not reasons to be suspicious of such a recapitulation? Are there not grounds for suspecting that it might pass over some things pertaining to other parts of the body?

Timaeus responds: what you said, Socrates, was very much "to our mind [κατὰ νοῦν]." The phrase can of course simply express agreement with what Socrates said yesterday, which—or the head of which—he is now to repeat.[11] Timaeus would, then, simply be declaring: what you said, Socrates, was in accordance with what we think about the constitution of the city. And yet, in a dialogue oriented almost single-mindedly toward νοῦς, it is difficult not to hear in this first occurrence of the word some resonance of what is to come; nor can one easily ignore the way in which this occurrence of νοῦς immediately echoes the reference to the head, in which eventually the νοῦς of certain living beings will prove to be housed. Proclus had no doubt but that this accordance to νοῦς refers both to the

---

9. The basis for this more specific metonymy, which substitutes *head* not just for *the main part* but for *the main part of a discourse,* is provided by a passage in the *Phaedrus* in which Socrates links the parts of discourse to the parts of the body: "Well, there is one point at least that I think you will admit, namely, that any discourse [λόγος] ought to be constructed like a living being, with its own body, as it were; it must not lack either head [μήτε ἀκέφαλον] or feet; it must have a middle and extremities so composed as to suit each other and the whole work" (264c).

10. In translating πόλις as *city,* it is imperative to recall in every instance that the Greek πόλις corresponds to nothing in modern political life, neither to the nation-state nor to the urban units that we call cities—even if the πόλις remains the basis to which all Western political thought is decisively linked. Heidegger, in particular, insists on the differentiation of the πόλις from all modern political forms (*Parmenides,* vol. 54 of *Gesamtausgabe* [Frankfurt a.M.: Vittorio Klostermann, 1982], 132f.).

11. This sense—the agreement of something (of something someone says or of some anticipated outcome) with what someone else thinks, believes, or expects—appears to be what is expressed by κατὰ νοῦν in a passage near the beginning of the *Euthyphro* (3e).

role that νοῦς will be accorded in the fabricating of the cosmos and to the noetic level at which the discussion will be pursued.[12] In any case, it is not at all out of the question to regard the phrase as posing a specific connection between Socrates' discourse and Timaeus' first discourse, which, by its own declaration, has to do with the works of νοῦς.

Repeating, recalling the head of yesterday's discourse, Socrates speaks of the constitution of the city. The best constituted city, the city that would be so constituted as to be the best, he describes as one ordered according to τέχνη. The city is to be divided into kinds (γένη), these kinds being determined by the differentiation between the various τέχναι. Thus, the city will be divided into those—that kind—who produce by letting things grow, by merely tending or cultivating what is generated by nature, *and* those who produce by making things, by fabricating them (ποιεῖν). Broaching this differentiation between farmers and artisans, though without developing it, Socrates alludes also to the further division into individual τέχναι. There is to be a strict division between the various τέχναι and a strict assignment of each citizen to a τέχνη; each is to practice the τέχνη proper to him, the pursuit to which he is suited by nature (κατὰ φύσιν), his one sole occupation. From the kinds who practice these various τέχναι, Socrates then explicitly distinguishes the kind whose occupation it is to defend the city, the guardians or soldiers. In their case, above all, the imperative must remain in force: they must pursue only this one sole occupation to which they are suited by nature. They must "be solely the guardians of the city" (17d).

The way in which Socrates articulates these divisions serves to give a preliminary delimitation of the range of the word τέχνη. Those who till the soil, the farmers, are to be included with those who practice the "other τέχναι" (17c). It is not insignificant that, while including both farmers and artisans under the rubric of τέχνη, Socrates nonetheless marks the difference. For whereas farmers tend and cultivate things that germinate and grow by nature, artisans fabricate things that could never come to be by nature. The difference between these two kinds foreshadows an opposition that will come more and more into play and into question in the course of the *Timaeus;* in its most general form it is the opposition between τέχνη and φύσις, between the order of fabrication (ποίησις) and that of procreation and birth. Yet in the present articulation both farmers and artisans are placed on the side of τέχνη and distinguished as such from the guardians of the city.

At this level of articulation, which stops short of developing an intrinsic determination of τέχνη, a certain reference can be ventured even across the lines determining the inviolable singularity of each dialogue. Reference especially to the *Sophist* is in order. For in a comparable articulation in this

<hr />

12. Proclus, *In Platonis Timaeum Commentaria,* 1:32.

dialogue, farming and the care of living things (of bodies subject to death) are included with—also, therefore, distinguished from—those τέχναι that put together or mold implements of various sorts. To these two forms of τέχνη a third is conjoined, that of imitation (μιμητική). What all of these share is an orientation to producing (ποιεῖν): "When something that previously was not is subsequently brought into being, we say that the bringer produces [ποιεῖν] and that the thing brought is produced" (*Soph.* 219b). All these τέχναι are directed to bringing something into being, whether it be a living thing, an implement, or an imitation. All these τέχναι are directed to production (ποίησις); they are directed to making something, either by tending what comes to be by nature or by composing and shaping materials taken from nature. Indeed, one might simply declare that τέχνη is ποίησις, were there not, in this very passage in the *Sophist*, a further development: all the τέχναι oriented to production are gathered under the word ποιητική, and this productive kind of τέχνη is then distinguished from another kind that includes learning and acquiring knowledge as well as money-making, fighting, and hunting. None of these involves working in the way an artisan works (δημιουργέω); rather than bringing something into being, they deal with something that already is, coercing things by words or actions or preventing themselves from being coerced by others. Thus positing an acquisitive kind of τέχνη (κτητική) over against the productive kind, the *Sophist* marks a reservation regarding the identity of τέχνη and ποίησις. The question may be left open whether this reservation is determined by the singularity of this dialogue. In any case there are ample indications of this identity given in other dialogues, most notably in the *Symposium*. Here again the sense of ποίησις is established: "For, of anything whatever that passes from not being into being, the whole cause is ποίησις" (*Sym.* 205b–c). All τέχναι are then said to be directed to such production: "so that the works of all τέχναι are productions [ποιήσεις] and their artisans [δημιουργοί] are all producers [ποιηταί]" (*Sym.* 205c).[13]

What, then, of the guardians? Since they are seemingly unproductive, are they to be excluded from the range of τέχνη, assuming that all τέχνη is production? Or are they to be included in that other kind of τέχνη that the *Sophist* distinguishes from the productive kind? Can they be said to practice an acquisitive τέχνη (along with others who fight or hunt—or learn)? Or is their pursuit something other than τέχνη? In the articulation given in the *Timaeus* Socrates designates all the pursuits mentioned (that of farmers, of artisans, and of guardians) by the general term ἐπιτήδευμα: pursuit, business, occupation. But in the *Republic,* which has a privileged

---

13. The word ποιητής also designates a poet. The *Symposium* goes on immediately to note that many who produce things are not called ποιηταί but have other names, while those whose productions have to do with music and meter commonly receive the name ποιητής, so that a part of the whole of ποίησις comes to have the name of the whole (see *Sym.* 205c).

connection to the *Timaeus,* Socrates refers to the struggle for victory in war as a matter of τέχνη and designates engagement in war by a word that suggests strongly that it is a τέχνη: πολεμική (see *Rep.* 374b). Indeed, one might well wonder whether it is only at the cost of disrupting the identity of τέχνη and ποίησις that the guardians can thus be regarded as pursuing a τέχνη. For in the *Republic* Socrates gives an indication that the guardians' pursuit does not entirely fail to produce something: they are, at least, "artisans [δημιουργοί] of the city's freedom" (*Rep.* 395b–c).

Among these various configurations of the identity of τέχνη and (of) ποίησις, a variation rooted, to some degree, in the singularity of the respective dialogues, there are two that need especially to be kept in focus in reading the *Timaeus.* According to one of these configurations, τέχνη and ποίησις would, in their virtual identity, designate the pursuit characteristic of the artisan, of those who make things by shaping and putting together natural materials; to pursue a τέχνη would be to fabricate things, and ποίησις would be fabrication. According to the other configuration, the range of τέχνη would be extended to include also the guardians (and perhaps others), either to the point of disrupting the identity of τέχνη and ποίησις (positing a nonproductive τέχνη) or by extending the sense of ποίησις to the point where it includes, for example, the production of the city's freedom. In the *Timaeus* there will be alternation and sometimes slippage between these two configurations, though as the dialogue proceeds to interrogate the opposition between ποίησις and φύσις, the narrower sense will prevail.

The imperative is that each pursue solely the occupation to which he is suited by nature. Thus, those to be assigned to each occupation must possess a specific natural suitability to the occupation, an ability that can then be realized and enhanced by appropriate rearing and training; they are then to pursue solely their one occupation, even to pursue it in precisely such a way as not to be distracted into any other pursuit. Socrates stresses the bearing of this imperative on those who are to defend the city, the guardians (φύλακες).[14] The characters of soul that they are by nature to possess in order to be suited by nature to be guardians are determined by the requirements that they be stern with enemies and yet mild with friends. To satisfy the former requirement they must exhibit exceptional spirit (θύμος), must be spirited; but in order that they not exercise sternness of spirit upon their friends but rather overrule it for the sake of mildness to those recognized as friends, the souls of the guardians must be such as are capable of bringing a certain cognition to overrule the fierceness of spirit, that is, they must be not only spirited but also philosophic. The souls of

---

14. Socrates uses the same word, φύλακες, when he first introduces the guardians in the *Republic* (374d–e). The brief description that the *Timaeus* offers of the nature required of the guardians and of their training parallels the more extended discussion in the *Republic* (374d–376e).

those suited to be guardians must be both spirited and philosophic, both at once (ἅμα). They are then to be brought up, to be given rearing and training (τροφή), in a way suited to develop these characters of soul that make them suitable by nature to be guardians. Among their forms of training are gymnastic and music.

The guardians especially are to pursue solely their one occupation. Indeed they are to pursue it in such a way that they remain oriented to it rather than being drawn aside into practices improper to their occupation. Thus, the form of community in which they are to live is to be such as to promote uninterrupted concentration on their occupation and devotion to practicing it with excellence (ἀρετή). This form of community is to be one that radicalizes community: the guardians—or rather, the auxiliaries, Socrates shifting at this point from φύλακες to ἐπίκουροι[15]—are to have no private property, to regard nothing as "their own property" (18b). Rather, receiving moderate compensation from those they protect, they are to spend their wages in common and lead a common life.

Socrates recalls also what was said about women: their natures are to be formed in about the same way as the men's. For women as for men the imperative that each pursue the occupation to which he—or she—is suited by nature is to be put in force regardless of whether that occupation has to do with war or with something else.

There is a slight change of tone as Socrates then asks: And what about procreation? Or, literally, what about child-production (παιδοποιία), the word itself hinting at a curious mixing that the *Timaeus* will put ever more into question, hinting that procreation is to be regarded as a matter of production, of making, perhaps even as in the pursuit of a τέχνη. At this point Socrates briefly interrupts the flow of remembrance in order to remark that the proposals made in this regard were novel, contrary to custom (ἀήθεια), and that precisely for this reason they are easy to recall. He recalls then the proposal that as regards marriage and children all should have all in common. It should be such that no one recognizes his or her actual offspring. Instead, all should regard all as their kinsmen, as belonging to the same family (ὁμογενής), to the same γένος. Thus, depending on their age, one should regard all others either as brothers and sisters, or as parents and grandparents, or as children and grandchildren. Timaeus confirms that, as Socrates had said, this is easy to remember.

Thus, the guardians or auxiliaries would be formed into a single family; all would be of the same kind, namely, such as to have everything in com-

---

15. In the *Republic* a distinction emerges between those who are to rule the city and those who are to defend it or go to war for it. Thus, among the guardians (φύλακες) Socrates eventually distinguishes between the rulers (ἄρχοντες) and the auxiliaries (ἐπίκουροι) (*Rep.* 414b). One could regard the shift in the *Timaeus* from φύλακες to ἐπίκουροι as alluding to the absence, in Socrates' account in this dialogue, of the discourse on the philosopher provided by the central Books of the *Republic*.

mon, nothing remaining private, neither property nor spouse nor children. The community into which they are to be formed would be determined by its lack or disregard of all differentiation on the basis of property ownership or of belonging to a particular family or to one or the other sex. The community would be such that there would be only the broad differentiation between generations. Yet even such broad differentiation is indicative that sexual difference will always come into play in mating and procreation. But, where it must come into play, it is to be controlled by the rulers. Thus, without calling attention to it, Socrates now puts in force the distinction between the guardians who rule and those who merely fight in defense of the city, the auxiliaries (ἄρχοντες/ἐπίκουροι [see *Rep.* 414b]).

Socrates continues. The rulers are to control the production of children in such a way that the best offspring are produced. To this end they will contrive means to control mating, while concealing this control from the auxiliaries themselves, who will then ascribe the outcome to mere chance. In particular, the rulers will contrive to insure that good men mate with good women and bad with bad. The offspring of the good are then to be properly reared, but those of the bad are to be sent off to other parts of the city, expelled, as it were, from the citadel of the guardians. And yet, by what he goes on to say, Socrates grants that not even these means will suffice for fully controlling the production of citizens, specifically, of guardians. For Socrates insists that the rulers must keep watch over the children as they grow up; if it turns out that children of bad parents prove to be worthy, then these worthy ones must be brought back to the citadel, and their opposites, those born of the good who have proved undeserving, must be transferred to the country or locality outside.

It is precisely in Socrates' reference to this country outside the citadel of the guardians, this locality to which the undeserving are to be sent, that the word χώρα occurs for the first time in the *Timaeus*.[16] One could say: from the outset what would be said in this word is posed at the margin of what can be fabricated, marking the limit of controlled production.

Socrates concludes by asking Timaeus whether they have now gone through the discourse of yesterday, at least in its chief points, in those

---

16. For reasons that will be developed at length later, neither *locality* nor *country* is an adequate translation of χώρα. Both words do, however, express connections that are significant in the prephilosophical sense of χώρα as it will be taken up and transmuted in the *Timaeus*. There is a parallel description in the *Republic*, which, though involving no reference to the χώρα, does refer to the nurse (τροφός), to which (though not by this name) the χώρα will be compared: "So, I believe, they will take the offspring of the good and bring them into the pen [σηκός] to certain nurses who live apart in a certain section of the city. And those of the worse, and any of the others born deformed, they will hide away in an unspeakable and unseen place, as is seemly" (*Rep.* 460c). Bloom calls attention to the word σηκός, a dwelling, an enclosure, a pen "where lambs, kids, and calves were raised." Bloom concludes: "This whole passage compares the mating and procreation of men to those of animals. The sacred marriages apparently take their standard, not from the gods, but from the beasts" (Allan Bloom, Notes to *The Republic of Plato* [New York: Basic Books, 1968], 459).

respects that pertain to the head (ἐν κεφαλαίοις). Timaeus agrees that they have. Nor is it difficult to agree in at least one respect: Socrates has presented a discourse on precisely the kind of city that is announced in the word κεφάλαιον. The entire city, as he has just described it, is to be ordered according to τέχνη. This means, first of all, that its divisions are determined by those of τέχνη and that its forms of community are determined by the requirements for excellence in the pursuit of τέχνη. But also it means that the city is *submitted* to a kind of τέχνη, that the city is one to be fabricated. Not only is it a site for the pursuit of the τέχναι, but also it is itself to be formed by the pursuit of a kind of fabrication that is at least analogous to that of the τέχναι. It is a technical city, one to be fabricated by and submitted to a certain know-how; it is a city of the head, as though other parts of the body and of the soul were not essential to production, fighting, and procreation. It is a capital city, a city in which ἔρως, birth, sexual difference, and much else would be submitted to a kind of technical order.

Particularly among the guardians there is to be produced a community of all having all in common, a community fabricated in such a way that all those aspects of life that one naturally shelters in the privacy, most notably, of hearth and home would now become open and common. This fabricated community is to supplement the natural, familial community, compensating for the ills that plague the latter on account especially of the role played in it by privacy. The fabricated community will thus tend to displace and replace the natural community, indeed so thoroughly that it will tend—with only minimal contrivance—to be taken as the natural community.

And yet, though doubly determined in accordance with τέχνη, there remains an essential respect in which the city is made according to nature: the division between the various τέχναι is linked to natural needs, and the assignment of men—and women—to their various respective τέχναι is determined in each case by their nature. Thus, it is especially remarkable that the city turn out to be most unnatural, not only in the sense of being fabricated in a way that would submit to control so much of what is taken to be most natural in human nature, but also in another sense so extreme as to suggest that an opposition may be at work in the very proposal to fabricate according to nature, an opposition between ποίησις and φύσις, at least with regard to the constitution, the πολιτεία, of the city.

This other, more extreme contrariness to nature goes unmentioned. But its threat is difficult to forestall if, as Socrates says, all are to regard all as their kinsmen. For according to this fabricated kinship system, one cannot but mate with a kinsman, indeed in every case. Hence, all mating will be tainted by incest: a man cannot but mate with daughter, sister, or mother. Furthermore, since the fabricated kinship system is to efface natural kinship (Socrates says that one is never to recognize one's own offspring), one *can* happen to mate even with a natural kinsman.[17] Without knowing that one has done so. Always the scene will be prepared, the scene on which to broach a tragedy. As in unknowingly marrying one's closest kin.

Nearly always it has been supposed that there is a determinable relation between Socrates' discourse in the *Timaeus* and that given in the *Republic.* Indeed there is a long tradition in which the *Republic* is taken to be precisely that discourse of yesterday that Socrates recounts in the *Timaeus.* Proclus, for example, observes that the events in the *Republic* take place on the Bendideia. Indeed this is explicit in the *Republic,* almost from the opening line, spoken by Socrates: "I went down yesterday to Piraeus with Glaucon, son of Ariston, to pray to the goddess; and, at the same time, I wanted to observe how they would put on the festival, since they were now holding it for the first time" (*Rep.* 327a). It is the day of the festival just imported from Thrace, the festival of the goddess later identified as Bendis (354c). Proclus notes, on the other hand, that the *Timaeus* is said to take place on the festival day of Athena (26e). Proclus takes this festival to be

---

17. The question of incest and of the possibility of preventing it is explicitly pursued in the *Republic.* Here, as in the *Timaeus,* the fabricated kinship system prescribes that all are to regard all as kinsmen. Thus, at one point in the course of Book 5 Glaucon says (and Socrates approves) the following: "With everyone he happens to meet, he will hold that he is meeting a brother or a sister or a father or a mother or a son or a daughter or their descendants or ancestors" (463c). The question of incest is most thoroughly pursued in a passage in which Socrates declares that men and women who are beyond the age of procreation will be free to have intercourse with whomever they wish except, in the case of a man, with a daughter or her children or with a mother or her ancestors, and correspondingly in the case of a woman. Glaucon asks how these people will be able to distinguish those kinsmen with whom they are forbidden to have intercourse. Socrates answers: "Not at all. . . . But of all the children born in the tenth month, and in the seventh, from the day a man becomes a bridegroom, he will call the males sons and the females daughters; and they will call him father; and in the same way, he will call their offspring grandchildren, and they in their turn will call his group grandfathers and grandmothers; and those who were born at the same time their mothers and fathers were procreating they will call sisters and brothers. Thus, as we were just saying, they will not touch one another. The law will grant that brothers and sisters live together if the lot falls out that way and the Pythia concurs" (461d–e). This system would mitigate the inevitability of incest, and by ordering the generations it would prevent incest across generational lines. But incestuous relations will still, under the specified conditions, be allowed within the same generation, that is, between those who, according to the fabricated system and perhaps according to nature, are brother and sister.

A. E. Taylor proposes the hypothesis that the prevention of incest between those who are brother and sister by nature is strictly controlled by contrivance of the rulers: "The authorities keep a register of 'marriages' and births. Hence *they* know accurately exactly who are in our sense the 'parents' of every child. The demand for the 'consent of the Pythia' to a 'brother-and-sister' marriage is plainly meant to *prevent* 'incestuous' intercourse between persons who are actual brother and sister by blood. (The Pythia would be instructed secretely by the authorities when to refuse her assent.)" (Taylor, *Commentary on Plato's Timaeus,* 47). Regardless of whether in the *Republic* these strictures can—despite all the questions that would have to be addressed (why, for instance, the tenth and seventh month?)—be construed in such a way that they would entirely exclude incest (construed, for example, as including all the conditions posited in Taylor's hypothesis), there is still no disputing that the city is haunted by the specter of incest. In the *Timaeus,* on the other hand, Socrates gives no indications whatsoever regarding any strictures that would curtail or prevent the occurrence of incest.

the lesser Panathenaea, since he is aware that the greater Panathenaea, celebrated on Hecatombaeon 28th (the day taken to be Athena's birthday), fell nowhere near the date of the Bendideia (Thargelion 19th).[18]

Thus, according to Proclus, there is a sequence of three days, a sequence punctuated by the occurrences of the word *yesterday* (χθές) at the beginning of the *Republic* and the *Timaeus,* respectively. On the first day, the events told of in the *Republic* take place. It is the day of the Bendideia, when Socrates and Glaucon go down to Piraeus and engage in conversation in the house of Polemarchus, talking on until way into the night. On the second day, Socrates narrates the events and discourses that took place on the previous day, repeating the entire discussion that occurred in the Piraeus, repeating it, back in Athens, to Timaeus, Critias, Hermocrates, and the unnamed fourth. This narration is what constitutes the text of the *Republic.* Then, on the third day, on the day of the festival of Athena, the today of the *Timaeus,* Socrates goes back over the narrative in its chief points, recapitulates it for Timaeus, Critias, and Hermocrates.

Such a three-day sequence is also supposed, for example, by Thomas Taylor.[19] Yet, more recent scholars have pointed out the difficulty of setting the dramatic dates of the two dialogues in such sequence: the lesser Panathenaea did not in fact fall just after the Bendideia but two months later, on the same date as the greater Panathenaea, which was held only every four years.[20] A conclusion may be drawn, then, in either of two directions. One possibility is to retain the three-day sequence and to assume that the festival of Athena to which the *Timaeus* refers is not the Panathenaea but some other festival of Athena such as the Plynteria, which was celebrated only a few days after the Bendideia. This alternative is proposed by A. E. Taylor.[21] The other alternative, supported by Corn-

---

18. Proclus, *In Platonis Timaeum Commentaria,* 1:26. See also *The Oxford Classical Dictionary,* 2nd ed., s.v. "Bendis" and "Panathenaea." The assumption that the *Timaeus* takes place on the day of the lesser Panathenaea is still found in Henri Martin, *Études sur le Timée de Platon* (Paris: Vrin-Reprise, 1981), 1:248.

19. "Socrates coming into the Piraeus for the sake of the Bendidian festival, which was sacred to Diana, and celebrated prior to the Panathenaea, on the twentieth of the month Thargelion or June, discoursed there concerning a republic with Polemarchus, Cephalus, Glauco[n], Ad[e]imantus, and Thrasymachus the sophist. But on the following day he related this discourse in the city to Timaeus, Critias, Hermocrates, and a fourth nameless person. On the third day they end the narration; and Timaeus commences from hence his discourse on the universe, before Socrates, Critias, and Hermocrates; the same nameless person who was present at the second narration being now absent from the third" (Thomas Taylor, "Introduction to *The Timaeus,*" in Plato, *The Timaeus and the Critias,* 42).

20. Eva T. H. Brann, "The Music of the *Republic,*" *The St. John's Review* 39 (1989–90): 23; Cornford, *Plato's Cosmology,* 5; *Oxford Classical Dictionary,* s.v. "Panathenaea."

21. Taylor, *Commentary on Plato's Timaeus,* 45. The Plynteria was an Athenian festival in which the image of Athena, stripped of its garments and adornments, was covered and brought to the seaside on the shore of Phaleron, the old harbor of Athens. The Plynteria took place around Thargelion 25th. See *Der Kleine Pauly: Lexikon der Antike,* 4:958.

ford and Brann,[22] is to abandon the supposition of a three-day sequence and to take the festival of Athena to be either the greater or the lesser Panathenaea. In this case there would be no connection between the dramatic dates of the *Republic* and the *Timaeus.* The discourse of yesterday that is recapitulated in the *Timaeus* would not be identifiable as that inscribed in the *Republic.*

Yet, regardless of whether a connection can be established between the dramatic dates of the two dialogues, there can be no question but that, as regards content, the discourse recapitulated in the *Timaeus* corresponds in considerable degree to that narrated in the *Republic.* Or rather, it corresponds to a portion of the *Republic.* For in the recapitulation several major discourses of the *Republic* are entirely omitted. In the recapitulation nothing corresponds to the beginning of the *Republic,* that is, to Socrates' narration of his descent (κατάβασις) to Piraeus-Hades, of his efforts to escape, and of his founding there in the house of Polemarchus a kind of miniature city. Nor does anything in the recapitulation correspond to the end of the *Republic,* to the story that Socrates tells of Er's descent to the underworld, the story in which Socrates tells in mythic guise of precisely that which he enacted at the beginning.[23] In the recapitulation in the *Timaeus* there is no trace of this mythic frame in which the rest of the *Republic* is enclosed.

Moreover, there is no reference to the discourse in Books 8–9 on the decline of the city, on the series of progressively more corrupt cities leading down to tyranny. In this regard it is not insignificant that the initiation of this decline is linked precisely to procreation and birth: there will be a failure to determine properly ("by calculation together with sensation" [*Rep.* 546b]) the right time for procreation, and the result will be children born out of season, children who thus turn out to be inferior rulers.

Socrates' recapitulation in the *Timaeus* omits also all reference to the discourse on the philosopher, which forms the center of the *Republic,* even though it is treated ironically as a kind of digression intervening between the building of cities in λόγος and the account of the corruption that cities undergo. The city of which Socrates speaks in the *Timaeus* is not the city of the philosopher but the city as constructed before the digression on the philosopher intervenes. This city is the outcome of an extended discourse in the *Republic;* within this discourse it is the third of the three cities built.[24] The first of these cities is the simple city of artisans in which each pursues his own

22. Cornford, *Plato's Cosmology,* 4–5. Brann, "Music of the *Republic,*" 23. Cornford points out, presumably in reference to A. E. Taylor's proposal, that no festival of Athena took place in Athens immediately after the Bendideia, that even the Plynteria came five days later.

23. I have developed this reading of the beginning and end of the *Republic* in *Being and Logos: Reading the Platonic Dialogues,* 3rd ed. (Bloomington: Indiana University Press, 1996), 313–20.

24. Brann writes: "The city Socrates recapitulates in the *Timaeus* is, in any case, not the city of the central books of the *Republic,* for, although his account is said to be complete (19a7), the philosopher kings are omitted; it is rather the 'third city' with all its notorious features" ("Music of the *Republic,*" 23).

τέχνη in such a way that the needs of all are satisfied. The second, the luxuri-ous city, is what results when the initially simple city comes to be swollen with unnecessary desires, for the satisfaction of which all sorts of refinements and luxuries will be required. For providing these refinements and luxuries, the land that previously sufficed proves insufficient. In Socrates' precise for-mulation: "And the land [χώρα] of course . . . will now be [too] small," so that we must "cut off a piece of our neighbor's land [χώρα]" (373d). It is a question of the χώρα, of several things that can be said in the word χώρα, that belong to its prephilosophical sense: it is a question of land, of the surrounding terrain, of the countryside that extends beyond the city proper. What comes to be required with the advent of the luxurious city is an expansion of the χώρα, that is, an expansion of the city itself as a whole, an expansion of the city by way of the χώρα. Such expansion will require going to war, for which, then, an army, a corps of guardians, will be required. The third of the three cities comes about when the guardians are added and the city ordered in such a way as to purge it of its excess, moderat-ing, though not eliminating, the need to go to war.[25]

Ordered according to τέχνη, fabricated in such a way as to submit erotic necessities to a kind of technical control, this city is posed at the threshold of tragedy. That it is also, in a certain respect, constructed in accordance with nature (each being assigned to the occupation to which he is suited by nature) only heightens the tension by pointing to a funda-mental opposition between technical production and nature. And yet, in the Platonic texts, in the *Timaeus* and especially in the *Republic,* the city is less a scene of tragedy than a subject of comedy.[26] The comedy of the city, of the city of the head, of the city that is nothing but head, is pre-sented in its most succinct form in a context remote from the political frame of the *Timaeus,* namely, in the course of Timaeus' account of the fabrication of the human body. The comedy is brief: it depicts the human head rolling along on the earth, coming upon heights and hollows of all sorts; it is unable to negotiate these, is at a loss as to how to climb over the heights and out of the hollows. Thus it was, declares Timaeus, that a body and limbs were attached to the head as its vehicles of transporta-tion (*Tim.* 44d–e).

In the *Republic* there is a proliferation of such comedy, especially on the subject of the city, the third city as it issues from that building of cities that occupies Books 2–4. One could say even that the building of cities culminates in an atmosphere of comedy that gathers around the discus-sion at the beginning of Book 5, leading in the course of this Book to a peculiar performance of a comedy.

25. I have discussed the building of these three cities in *Being and Logos,* 354–59.
26. An incisive philosophical discussion of the sense and role of comedy in the dialogues is presented by Drew A. Hyland, *Finitude and Transcendence in the Platonic Dialogues* (Albany: State University of New York Press, 1995), 128–37.

Having apparently completed the task of building in λόγος the most excellently constituted city, Socrates begins, at the outset of Book 5, to speak of the various kinds of bad constitutions and the corrupt cities produced by them. But Polemarchus interrupts him and refuses to let him go on until he discourses on the begetting of children. Polemarchus insists on hearing how it is that the guardians are to have women and children in common and how the begetting and rearing of children is to occur. Polemarchus underlines the significance of the question of begetting: "We think it makes a big difference, or rather, the whole difference, in a constitution's being right or not right" (*Rep.* 449d). Yet Socrates resists, referring to the swarm of λόγοι that are likely to be stirred up if he is forced to address this question. He pleads that there is much room for doubt in such matters and acknowledges his fear that whatever λόγος he might present about such matters might seem more like a prayer. Among the things he says as he is resisting Polemarchus' demand (reinforced by Adeimantus, Glaucon, and Thrasymachus) is the following: "It's not because I'm afraid of being laughed at . . ." (*Rep.* 451a). The suggestion is that what is to follow may indeed be laughable and that Socrates is not afraid to play out the comedy. Immediately after this remark, the text continues (that is, Socrates the narrator narrates): "And Glaucon laughed. . . ."

The comedy is then literally played out by Socrates and Glaucon. Socrates even virtually announces that they are about to begin the performance of a drama: "Having completely finished the male drama," now it would be right "to complete the female" (*Rep.* 451c). He begins by speaking of male and female guard dogs. Then, having just begun speaking of how they are to be used for the same tasks and hence to be trained in the same way, having shifted imperceptibly in the course of this speech from female dogs to women, Socrates suddenly interrupts himself and observes that "many of the things now being said would look ridiculous [laughable—γελοῖα] if they were to be done as said" (*Rep.* 452a). Socrates mentions as most laughable the sight of women exercising naked with the men in the palaestras. Glaucon replies: "By Zeus! . . . that would look ridiculous [γελοῖος] in the present state of things" (*Rep.* 452b). Socrates refers to all the jokes (σκώμματα) that witty people would tell about such sights; with a kind of mock heroism Socrates declares that they must not be afraid of all these jokes. He goes on to refer literally to the *comedies* that used to be made even about men exercising naked in the gymnasiums, and then he proceeds to set down a kind of mock standard for comedy, delivering it with a seriousness of tone that already tips over into comedy: "He is empty who believes anything is ridiculous other than the bad, and who tries to produce laughter looking to any sight as ridiculous other than the sight of the foolish and the bad" (*Rep.* 452d). Then, with their prologue finished, Socrates and Glaucon openly begin their performance, pretending to carry on a dialogue with those on the other side of the question, thus generating a dialogue within the dialogue. In the course of the drama there is a demand for "a community of pleasure and pain" (*Rep.* 462b), since such community would bind the city together in contrast to the privacy that tends to dissolve its unity. And yet, such a demand can be made only by disregarding the utter singularity of the body and of the pleasures and pains that befall it, that is, by comically disregarding what can never in deed be disregarded. In saying, just a bit later, that there is "nothing private but the body, while the rest is common" (*Rep.* 464d), Socrates only underlines the comic character of the demand. Sexual difference also plays a role in the comedy that Socrates and Glaucon enact. At the beginning, sexual difference is openly and without hesitation affirmed. Asked by Socrates whether woman differs in her nature from man, Glaucon replies: "But of course she differs" (*Rep.* 453c). Socrates notes that the implication of this difference was one of the things that made him hesitant to speak on such matters, that it was one of the things that he "was frightened of" (*Rep.* 453d). And then, when he goes on to press the question as to what the difference of nature is between men and women, venturing thus to differentiate between differences, he ends up—comically—reducing the difference between men and women to something analogous to the difference between bald and long-haired men (*Rep.* 454c). This difference proves—comically—to be only a matter of the *head!* Even when it is asserted that the two sexes have the same nature as regards what makes one suited to be a guardian, the assertion proves to undercut itself. Thus, Socrates asserts: "Men and women, therefore, also have the same nature with respect to guarding a city, except insofar as the one is weaker and the other stronger" (*Rep.* 456a). As if being weaker or stronger were not a decisive determinant of one's suitability to fight in behalf of the city.

What the comedy of the city brings to light is the failure, the incapacity, of the fabricated capital city to incorporate ἔρως and all that is linked to the erotic: procreation, mating, birth, sexual difference, corporeity itself in its singularity. The comedy exposes this incapacity precisely by playing out the comic disregard for the erotic that such a city involves, the disregard that makes it possible to suppose a community of pleasure and pain and the disregard for sexual difference. The comedy plays out such disregard in such a way as to expose it as comic. What is thus marked by the comedy and suggested by the recapitulation of it in the *Timaeus* is the limit of τέχνη, of ποίησις, of political fabrication, with respect to ἔρως.[27]

There is one other indication that needs to be stressed. It, too, occurs in the comedy in Book 5 of the *Republic.* Socrates is speaking about how the men and women guardians will be gotten together for mating. He says:

---

27. The peculiar way in which ἔρως enters into the discourse on the city has been analyzed along similar lines by Stanley Rosen, *The Quarrel between Philosophy and Poetry* (London: Routledge, 1988), 102–18.

"And, mixed together in gymnastic exercise and the rest of the training, they will be led by an inner necessity to have intercourse with one another. Or am I not, in your opinion, speaking of necessities?" Glaucon answers: "Not geometrical but erotic necessities, . . . which are likely to be more stinging than the others when it comes to persuading and attracting the many" (*Rep.* 458d). The word translated by *necessity* is ἀνάγκη. It is a matter not of necessities of the head but of erotic necessities at the limit of what can be calculated, controlled, fabricated. In the *Timaeus,* too, the discourse will turn to necessity, at precisely the point where Timaeus interrupts himself and launches his second discourse. There, too, but with regard to the cosmos rather than the city, it will be a matter of what is at the limit of fabrication.

Once Socrates has finished recapitulating the discourse of yesterday, he sets about proposing what he would now like to hear in return, now that he is a guest and the others his hosts. The moment he begins to present this proposal, his words become highly erotic. He speaks, not of what he thinks about the city, but about his feeling, his affection, his passion (πάθος). He likens his passion to that of one who sees beautiful living beings (ζῷα καλά), whether in drawings or truly living but in repose. Socrates' passion is like that of one who, seeing these living beings, is then moved by the desire (ἐπιθυμία) to behold them in motion and vigorously engaged in some such struggle (ἀγωνία: struggle for victory, as in a contest or in war; gymnastic exercise) as seems suitable to their bodies. This is how he feels about the city: he would gladly hear a discourse about this city contending in the struggle against other cities, entering into war (πόλεμος) with other cities.

Socrates thus proposes a discourse that would set in motion the city whose constitution he has just drawn in the words of his recapitulating discourse. Yet the question is: Why does setting the city in motion require sending it to war? How is it that beholding it in motion even means primarily attending to it as it engages in war with other cities? Could it not be in motion without going to war? Could it not be in motion simply by having all the τέχναι properly ordered and actually being pursued within the city? Would the wheels of production not suffice to set it in motion and to keep it moving? Why must it, as Socrates passionately insists, go to war?

Several considerations are pertinent here. Most obviously, war is necessary because there is one occupation that cannot actually be pursued except in war, namely, that of the guardians. As long as the city is not at war, the guardians will remain idle as regards their actual pursuit, no matter how engaged they may be in their preparation and training. At least with regard to this occupation, the city will remain in repose.[28]

---

28. Proclus observes in this connection that even if war is not the τέλος of the city, it "exhibits the greatness of virtue [ἀρετή] to a greater degree than peace, just as mighty waves and a storm show in a stronger light the skill of the pilot" (Proclus, *In Platonis Timaeum Commentaria,* 1:56).

But how is it that going to war has such paradigmatic significance as Socrates suggests? How is it that beholding the city in motion means primarily attending to its polemical struggles? How is it that Socrates' desire is focused exclusively on the city at war, either in its military actions or in its negotiations with other cities?

Consider more closely the implications of Socrates' formulation of his proposal. In effect, he is admitting that his presentation of the head of the discourse has portrayed the city either as lifeless (a mere drawing) or else as not displaying its vitality (as in repose). This admission is corroborated by reference to the *Republic:* the city is one that disregards much that belongs to life, that attempts to submit to technical control all that pertains especially to ἔρως. Setting it in motion means releasing all that belongs to life, either bringing to life what are merely figures in a drawing or vitalizing those who lie in repose. It would be a matter of letting all that belongs to life come into play, of releasing especially all that belongs to ἔρως and to desire. Thus it is that, as Socrates calls for setting the city in motion, his very discourse becomes erotic and affective; it becomes a discourse of desire, mirroring precisely that for which it calls. Yet, when the city comes alive, when those unnecessary desires spoken of in the *Republic* are released, it will become necessary to cut off a piece of another city's land in order for the means of satisfying these desires to be made available. As a consequence the city, thus brought to life, will have to go to war. Once the city comes alive, it can no longer remain merely a self-enclosed ordered totality of artisans but will be related polemically to other cities, engaged with an other, with an outside.

Setting in motion in the sense of vitalizing calls up the passions and desires that inevitably set the city on the course of warfare. To say almost nothing of the still more intrinsic relation between war and motion that can be found at work in the *Republic:* war is the most extreme figure of motion, the figure of motion brought to its traumatic extreme in such a way that at its very moment of completion it reverts into the withdrawal of all movement, the rigor of death, the silent immobility of lifeless bodies lying on the battlefield.[29] As when Er died in war and on the tenth day, when corpses, already decayed, were picked up, was found preserved and came back to life (ἀναβιόω) to tell his story (*Rep.* 614b).

Behind the need to go to war, there is a decisive material dependence. For every τέχνη depends on resources it does not itself produce; ultimately it depends even on materials that lie completely outside the order of production (ποίησις). Each τέχνη takes its materials either from an inferior τέχνη (the shoemaker gets leather from the tanner) or, finally,

---

29. The role played by the figures of motion and of war in the *Republic* has been thoroughly and incisively investigated by Claudia Baracchi, "Of Myth and Life: On the Question of Genesis in Plato's *Republic*" (Ph.D. dissertation, Vanderbilt University, 1996).

from nature (the tanner gets hides from hunters and trappers who get them from animals found in nature).

In this connection it should be noted how the comedy of the city is briefly resumed at the end of Book 7 of the *Republic.* Glaucon likens Socrates to a sculptor who has produced ruling men who are wholly fair (πάγκαλος). Alluding to the discussion of sexual indifference, Socrates adds: And ruling women too. Then Socrates proposes finally that the founding of the new city will require the expulsion of everyone over the age of ten; these are to be sent off to the fields, the countryside (ἀγρός), so that the children can be taken over and reared without acquiring those dispositions they otherwise would receive from their parents (*Rep.* 540c–541a). Thus, in order that the ruler-sculptor be able to shape the city in the image of the paradigm constructed in discourse, it is necessary first to make it a city of children. Not only will they be erotically undeveloped, but also in all other respects they will be, like the sculptor's marble, sufficiently unformed as to provide the requisite human material for the political ποίησις that the founders and subsequently the rulers will carry out. It is as if the citizens to be were mere raw material, for example, various metals dug up from the earth, as in the noble lie that the rulers are to tell.

Suppose now that Socrates' discourse on the city, his recapitulation of yesterday's discourse, is set within its primary context, that is, taken along with its reference to Books 2–5 of the *Republic* and with what, in his subsequent proposal, Socrates says about the lifelessness of the city outlined in the discourse. Then, one might say that Socrates' discourse serves to mark certain *limits* that impose themselves on the fabrication (ποίησις) of the city, limits that limit the extent of the technical order that could be imposed on the city. Three kinds of limits can be distinguished. There is, first of all, the limitation by ἔρως and all that is linked to ἔρως, that is, mating, procreation, birth, sexual difference, corporeity itself in its singularity. The comedy of the city is played out in such a way as to disclose how these aspects and forces of life escape technical closure. Indeed, in the very formulation of his proposal regarding what he desires now to see depicted, Socrates grants the lifelessness of the city sketched in his discourse; he admits, in effect, that the vital forces have been left out. Secondly, there is limitation by the relation to other cities, to an outside. This relation is necessitated by the release of vital forces and the warfare that inevitably follows.[30] Thirdly, there is the limitation that results from dependence on materials that are not produced. Each of the τέχναι pursued in the city has such a dependence on materials from outside its own sphere of production. But also, more significantly, the political ποίησις, the fabrication of the

---

30. War, it seems, is so inevitable that it can be said always to exist among cities, whether openly declared or not. Thus, in the *Laws* Clinias says: "There always exists by nature an undeclared war among all cities" (*Laws* 626a).

city, requires material that it does not fabricate, as becomes especially evident in the discussion, at the end of Book 7 of the *Republic,* of how the city built in λόγος could be established most quickly and easily. Producing the city requires living human beings, who are *born, not produced.* These same three limits will reappear later, in Timaeus' first discourse, where they will be transposed from the fabrication of the city to that of the cosmos.

In the *Timaeus* the entire Socratic discourse on the city is a remembrance, and not only in the sense that it recalls what was said yesterday. To remember is to bring back before one's vision something that, as past, is—and remains—absent. In a more radical sense, to remember is to bring and hold before one's vision things that in and of themselves pass away, things that are always already past as soon as they come to presence, things that are not just singularly past but rather are determined as such by their becoming-past, things that even before becoming singularly past are already stamped by passingness. In the Platonic texts such remembrance is thought as vision of the εἶδος that shines through and gathers such things. Here the word εἶδος (from εἴδω: see) has the sense: that which is seen, the look that something presents when one looks at it, the look that things of the same kind have in common so as to look alike, the look that can still be envisioned even when the things that had that look have passed away. In coming to have before one's vision the enduring look of things that come and go, one brings those things back in their full presence, indeed in a presence of which they themselves, stamped by passingness, are incapable. By envisioning the look of things, one remembers those things in the most radical way.[31]

The Socratic discourse in the *Timaeus,* recapitulating another of the same kind, has the character of a remembrative turn to the εἶδος: in the vision of the εἶδος of the city, Socratic remembrance would bring to full presence that which shines through and gathers all passing cities. The city remembered in the Socratic discourse would be "a paradigm laid up in heaven," one that is "nowhere on earth" (*Rep.* 592b). And yet, the Socratic remembrance does not merely attend to the vision of this paradigm. It also *recoils* from it, back toward another kind of city, one made in its image and yet capable of being established on earth, a city exposed to the forces of ἔρως and lineage, of exteriority and alterity, of materiality and scarcity. It is this movement of recoil from the εἶδος that generates the comedy in which the limits of the paradigmatic city come to be exposed; indeed one could say that the comedy *is* the recoil enacted. Thus, in the comedy the Socratic remembrance of the city issues in a remembrance of these limits.

Having expressed his desire to hear a discourse depicting the city in vital motion, Socrates turns to the question of who might be capable of

---

31. In a passage in which the εἶδος is systematically replaced by the *whole,* Proclus makes the same connection: "But to retain in memory things that are absent is to behold wholes separately and stably" (Proclus, *In Platonis Timaeum Commentaria,* 1:105).

presenting such a discourse. Who would be able to depict the city vitalized in war with other cities? Who could speak in the appropriate fashion about the city in its polemic relation to other cities beyond its boundaries, beyond even its surrounding countryside, completely outside all its territories? Socrates immediately disqualifies himself, though without offering any reason why he could not present such a discourse. He says merely that he judges himself not to be capable (δυνατός) of praising sufficiently (ἱκανῶς ἐγκωμιάσαι) the men and the city; he adds that his incapability is not to be wondered at (οὐδὲν θαυμαστόν) (19d).[32]

At just the moment when Socrates declares himself incapable of presenting a sufficient encomium, he addresses Critias and Hermocrates, calling them by name and addressing his declaration to them. These other two, counted at the outset and now called by name, are about to enter the discussion. But not before Socrates disqualifies two kinds of men that might otherwise be thought qualified to give an encomium on the city come alive. One kind consists of the imitative tribe (τὸ μιμητικὸν ἔθνος), the poets. Socrates disqualifies the poets by speaking of the scope of imitation: one will imitate best and most easily the things among which one has been reared, whereas it is hard to imitate what lies outside that range, and harder in λόγος than in deeds. The implication is that the poets, reared in the city and carrying on their pursuit there, their vision restricted thus to what lies within the range of the city, are not prepared to produce an imitation of the city at war; that is, they cannot depict in words the relation of the city to the outside, to another city. It is for precisely the opposite reason that the sophists, as Socrates explains, are unfit to give an encomium on the city at war. Wandering (πλανητόν) from city to city (like the wandering stars, the planets that Timaeus will locate in the circle of the different), the sophists have no settled habitation of their own. The implication is that their ambit is too external to the city for them to be capable of depicting the city at war, that is, the polemical relation of inside to outside, of the selfsame city to its other. As he is speaking of the sophists' inability, Socrates slips in an indication of just what kind of men would need to be depicted: men who are at once philosophers and statesmen. Then, turning to his hosts, describing them as of a kind that shares both qualities, speaking briefly of each of the three in turn, Socrates admits that yesterday when he agreed to speak of the city he had it already in mind that they would be preeminently capable of following up with a discourse on the city at war.

32. In reference to this passage, Proclus argues against those ancient interpreters who take Socrates' remark to indicate either that the encomiastic form of speech is alien to Socrates' manner of speaking or that Socrates was too inexperienced in war to be able to speak adequately on this subject. To the first supposition Proclus offers as counterexample Socrates' encomium in the *Phaedrus;* in reference to the second he recalls that Socrates fought at Delos and Potidaea. Proclus insists also that Socrates is not speaking ironically: "But the irony of Socrates was employed against sophists and young men, not against those who [as in the *Timaeus*] were wise and knowledgeable" (ibid., 1:62).

Socrates identifies Timaeus as a native of Locri in Italy. Locri was a Greek colony founded around 700 B.C. The city possessed the earliest written legal code in Europe, and reputedly it was excellently governed; it was successful in war and even founded colonies of its own.[33] Socrates describes Timaeus as a wealthy and highborn citizen who not only has occupied the highest offices in Locri but also has become eminent in philosophy (20e). Beyond what is said of him in the dialogue, nothing is known, not even whether such a person existed historically,[34] even though his signature was found on another text, which I will examine later, a text that so decisively reinscribes Timaeus' long discourse in the dialogue that for a long time it was thought (by Proclus, for instance) to be the original that Plato had merely reinscribed and prefaced with an introductory exchange.

Socrates describes Critias more briefly: to all here it is known that as regards the subjects under discussion he is no novice (ἰδιώτης: someone uninformed, a layman as opposed to a professional; also, a private person, an individual) (20a). Critias is an Athenian, and the other two hosts are said to be staying with him (20c); he is the original host, having already hosted the other two before all three, in turn, play host today to Socrates. He is quite an old man. Later, after he recounts the story of the original Athens, a story heard when he was ten (21b), Critias wonders at the way one can recall the lessons of one's childhood: he is confident that not a single detail of the story has escaped him, even though, as he says, he does not know whether he could recall all he heard yesterday (26b). Most commentators now agree that he is to be identified, not—as Proclus and others assumed[35]—as the Critias who was Plato's mother's cousin and a leader among the thirty tyrants, but rather as the grandfather of that Critias and Plato's great-grandfather.[36] Still another Critias will soon be invoked: the Critias who speaks in the dialogue refers to his grandfather Critias, from whom as a youth he first heard the story of the beginning of Athens (20e–21b).

Of Hermocrates, Socrates says very little, only that one can trust the many witnesses who attest that both by nature and by nurture he is competent for the discussion to come (20a–b). From Proclus on, the Hermocrates of the dialogue has generally been identified as the Syracusan who played a major role in the Sicilian struggle against the Athenian expe-

---

33. *Oxford Classical Dictionary,* s.v. "Locri Epizephyrii."
34. Cornford, *Plato's Cosmology,* 2–3.
35. Proclus, *In Platonis Timaeum Commentaria,* 1:70.
36. Cornford, *Plato's Cosmology,* 1–2; Taylor, *Commentary on Plato's Timaeus,* 23; see the genealogical table in John Burnet, *Greek Philosophy: Thales to Plato* (London: Macmillan, 1964), 286.

dition to Sicily in 415–413 B.C.[37] Thucydides mentions him often in connection with this conflict. He first appears on the scene a decade before the Athenian expedition; Thucydides portrays him as having warned the Sicilian cities that they should make peace among themselves in order to repel the growing threat of Athenian invasion. For instance, when, in 424, the two Sicilian cities Camarina and Gela made an armistice and this led to an assembly of various cities at Gela: "Hermocrates, son of Hermon, a Syracusan, the most influential man among them, delivered the following speech to the assembly."[38] In his speech, as reported by Thucydides, Hermocrates said that his purpose was "to state publicly what appears to me to be the best policy for Sicily as a whole." He warned the Sicilians: "There is also the question whether we still have time to save Sicily, the whole of which in my opinion is menaced by Athenian ambition" (*Thuc.* 4.59). He exhorted the Sicilians not to remain absorbed in local quarrels while neglecting the common enemy, but to unite "in a common effort to save the whole of Sicily" (*Thuc.* 4.61). Even at this early stage, one thing that becomes clear from Thucydides' account is that Hermocrates was not just an orator set on persuading the cities to join a common fight against the Athenians, but that he was also a wily, practical military man. Thus Thucydides represents him as having said: "Vengence is not necessarily successful because a wrong has been done, or strength sure because it is confident" (*Thuc.* 4.62). Thucydides concludes: "Such were the words of Hermocrates. The Sicilians took his advice and came to an understanding among themselves to end the war. . . . The peace was concluded, and the Athenian fleet afterwards sailed away from Sicily" (*Thuc.* 4.65).

But this was only the beginning of the Syracuse affair. A decade later the Athenians sent a huge expedition to Sicily. News of the expedition reached Syracuse, but many doubted the reports. Thucydides tells how in an assembly Hermocrates came forth to warn his fellow Syracusans that the Athenians were coming, indeed with the aim of conquering Sicily. In addition, he advised them how to prepare for the attack by seeking allies, by sending out false reports exaggerating the size of their own force, and by intercepting the Athenian ships before they reached Syracuse (see *Thuc.* 6.32–35). This time Hermocrates' advice was not heeded; soon the Athenians arrived, and in an encounter at Syracuse the Syracusans were routed, though not thoroughly defeated. Thucydides tells of the events after the battle: "Meanwhile the Syracusans burned their dead and then held an assembly, in which Hermocrates, son of Hermon, a man who was

---

37. Proclus, *In Platonis Timaeum Commentaria,* 1:71–72; Cornford, *Plato's Cosmology,* 2; Taylor, *Commentary on Plato's Timaeus,* 14.
38. Thucydides, *The Peloponnesian War,* 4.58. In further references: *Thuc.*

in general second to none in intelligence and who had given proofs of military capacity and brilliant courage in the war, came forward and encouraged them" (*Thuc.* 6.72). Again Hermocrates offered specific military advice; this time the Syracusans listened and voted to do exactly as he had said. Along with two others, he was elected general.

As a general, Hermocrates continued to demonstrate his prowess at military strategy. Thucydides tells of one incident that occurred just after the Syracusans had inflicted a considerable victory at sea on the Athenians. Discouraged by their defeat at sea, the Athenians decided to retreat by land. But Hermocrates suspected their intentions and foresaw the danger that they might reestablish themselves elsewhere in Sicily and from there renew the war. He convinced the authorities that they and their allies should immediately block the roads and passes, but the Syracusans were so engaged in celebrating their victory that there was little hope of persuading them to take up their arms and march out again. Thucydides tells of the cleverness and resourcefulness with which Hermocrates handled the situation: "Hermocrates, finding himself unable to do anything further with them, now had recourse to the following stratagem of his own. What he feared was that the Athenians might quietly get a head start on them by passing the most difficult places during the night; and he therefore sent, as soon as it was dusk, some friends of his own to the camp with some horsemen who rode up within earshot and called out to some of the men, as though they were well-wishers of the Athenians, and told them to tell Nicias (who had in fact some correspondents who informed him of what went on inside the town) not to lead off the army by night as the Syracusans were guarding the roads, but to make his preparations at his leisure and to retreat by day. After saying this they departed; and their hearers informed the Athenian generals, who put off going for that night on the strength of this message, not doubting its sincerity" (*Thuc.* 7.73–74). This stratagem gave the Syracusans time to block the roads and passes. Then it was only a matter of time until the Athenian army was reduced to such a desperate state that Nicias surrendered. By the fall of 413 the entire Syracusan exploit had come to an end.

Little wonder, then, that Hermocrates is proposed as one capable of presenting an encomium on the city at war. Little wonder that he would be thought capable of depicting in discourse the city at war with other cities. For, as Thucydides describes him, he is a man of proven military skill, one who is a master of military strategy, one who is adept at foreseeing the intentions of the enemy, at anticipating dangers hardly suspected by others, and at heading off threats before they strike, countering them with cleverness, resourcefulness, and whatever stratagems might be needed. He is one whose ability goes beyond merely planning battle strategies; as he spoke before the assemblies and advised his countrymen in the face of the

Athenian threat, he assumed the aura not only of a general but of an orator and statesman. To an Athenian of the mid-fourth century he would be recognized above all as one of those most responsible for repulsing the greatest effort Athens had ever made at imperialist expansion.

Socrates reiterates that his three hosts are most qualified to depict the city at war. He reminds them of the agreement that in exchange for his speech of yesterday they are now to offer him a feast of λόγοι, a feast (ξένια) on the occasion of this hospitable reception (ξένια can also mean: hospitable reception). He declares: Here I am, all prepared, or rather, all adorned for the feast, all dressed up (he slyly uses the word κεκοσμη-μένος, related to κόσμος). Here I am all dressed up and most eager to receive (δέχεσθαι).

Then Hermocrates speaks. It is his only speech in the *Timaeus.* In a sense it is not a speech at all but only some references to speeches of others: he assures Socrates that, as Timaeus has said, they are eager to offer Socrates the speeches promised; then he recalls that yesterday, while returning to the guest chamber at Critias', Critias told them an old story; he requests that Critias now tell it to Socrates. One could say, then, that in the *Timaeus* Hermocrates really gives no speech proper. In the dialogue *Critias* it is much the same: he speaks only once, and then only to exhort Critias to go ahead courageously and present his discourse (*Crit.* 108b–c). Whether there was to have been a dialogue called the *Hermocrates*—a supposition that is not mentioned at all when in the *Timaeus* Critias sets out the speeches to come, a supposition based on a single, quite undecisive remark in the *Critias* (108a–b)—is a question that remains open. So, too, does the question whether even in the *Hermocrates* Hermocrates would really have presented a proper speech. Or remained mostly silent.

In the *Timaeus,* in any case, Hermocrates presents no proper speech. Aside from the brief hermeneutical intervention in which he ties together the threads of other discourses, he remains a silent auditor. But this is not to say that he is a mere stage prop, that his presence is without significance. Indeed, silent audition, silent apprehension, will prove to belong to, to be called for by, some of the things that the *Timaeus* will nonetheless address, certain things, for instance, that are not yet things but only traces that flee from the λόγος that would seek to capture them with such words as *fire, air, water,* and *earth.* Silence will thus prove to be a decisive moment in the *Timaeus.* Even Socrates, who was notorious for his incessant interruptions and interrogations, remains silent throughout most of the *Timaeus.* This moment of silence is embodied in Hermocrates. Thereby the sense of his name is inverted, though it is, in a sense, also exemplified by the single quasi-speech he gives in the *Timaeus:* in what he says he is a mere messenger, mediating between the discourses of others.

THE ARCHAIC CITY

The feast is ready to begin. A feast of discourses. Also of reception and of remembrance.

Critias remembers another city, a different city: ancient, archaic Athens. Or rather, he remembers—and is to repeat—a discourse about this city. It is not a discourse that occurred only yesterday or the day before, but, like the ancient city of which it tells, it belongs to the remote past.

Critias introduces this discourse by saying something about it in advance, beginning with a discourse on this ancient discourse: "Listen, then, Socrates, to a discourse [λόγος] that is very strange but entirely true, as Solon, wisest of the seven, once declared" (20d–e). It should be noted that Critias does not call what he is about to present a story or myth (μῦθος) but a λόγος, indeed a *true* λόγος. He says also that it is very strange, using the word ἄτοπος, which means, more literally: without place, out of place. This is the first of several references to place (τόπος) that will occur as Critias speaks. As guarantor of the truth of the discourse, Critias appeals to Solon, the Athenian statesman who in the early sixth century, as chief archon, introduced sweeping reforms that promoted economic development, established a more humane code of justice, and secured the rights of citizens to some share in government. It is generally believed that after introducing his reforms Solon traveled for some ten years, visiting Egypt along the way, but returned finally to find Athens riddled with strife and intrigue. In commenting on the present passage of the *Timaeus,* Proclus mentions Solon's political activities, especially his establishment of laws. Proclus continues with a story: "And a story [ἱστορία] is told of a tripod that was dragged up in a net by certain young men . . . ; the oracle [of Apollo] was consulted on this occasion, and the god answered that it should be given to the wisest one. Thus it was offered first to Thales, but he sent it to another of the seven wise men, and this one again to another, until finally it came to Solon, all of them yielding to him. Solon, however, sent it to the god, saying that he was the wisest of beings."[39] Proclus' point in telling the story is to explain why Critias calls Solon the wisest of the seven. But also, though Proclus does not draw the parallel, one can be drawn between this story and the one that Socrates tells about himself in the *Apology,* about his involvement with Apollo's oracle regarding who is wisest of all.[40]

Critias proceeds to tell how the ancient discourse came to be handed down. Its origin is Solon himself—or rather, it is, in the beginning, traced back only to Solon, though soon it will be mentioned that Solon brought it from Egypt. At that point there will be a demand to recount it from the

---

39. Proclus, *In Platonis Timaeum Commentaria,* 1:81.
40. See *Apol.* 21a–24b, together with my discussion in *Being and Logos,* 46–54.

beginning (ἐξ ἀρχῆς) (21d), to recount from the beginning the discourse about how the ancient discourse got handed down, to give from the beginning the account of how the account of the beginning was transmitted.

But, for now, Critias takes Solon as the origin of the discourse. Solon is said to have told it to his relative and dear friend Dropides. In turn, Dropides told his son Critias, who then, when ninety years of age, told it to his grandson, another Critias, who at the time was only ten years old but who now, in the *Timaeus,* is telling Socrates of the lineage of speech, not just freely but in exchange, in repayment, for the discourse offered yesterday by Socrates. Thus, the discourse that Critias would offer in exchange to Socrates is a legacy, something handed down to him from previous generations, a kind of discursive inheritance.

What is the discourse about? Initially Critias identifies its content as: the ancient deeds of the city, which were great and wonderful (μεγάλα καὶ θαυμαστά) but which have been effaced (ἠφανισμένα: have disappeared, have been made unseen, made not to appear) by time and the destruction of the people (20e). Socrates compliments Critias and then, in encouraging Critias to tell about these deeds, refers to them as something not said, not told of (οὐ λεγόμενον) (21a). This reference gives a hint that, even if verbally handed down from Solon on, there will somewhere have been a discontinuity, a break in the chain of verbal transmission; there will have been some point where they were not transmitted by being told of, not handed down by word of mouth.

Critias tells of the setting and circumstances in which the other Critias, his grandfather, passed along the legacy of discourse. This occurred during the Apaturia, a three-day festival of the sons of the same ancestor, celebrated in Athens in the month of Pyanopsion. On the first day there was feasting, and on the second day sacrifices; then on the third day, called kureotis (κουρεῶτις), the youth were enrolled in the phratry (φράτρη), the kinship group descended from the same ancestor.[41] It was on the third day, kureotis, that the aged Critias passed along the discourse that, as grandson Critias now reveals, Solon had brought from Egypt hoping to apply to it his poetic talents. By marking this day as the day of transmission from his grandfather, Critias underlines the character of the discourse as legacy, its link to family, parentage and birth, the succession of generations, lineage. It is not a discourse fabricated only yesterday or the day before; it is not a discourse constructed in the recoil from a vision of presence and separated from that presence only by the interval setting the

---

41. According to the *Oxford Classical Dictionary* (s.v. "Apaturia"), those enrolled in the phratry on kureotis consisted of three groups: children, young adult men, and newly married wives. Taylor takes them to be only the children born in the preceding twelve months (*Commentary on Plato's Timaeus,* 51). Martin takes them to be young boys and girls of three to four years of age (*Études sur le Timée,* 1:248–51). Following Proclus (*In Platonis Timaeum Commentaria,* 1:88), Martin takes the Apaturia to be a festival in honor of Bacchus.

image apart from the paradigm. Rather, it is a legacy handed down to Critias from those to whom he is linked by bonds forged in and through the fire of ἔρως, by the lineage remaining as trace of ἔρως.

But now, as he speaks in the *Timaeus,* Critias is quite old. After he has recounted what he heard from the older Critias, the previously younger but now quite old Critias remarks at how wondrous (θαυμαστόν) it is that something learned in childhood can be remembered in every single detail, even when one can no longer remember what one heard yesterday. What Critias heard yesterday was of course Socrates' discourse on the city, the discourse of which he had, today, to be reminded. Indeed, he notes that when, hearing Socrates' discourse on the previous day, his wonder was aroused as he began to remember the other discourse on the city, he was nonetheless hesitant to speak of it immediately, since, owing to lapse of time, his remembrance of it was not sufficient. He goes on then—in the present—to tell Socrates how he went about recovering his memory of his inherited discourse, reclaiming, as it were, his discursive inheritance. He tells how, as soon as he, Timaeus, and Hermocrates left Socrates on the previous day, he began telling it to the others as he remembered it, fixing it thus in discourse, by repetition. He continued alone through the night— one wonders: could it have been in a dream?—until finally he recovered the entire discourse, which he then told to Timaeus and Hermocrates immediately after daybreak, thus repeating it a third time. And so, says he, it would be most wondrous if any part of the discourse whatsoever had escaped him.

And yet, Critias' ostensible success in closing the circle of memory so quickly, in bringing his remembrance back to that discourse handed down memorially from Solon, in doing so, it seems, from one day to the next— this only serves by contrast to underline the radical character of the further withdrawal that Solon's discourse on the city undergoes. For one might almost regard Critias' recovery of his memory as a simulacrum of the turn to the εἶδος, in which those gathering wholes that were—and had to be—dimly present to one's vision are brought to full presence, indeed as a kind of ideal legacy reclaimed. And yet, there can be no question but that Critias' discourse on the city is anything but a turn to the εἶδος; nor can one suppose even that it is a discourse generated in and through the recoil from the εἶδος to the image. For the city that Critias remembers, the city that had already to be remembered when Solon first told of it in Greece—that city is ancient Athens, the original Athens, an ἀρχή distinct from the eidetic ἀρχή and from its mere image, another kind of beginning, a kind beyond kind, a third kind.

And yet, granted the distinction, the city that Critias remembers must be declared the *same* city as that presented in the Socratic remembrance. For several reasons. The first is that Critias sets about recovering his memory of the discourse on the ancient city precisely *in order to* satisfy Socrates' desire to behold in motion, at war, that city of which he spoke on the previous day. Second, when Critias tells how, on hearing Socrates tell of this city yesterday, his wonder was aroused as he began remembering the other discourse on the city, he suggests that precisely what aroused his wonder was that the two accounts coincided so exactly in most respects (25e). And, third, when, after the preliminary version, Critias sets forth his proposal to give the full version, he says explicitly that the city spoken of by Socrates will be taken to be that ancient city of which he, Critias, has just spoken (26c–d).

It is, then, the same city, and yet, in the discourse handed down from Solon and to be repeated by Critias, this city is to be *told of differently.* One difference is alluded to in the word Critias uses when he refers to the short account he has given in contrast to the full account he promises for later. For the short account he does not use the word κεφάλαιον (of the head), as did Socrates, but rather συντόμως (concisely) (25e). The word κεφάλαιον occurs in this context only in the negative, namely, when, referring to the full account promised, he says that he will not tell merely of what pertains to the head (μὴ μόνον ἐν κεφαλαίοις) (26c). This suggests that even in the short account, Critias is telling of more than just the head of the city, that he is telling of a city that is vital and embodied.

But there is another, more conspicuous difference between the ways in which Socrates and Critias tell of this same city. Critias formulates this difference by declaring that he will tell of the city, not in μῦθος (ἐν μύθῳ), as was done yesterday, but in truth (ἐπὶ τἀληθές) (26c–d). Accepting Critias' proposal, Socrates reformulates the distinction as that between an invented μῦθος and a true λόγος (26e). Thus, it is the same city, but, in the transition from Socrates' discourse on it to Critias', in the transition from the first to the second remembrance of it, a transition is to be made from μῦθος to true λόγος. Indeed, one could regard this transition from one political discourse to another as the locus of a reconstitution of the very opposition between μῦθος and λόγος, its reconstitution beyond the traditional form that is recalled within Critias' discourse as the difference between the story of Phaethon's fateful voyage across the sky, burning up all that was on earth, and the truth that a shifting of bodies in the heavens once caused destruction of things on earth by fire (22c–d). Against this background, the reconstitution in play here can only appear paradoxical: what is now to be called μῦθος is precisely a discourse that turns to the εἶδος, whereas what is called true λόγος is an old story about some largely forgotten ancestors.

But what, then, is the precise character of the transition from the Socratic city to ancient Athens, from the eidetic city to the archaic city? An indication is given at that point in Critias' discourse where the constitution of ancient Athens is described by comparison with the Egyptian city Sais visited by Solon (24a ff.). The description mentions the various kinds, artisans, hunters, farmers, the military, each of which is to pursue its own occupation without mixing in that of the others—thus forming an ordered city, one ordered to this extent by reference to τέχνη. But what is not mentioned at all in the description are the regulations by which mating and so-called child-production were to be technically controlled, the very feature that was most obtrusive in Socrates' recapitulation of yesterday's discourse and to which he explicitly called attention as something easily remembered. In the description given in Critias' discourse, what one finds in place of the comic exclusion of ἔρως is reference to the goddess Athena, who established archaic Athens and provided its soldiers with shields and spears, equipping them for warfare, enabling the city to go to war. Furthermore, in place of the technical rulers of the Socratic city, the ancient city has a class of priests, presumably in service to the founding goddess Athena. Critias declares—and then immediately repeats the declaration, underlining it—that the goddess was careful to choose a fruitful place (τόπος), one with a temperate climate, one that would bring forth the wisest men, one that would produce men who, like Athena herself, would be lovers of war and of wisdom (24c–d).[42] Thus, the transition from the eidetic city to archaic Athens is a transition to a city that would be somewhere, in some singular *place.* Whereas the eidetic city is "nowhere on earth" but rather is "a paradigm laid up in heaven [ἐν οὐρανῷ]" (*Rep.* 592b), archaic Athens is in that singular, fruitful place chosen for it by the goddess, a city with "the finest constitution of any under heaven [ὑπὸ τὸν οὐρανόν]" (23c).[43] Considering the affinity of place (τόπος) with the χώρα, it is thus appropriate that in Critias' discourse on the city in place the word χώρα occurs. Indeed, it occurs twice, first in reference to Sais

---

42. Thucydides also stresses how decisive the place of a city is. In his opening description of the situation in Greece before the Peloponnesian War, he mentions several regions such as Boeotia and Thessaly where the land is very fertile. Such places were not entirely favorable to the development of the cities: "The goodness of the land favored the aggrandizement of particular individuals, and thus created faction which proved a fertile source of ruin. It also invited invasion. Accordingly, Attica, from the poverty of its soil [διὰ τὸ λεπτόγεων] enjoying from a very remote period freedom from faction, never changed its inhabitants" (*Thuc.* 1.2). In reference specifically to the comparison drawn between ancient Athens and Egyptian Sais, Proclus declares place (τόπος) to be one of the major factors that bring about differences between cities (*In Platonis Timaeum Commentaria,* 1:99).

43. Proclus marks this contrast: archaic Athens is "the best of those under the heavens; for the paradigm of it is in the heavens" (*In Platonis Timaeum Commentaria,* 1:129). Proclus also insists that that which is truly place (τόπος) is interval (διάστημα), though this word occurs in the *Timaeus* only much later and in the quite different context of Timaeus' account of how the god installed proportional intervals in the cosmic soul (36a–b). On the basis of the identification of true place as interval, Proclus distinguishes place as interval from earth and air: "By *place,* therefore, we must not understand the earth or this air, but prior to these, the immovable interval, which is always illuminated in the same way by the gods and divided by the allotments of Δίκη" (ibid., 1:162). This gestures in the direction of the distinction that will be drawn in Timaeus' second discourse between the likes of air and earth, on the one hand, and the χώρα, on the other.

(22e), then in reference to archaic Athens (23b). Its occurrence in reference to Athens is most remarkable, serving to link—even if formally—race, generation (γένος), procreation to the χώρα. The word is addressed to Solon by an Egyptian: "You do not know that the best and most beautiful race among men were born in the χώρα where you now dwell, and from them both you yourself are sprung and the whole of your city, from a little seed [σπέρμα] that happened to be left over." This third kind of city, neither paradigm nor image, has its own singular place; it is a place where humans are born, not fabricated, where a race and a lineage are established. It is a city of the third kind, a choric city.

The role of Athena in the *Timaeus* is not limited to her having founded both Athens and Sais and equipped them for war. Indeed, Critias declares that he will deliver his discourse both as payment of debt to Socrates and as a tribute of praise to the goddess on this her festival day, singing it justly and truly in her honor. If one assumes that the festival is the Panathenaea, then some remarkable connections begin to take shape. The Panathenaea was primarily a celebration of the Athenian victories by land and sea in the Persian wars,[44] the wars in which Persia sought to expand into the eastern Mediterranean by subjugating the Greek cities. But the Persians are most certainly not the only ones to have gone to war in hopes of expansion. Any city that is in place is set in a certain opposition to the other cities outside it, and this opposition can always erupt into a war of expansion. If, moreover, the city is swollen by the release of unnecessary desires, it will be most strongly tempted to venture war in order to expand into places occupied by other cities, taking their land so as better to satisfy the desire for luxury. The figure of the expansion of the city in which it comes into polemic relation to other cities outside it is drawn in three different connections engaged by Critias' discourse. The first draft is connected with Athena's festival: the expansion of the Persians into the Greek world, bringing them into conflict with Athens. The second is drawn by the account Critias gives of the great and wonderful deeds of the ancient city: the expansion of Atlantis against the cities of the Mediterranean, bringing it into conflict with ancient Athens. The third is drawn by the silent presence of Hermocrates, who will lead the Syracusans to victory against the expansionist exploits of Athens. In these various dimensions, then, there are three drafts of the same kind of polemic expansion, or rather, of victory against such expansionist adventures, the victory prefigured in deed by the presence of Hermocrates, that told of in the true λόγος delivered by Critias, and that celebrated by all at the festival of the goddess.

In Critias' discourse it is not only the city that proves to be related to externality and alterity but also the discourse itself in which he tells of that city. The discourse remembered by Critias, which he promises to relate

---

44. Cornford, *Plato's Cosmology,* 5. On this point Cornford refers to Proclus' account.

later in detail, did not originate with Critias' ancestors. Rather, this discourse on the great and wonderful deeds of archaic Athens was presented to Solon only when he traveled *outside* Greece, to another land, a foreign place. In particular, the story was told when he visited the Egyptian city of Sais, a city said also to have been founded by Athena, but by an Athena with another name, the foreign name Neith. Thus, the discourse on ancient Athens was brought from a foreign land, from a kind of foreign double of Athens. The true λόγος that Critias promises to repeat is a foreign λόγος, one preserved in the receptacle of a foreign civilization. But in a foreign place speech is foreign; indeed, speech is what, above all, distinguishes the foreign, differentiates the Egyptian from the Greek. Hence, one cannot but assume that in bringing the λόγος back from a foreign place Solon would have been faced with the question of translation. Indeed, in the *Critias* Critias tells about the way in which Solon dealt with the question of translating this λόγος. Critias introduces the pertinent discussion in order, as he explains, to forestall his listeners' surprise at hearing Greek names given to foreigners. Noting that Solon planned to use the λόγος for his own poetry, Critias explains that, through questioning, Solon sought out (διαπυνθανόμενος) the force (δύναμις) of the words (ὄνομα) and found that the Egyptians who had first written them down had transferred them, transported them (μετενηοχότας—from μετα-φέρω) into their own sounds or voice (φωνή). Then, taking back, recovering, the thought, intention, sense (διάνοια) of each word and bringing it into his people's φωνή, he wrote it down. Thus, the λόγος that Solon brought back was a translation, a written-down translation.

While in Egypt, Solon was told not only about ancient Athens but also about the Greeks' lack of memory of it, that is, why neither he nor any other Greek remembered archaic Athens, that is, why the ancient deeds had, in Greece, been effaced. Solon was told this on an occasion when he ventured a discourse on ancient things, repeating the discourses that the Greeks took to be discourses on original things, on beginnings, for example, the story of Phoroneus, the first man, and his daughter Niobe, and the story of Deucalion and Pyrrha, who survived the flood and generated a new race of men, a new beginning of mankind. As he was relating these stories, Solon was interrupted by a very old Egyptian priest, who told him that all Greeks are children, that there is no such thing as an old Greek, that is, that the Greeks do not possess memory capable of extending to— of bringing back to mind—the truly ancient things. They are oblivious even to their own ancient origin, archaic Athens, of which they know nothing whatsoever. The old priest explains why the Greeks are lacking in such memory: it is because of their repeated loss of *writing* (as a result of floods, which are survived only by the illiterate herdsmen in the mountains) *and* because memory of ancient things is linked inseparably to writing. In Sais, on the other hand, the country, the terrain, is different; its region is such that Sais is not exposed to the destructive natural forces that the Greeks must endure. As a result of this difference, one based precisely on difference of *place,* it has been possible for the discourses on ancient things to be written down and preserved. In particular, the discourse on Athens as it was in the beginning has been sheltered in this foreign receptacle. Thus it is that the Egyptians can remember this discourse and can repeat it for Solon. Indeed, as the old priest begins to tell Solon something about ancient Athens, he promises (according to Solon's account, handed down, it seems, by word of mouth) that later they will take the actual writings and go through everything in detail.

The Greeks are children. They are capable of remembering only what is recent, only what still has a living connection to the present so that it can be brought back to mind, brought to presence before one's present vision. Or, at most, the Greeks can remember only what is linked to the present through some direct lineage of speech, so that, as Critias seems to do, one can recover one's memory of a discourse handed down through the lineage. Where such connections—*living* connections, even if handed down in speech—are lacking, remembrance requires writing. Remembrance requires the marking of time by writing; without writing, differences would be effaced, different times would be conflated, just as Solon, repeating the stories brought from Greece, conflated the many diverse destructions by fire and water and numerous other means. Because of their repeated loss of writing, the Greeks are incapable of memory of truly ancient things, whereas the Egyptians, because their writing is preserved, have such memory and indeed can pass it on to Solon so as to interrupt, from without, the Greek forgetfulness of the beginning.

Where living connections are lacking, where, as with ancient things, what one would remember is withdrawn outside all such connections, there remembrance requires writing, the externality of which—that one does not bear it within oneself, that it can be lost without a trace remaining—corresponds in a sense to the exteriority of those things that can be remembered only through writing, those things that can have disappeared without leaving a trace, as the ancient Athenian warriors were swallowed up by the earth and Atlantis by the sea.

More radically, it is a question of remembering something so ancient that it escapes even the Socratic remembrance that turns to the εἶδος, the remembrance that would bring back in the presence of the εἶδος everything that comes and goes, the remembrance that could even recoil from the εἶδος and, from the comedy, unfold an imaginal discourse. It is a question of remembering a beginning whose withdrawal outside presence is hardly less interruptive than that of the third kind, a beginning whose exteriority—marked by the repeated cataclysmic destructions and the resulting loss of writing—cannot but make it difficult to catch, not unlike the very advent of exteriority as such, that is, the χώρα. Such a fugitive beginning can be caught and held only by writing, by its marking of time.

It is with Critias' discourse that the *Timaeus* makes the transition from dialogue to monologue, that is, from a discourse that openly imitates the conversation of living speech to a writing that no longer imitates living speech, a writing that, in its form, is almost just writing, that would be just writing were it not presented as inscribing what Critias says. In this transition there is mirrored in the form of the text the transition effected in what is said, the transition from a city that can be held in living memory to a city whose remoteness is such that its memory requires writing.

Critias' discursive legacy, passed along and repeated in living speech, is thus finally linked to writing, namely, at the point where Solon is instructed by the Egyptian priest, who knows of Athens as it was in the beginning only because the memory of its great and wonderful deeds has been preserved in writing. Yet in the *Critias* it comes to light that Critias' discourse is even more entangled with writing than might be supposed on the basis of the *Timaeus* alone. For there (*Crit.* 113b) he admits that the written text, which Solon produced by translating the Egyptian writings, was passed along to his grandfather and is now *in his own possession.* Thus, Critias' legacy is not only one of living speech passed down through the generations but also includes—and not only as a remote source—a written text, a book, indeed a translation. Critias' speech and his memory are from the outset invaded by writing, inseparably intricated in a graphic legacy.

When Critias has finished, Socrates speaks again briefly. It is his third-from-last speech in the entire dialogue, and it announces the silence into which Socrates will soon, even more decisively, withdraw. He applauds Critias' discourse both for its appropriateness on the festival day of the goddess and for its being a true λόγος rather than an invented μῦθος. Socrates urges Critias to go ahead and deliver his discourse, wishes him good luck, and then, referring again to yesterday's speech, vows now to keep quiet and to listen (26e–27a).

Critias proposes the order (διάθεσις) of the feast of λόγος that is about to commence. He says: since Timaeus is the most astronomical of us and has made it, most of all, his business to know about the nature of the universe (περὶ φύσεως τοῦ παντός), let him speak first, beginning with the generation of the cosmos (ἀρχόμενον ἀπὸ τῆς τοῦ κόσμου γενέσεως) and ending with the nature (φύσις) of mankind (27a).

As the discourse by Timaeus the astronomer is announced, one readily recalls another, a discourse not recapitulated in the *Timaeus* but not unrelated to what Socrates does recapitulate there: the discourse in the *Republic* that prescribes the course of studies to be followed by the prospective philosopher-rulers. One recalls especially the position of astronomy in that course: on the one hand, the discussion of astronomy is the site of a double interruption, first, in order to replace it with solid geometry as third (after arithmetic and geometry, that is, plane geometry) in the course of studies (*Rep.* 528a–b), and then, in order to replace visual apprehension of the things above with an astronomy pursued by discourse and thought (διάνοια), not by sight (*Rep.* 529a–d); on the other hand, thus realigned and reordered, astronomy proves to occupy the highest position among those studies that lead up to dialectic, sharing that place only with its aural counterpart, harmonics. Socrates says, speaking to Glaucon: "It may be ventured, I said, that as the eyes are fixed on astronomy, so the ears are fixed on harmonic movement, and these two kinds of knowledge are in a way akin, as the Pythagoreans say and we, Glaucon, agree" (530d). This could almost serve as a description of where Timaeus' discourse—or rather, his *first* discourse—will end, with eyes and ears attuned to the harmonic circlings in the heaven.

Critias continues with his proposal regarding the order of the feast of λόγος: once Timaeus has finished his entire account leading up to the generation of mankind, Critias himself will take over the mankind to which Timaeus' discourse will have given birth; from Socrates he will take over a select portion who are well-educated. Then, in accordance with the speech and law of Solon, Critias will bring them, as he says, "before us as before a court of judges and make them citizens of this city of ours" (27b), that is, citizens of archaic Athens.[45] Once Athens (as it was in the beginning) has thus, in λόγος, acquired its citizens, Critias will deliver his discourse about the ancient deeds great and wonderful.

But why only then? Why does Critias, having begun to tell of archaic Athens, not just continue and give the entire account? Why is it necessary to interpose Timaeus' discourse on the generation of the cosmos and thus to defer the true λόγος on archaic Athens? It is necessary only if one would *begin at the beginning.* Thus, what determines the order proposed by Critias is the demand to begin at the beginning. Indeed, Timaeus will soon proclaim openly this decisive exigency: "With regard to everything it is most important to begin at the natural beginning" (29b). Here, as repeatedly in the *Timaeus,* it is a matter of a palintropic move, of a turn through which one beginning (archaic Athens) is referred back to a still earlier beginning (the generation of the cosmos).

---

45. Regarding this process Proclus explains: "However, the men are introduced by Critias in accordance with the law and speech of Solon, because Solon narrates that the Athenians were once thus governed and established laws concerning the way in which children were to be introduced into the city [εἰς τὴν πολιτείαν] and into the phratries and concerning the way they were to be registered; and likewise, concerning the kind of judges by which they should be tried. . . . As Critias therefore admits that the men educated by Socrates were Athenians, he follows the speech and law of Solon in accordance with which certain persons are introduced into the city" (*In Platonis Timaeum Commentaria,* 1:203).

2

Production of the Cosmos

PRELUDE

Socrates' penultimate speech praises, as from the threshold, the reception he is to be given in return, the feast of discourses with which he is about to be, as he says, perfectly and brilliantly entertained. Addressing Timaeus by name, Socrates declares that it will be his turn to speak as soon as he has invoked the gods as prescribed by custom (κατὰ νόμον). As if a discourse on nature required that one first turn away, that one begin in the opposite direction, in accord with νόμος rather than φύσις. As if one could only turn *back* to nature. As if the return to nature, the return of nature, could take place only after one had turned from it, only from out of that turn, that δεύτερος πλοῦς. As if discourse on nature were necessarily palintropic.

Timaeus' response confirms the appeal to custom: everyone with even the slightest prudence (σωφροσύνη) invokes the gods, and so too must we, praying that what we say will be approved, above all, by them and, secondly, by us. Timaeus adds: so much, then, for invoking the gods; ourselves we must also invoke. The self-reference hints at a kind of impious piety in which referral to the gods would, even if aporetically, be paired with reliance on one's own powers rather than precluding such reliance; thus is the bearing exemplified in Socrates' questioning response to what the god proclaimed, through the Delphic oracle, about his wisdom.

The peculiar performative character of this invocation was marked already by Proclus.[1] In effect, Timaeus declares the necessity (ἀνάγκη) of

---

1. "But why does Timaeus say that it is necessary to pray and magnificently proclaim that the gods and goddesses should be invoked, and yet does not pray, though the opportunity is there, but immediately turns to the proposed discussion? We reply that it is because some things have their end comprehended in the very will itself [ἐν αὐτῇ τῇ βουλήσει]" (Proclus, *In Platonis Timaeum Commentaria*, 1:221).

invoking the gods (a necessity of custom, not of nature) and then immediately declares that the gods have been invoked, yet without ever in deed invoking them. As if merely declaring that they must be invoked and then declaring that they have been invoked were sufficient. As if these λόγοι that might be expected to frame the invocation proper could instead replace it and constitute the invocation in deed.

In the midst of this peculiar performative, Timaeus announces his intention: discourses are to be produced (ποιεῖσθαι) about the all, the universe (περὶ τοῦ παντός), discourses telling how it was generated or else is ungenerated. It will turn out that these discourses on how the universe was made—for its generation proves to have been fabrication—will also analyze making as such (ποίησις). Thus, the discourses on making, on production, will recoil upon themselves as produced, as made. Timaeus' discourses on the universe will also incorporate discourse on discourse. Even when it is a question of the limits of production and of discourse. Even when it is a question of the limits beyond which discourse can no longer be produced, can no longer be simply made.

Timaeus speaks: "In my opinion there is first to be distinguished the following. What is that which is always being [τί τὸ ὂν ἀεί], having no genesis, and what is that which is [always]² generated, but never being? On the one hand, that which is comprehended by intellection with discourse [νοήσει μετὰ λόγου], being always according to the same [ἀεὶ κατὰ ταὐτὰ ὄν]; on the other hand, the opinable grasped by opinion with non-discursive sense [δόξῃ μετ' αἰσθήσεως ἀλόγου], being generated and perishing, never being in the manner appropriate to being [ὄντως δὲ οὐδέποτε ὄν]" (27d–28a).

On one side, then, Timaeus sets τὸ ὂν ἀεί: that which is always being, that which *always* is (which does not come to be) and which is always *being,* which *is* in the manner appropriate to being (ὄντως ὄν). Such always being, perpetual being, is always according to the same (ἀεὶ κατὰ ταὐτὰ ὄν): it remains in oneness with itself (see 37d), is always one with itself, always the same as itself, selfsame. Timaeus declares that such perpetual being is comprehended by intellection with discourse (νοήσει μετὰ λόγου). This is to say that one approaches perpetual being only on the δεύτερος πλοῦς (the second sailing or, more precisely, taking to the oars in the absence of wind) that consists in turning away from things as they are manifest to sense, that is, away from nature, turning toward discourse, having recourse to λόγοι in order to behold (σκοπεῖν) in them the truth of

2. In the phrase τί τὸ γιγνόμενον μὲν ἀεί the word ἀεί is omitted by Proclus and Simplicius as well as by Cicero and Chalcidius in their Latin translations. Whittaker has shown that this omission is even more widespread than earlier commentators had indicated. He maintains "that in later antiquity the accepted reading was τί τὸ γιγνόμενον μέν without the ἀεί" More generally, he concludes: "The correct reading is, I believe, τί τὸ γιγνόμενον μέν without the ἀεί" (John Whittaker, "*Timaeus* 27D 5ff.," *Phoenix* 23 [1969]: 181–85).

beings. In telling of this turn in the *Phaedo*, Socrates describes it as commencing with the posing of a ὑπόθεσις; that is, one begins by setting something under sensibly manifest things, under them as their basis, their origin, their original. Thus, one sets under the manifold of sensibly manifest beauties something that would be named the beautiful itself (αὐτὸ τὸ καλόν). The naming is not fortuitous but intrinsic to the turn, to its commencement with the posing of a ὑπόθεσις. For what is posed over against the sensible manifold is a *one,* and it is posed precisely from λόγος. It is set forth from the sphere of discourse in which it—along with all other such *ones*—is always already operative, even before being set forth as a ὑπόθεσις. For as one utters the word *beautiful,* there comes into play a certain unifying, a gathering, of the manifold of things that can be called by this one name. To open the space of the distinction is to set over against—and yet, under—sensibly manifest things the *ones* that are always already operative in discourse.[3] This is why the intellection, the noetic vision (νόησις), that would comprehend that which is always one with itself must be μετὰ λόγου, with discourse, by way of discourse.

Having no genesis, perpetual being is to be distinguished from τὸ γιγνόμενον: that which has been generated, that which has come about through generation, that which has come to be either by being born or by being produced or perhaps by some other way if there be such. But whatever is generated is also—with only one partial exception, to be detailed later by Timaeus—subject to perishing. As perpetually being generated and perishing, as never being in the manner appropriate to being, the generated is always becoming different from itself. The generated is not simply the sensibly manifest; Timaeus designates it, rather, as the opinable (τὸ δοξαστόν), as that which is grasped by opinion with sense devoid of λόγος. The word *opinion* (as well as such alternatives as *belief* and *judgment*) is insufficient, if not misleading, as a translation of δόξα. The verb δοκέω means, on the one hand, to opine or suppose but, on the other hand, to seem, to appear to be something or other. Thus, one opines as things seem; one supposes them to be that which they appear to be. Nothing could be more alien to Greek thought than to regard δόξα as a kind of belief produced and retained within the interiority of a subject without regard for the way things *seem.*

This distinction, set down at what seems the beginning of Timaeus' speech, has for us today the appearance of utter familiarity: one will readily translate it into a discourse about forms, even into a theory of forms, which Plato is alleged to have held. Yet in the face of such translation, which not only translates Plato's text but also translates back into—onto—Plato's text something remote from it, there is need for the utmost caution and reserve. Does one know *what* the so-called forms are, even if

---

3. See *Phaedo* 99d–100b, along with my discussion in *Being and Logos,* 38–43.

such Greek words as εἶδος and ἰδέα are retained and, through them, the link to vision, to the *look* of things? Does one know even how to ask the question? As soon as one asks *what,* one has already broached—that is, assumed—precisely that which is thought as εἶδος. The εἶδος is *what* something is. It answers the question: τί ἐστι . . . ? Thus, if one asks what a form is, one is asking: What is the what? That is, one just doubles the question and risks being ensnared in mere double talk. One would have to ask also what theory means, and yet all three words *(what, theory, means)* would lead one right back to that which the Platonic text undertakes to think and to determine in the words εἶδος and ἰδέα. Here the utmost vigilance is called for. Here one needs, above all, to be on guard against naively projecting back into the Platonic texts a conceptuality and a language that were forged only in and through those texts—or on the basis of what they achieved and at the cost of moving away from them.

One needs at least to hold the distinction in a certain suspension rather than taking it to be an established principle set down here at the beginning. Especially considering how Timaeus himself leaves it suspended: for he introduces it both as his opinion (κατ' ἐμὴν δόξαν), that is, as something that to Timaeus *seems* to hold, and *as a question.* Whether one takes the immediately following statement as appositional elaboration of the question or as a kind of answer to it (at best, only the beginning of an answer), one cannot but be struck by the apparent displacement of the distinction itself. Even before elaborating the distinction as setting apart that which is comprehended by intellection and that which is grasped by opinion, Timaeus has already placed the distinction itself on the side of the opinable. Rather than simply reasserting an established distinction, the *Timaeus* reopens the *question* of the distinction.

Thus, a certain suspension is operative here at what seems to be the beginning of Timaeus' speech, here where he seems to make a beginning, to begin with the beginning. Yet it is questionable whether—with this distinction, by the way he introduces it—he has made a beginning. Indeed, as soon as he has drawn out the general consequences of the initial distinction for the question of the cosmos, he marks the transition and the continuity with these words: τούτων δὲ ὑπαρχόντων αὖ . . . (29b). The clause can mean: "And, moreover, beginning with these things. . . ." But it can also mean: "And, moreover, granted these things. . . ." Thus, in its possible meanings, the clause slides between saying that these things (that is, the distinction and its immediate consequences) constitute the beginning *and* saying that they are *merely granted* (merely laid down in the sense of ὑποκείμενον, with which ὑπάρχω in this signification is associated), that is, saying that the distinction is merely granted because it is not established but merely says how things seem. The clause hovers, then, between saying that the distinction is the beginning *and* saying that it is something merely granted in order *then* to begin indeed, to make actually a beginning.

Leaving the distinction suspended at the apparent beginning of his discourse, Timaeus continues: "And, moreover, everything generated is of necessity generated by some cause [ὑπ' αἰτίον]" (28a). It goes almost without saying that the sense of *cause* needs to be determined from the Platonic text itself and not predetermined by post-Aristotelian or even modern conceptions. In the present case this requires only that one adhere to what Timaeus says, for almost immediately he will identify the pertinent cause and describe quite precisely the mode of causality involved.

It is most remarkable that Timaeus ascribes necessity to the connection joining the generated to a cause: the generated is of necessity, from necessity, by the force of necessity (ἐξ ἀνάγκης), generated by some cause. Furthermore, when he reiterates this connection in order to set the stage for the appearance (or nonappearance) of the maker who is cause, he again names necessity as securing the bond between the generated and its cause (28c). Indeed the entire passage that serves to introduce Timaeus' discourse and that is punctuated at its limits by Socrates' last two speeches (27c–29d) is replete with references to necessity (see also 28a–b, 29b). The role given here to necessity is especially remarkable in view of what will be said of it at the outset of Timaeus' second discourse: that the first discourse has, except for a small part, dealt with what is brought about by νοῦς, whereas the second discourse is to address what comes about through necessity (δι' ἀνάγκης) (47e). Yet from its outset the first discourse too, at least in small part, will have been engaged with necessity: the workings of νοῦς will already have been contaminated by ἀνάγκη.

Timaeus describes the pertinent mode of causality: "When the maker of something forms its look and capability [while] looking to what is always selfsame [τὸ κατὰ ταὐτά], using a paradigm of this sort, all that is accomplished in this way is of necessity beautiful" (28a–b). The conditional clause outlines the determination or structure of making or production (ποίησις). The word here translated as *maker* (δημιουργός) means primarily a craftsman, an artisan, someone who makes (ποιεῖν) things by pursuing a τέχνη. In Timaeus' discourses this designation will often be used for the god who makes the cosmos; it is the same word that Socrates uses in the *Republic* to refer to the artisans who, for instance, make up in its entirety the first of those cities built in λόγος (see *Rep.* 370d). The god who makes the cosmos is preeminently an artisan god, a god who pursues a certain cosmic τέχνη, though he is also called *the god* (ὁ θεός), as well as *producer* or *maker* (ποιητής) and *builder* (ὁ τεκταινόμενος), which has the appropriateness of referring both to building or making and also to the devising or planning that the god in effect carries out in looking to a paradigm.

The maker of something forms its look and capability. He forms it (ἀπεργάζομαι) by *working* on it, by bringing about a work (ἔργον). He forms its look (ἰδέα). Like εἶδος, the word ἰδέα is derived from εἶδω, *see,* and the connection with seeing is of utmost consequence.[4] Whatever the layers of sense that later come to enshrine these words, the ἰδέα or εἶδος of something signifies first of all—that is, at the point from which philosophical determination begins—the *look* of that something, how it looks when one looks at it, the look that two things share when they look alike. The maker of something also forms its capability (δύναμις—from δύναμαι: *be able* or *capable*), that by which it is capable of performing the functions that belong to such a thing.

Timaeus' description of ποίησις (making, fabricating, production) brings to light its mimetic structure. In fabricating something, the maker looks to the model or paradigm (παράδειγμα) in order to form the product, to fashion its look and its capability, in such a way that it looks like the paradigm and has the capability for whatever functions belong to something with such a look. Looking in advance to the paradigm, the maker gives the work the same look; he fabricates it in imitation of the paradigm, that is, as an image of the paradigm.[5] This is the way a work is to be executed, accomplished, or, more precisely, brought completely to its end (ἀποτελεῖσθαι), brought into its τέλος. Indeed when the maker sights in advance the look of the work (how it is to appear, the *how* of its appearing), such sighting has in view what the work is to come to in the end, when it is finished. In looking to the ἰδέα or εἶδος, the maker looks ahead to the τέλος into which the work, by being fully fabricated, is to be brought.[6]

What the artisan produces is an image (εἰκών) of the paradigm to which he will always have looked as he comes to shape the image. In the case of the artisan god, the image produced is the cosmos itself. This is to say, conversely, as Timaeus does say, that the cosmos is an image. More precisely, what Timaeus says is: "It is wholly necessary for the cosmos to

---

4. The word εἶδω is obsolete in the present active, which is supplied by ὁράω. The importance of this link to seeing for interpreting the philosophical determination that these words undergo beginning with the Platonic texts is stressed by Martin Heidegger ("Platons Lehre von der Wahrheit," in *Wegmarken,* vol. 9 of *Gesamtausgabe* [Frankfurt a.M.: Vittorio Klostermann, 1976], 214).

5. In the *Gorgias* (503e) Socrates refers to the δημιουργός who, "looking to his own work, selects the things he applies to that work of his, not at random, but so as to give a certain εἶδος to whatever he is working on."

6. In his interpretations of Plato and of Aristotle, Heidegger repeatedly and in various specific connections discusses the structure of ποίησις and its bearing on such fundamental philosophical determinations as εἶδος, μορφή, τέλος, and πέρας. See *Die Grundprobleme der Phänomenologie,* vol. 24 of *Gesamtausgabe,* 149–53; *Aristoteles, Metaphysik Θ 1–3,* vol. 33 of *Gesamtausgabe,* 136–44; *Platon: Sophistes,* vol. 19 of *Gesamtausgabe,* 40–47. According to Heidegger, Plato—and indeed ancient philosophy at large—interprets being as such within the horizon of production (ποίησις) (see *Grundprobleme der Phänomenologie,* 405). The question, addressed by the present study, is whether in the Platonic texts the general orientation to production is not accompanied by a critique of production, that is, a marking of its limits, as noted already in specific reference to the city.

be an image of something" (29b). Thus, not only is the cosmos an image of something, but also this very bond is a matter of necessity (ἀνάγκη), that is, in the character of the cosmos as an image and hence as bound to a paradigm, necessity is involved.

But what of the god himself? Initially, at least, Timaeus draws back from speaking of him, focusing instead on the structure of ποίησις and on the cosmos as a product of divine ποίησις. Timaeus says: "To discover the maker and father of this universe would be a task [ἔργον], and, having discovered him, to declare [λέγειν] him to all would be impossible [ἀδύνατον]" (28c). It would be a task, says Timaeus, to discover (εὑρεῖν) the artisan god. One could also translate εὑρεῖν as *to devise* or even *to invent*. One wonders whether perhaps the god is so elusive, so difficult to discover, that one must invent him; or whether perhaps when he turns up in the discourse one might never quite be sure whether one has discovered him or invented him. In any case, having thus declared that the capability of discoursing on the god is lacking, Timaeus himself—in his own discourse—then turns away from declaring the god: "Therefore, let us go back to inquiring about the cosmos" (28c). Yet in what Timaeus does say of the god, in the names by which Timaeus calls him, one peculiarity should be noted: Timaeus calls him both maker (ποιητής) *and* father (πατήρ) of the universe. In this double naming Timaeus broaches the primary opposition that emerged in the previous discourses: the opposition between the order of ποίησις and τέχνη and that of ἔρως (birth, procreation, etc.), or, more generally, between ποίησις and φύσις. For surely to be the maker is not the same as to be the father. Surely it is not the same for the universe to be made as for it to be fathered and born.[7]

From the outset one can anticipate that the structure of ποίησις, specifically, the distinction between paradigm and image, will be submitted to the distinction between perpetual being and that which is generated. Indeed, Timaeus is not long bringing the latter distinction into play; yet initially he brings it to bear in such a way as to distinguish between two kinds of mimetic production. The distinction supplies the

---

7. Plutarch poses the question provoked by this double naming: "Why did he call the supreme god father and maker of all things?" Though mentioning other explanations, Plutarch regards the following as most correct: "Or is there a difference between father and maker and between birth and genesis? For what has been born has thereby been generated, but, on the other hand, it is not so that he who has begotten has thereby made, for birth is the generation of an animate thing. Also in the case of a maker, such as a builder or a weaver or one who produces a lyre or a statue, his work, when done, is separated from him, whereas the origination and force [ἀρχὴ καὶ δύναμις] emanating from the parent is blended in the offspring and remains with its nature, which is a fragment or part of the procreator. Since, then, the cosmos is not like products that have been molded and fitted together but has in it a large portion of vitality and divinity, which god sowed from himself in the matter and mixed with it, it is seemly that, since the cosmos has been generated as a living being, god be named, at once, father of it and maker" (*Platonic Questions*, II, 1).

two kinds of paradigms to which an artisan can look: if he looks to a paradigm that is selfsame, then the work brought into its end in this regard will be of necessity beautiful (καλὸν ἐξ ἀνάγκης), but if he looks to a paradigm belonging to what is generated, the work will not be beautiful. But what is to be understood here by *beautiful*, and how is it that one kind of ποίησις produces a beautiful work while the other does not? In the *Phaedrus* Socrates declares that what distinguishes the beautiful from all else is that it is the most shining forth (ἐκφανέστατον) and the most beloved (ἐρασμώτατον).[8] Leaving the latter determination aside (as expressing the link between the beautiful and ἔρως), one can say: the beautiful is that which shows itself (φαίνεσθαι) forth; it is the being that most shines forth in its self-showing, that shines forth into and in the domain of the visible, the generated. *The beautiful* names the shining-forth of being in the midst of the visible, and whatever among generated things can be called beautiful are such precisely by their capability for letting such shining forth occur. Because those works made in the image of selfsame being are the ones most capable of letting being shine forth, the paradigm showing itself in their very imaging, such works are to be called beautiful.

Timaeus grants a certain latitude regarding the name by which to call that which already he has called τὸ πᾶν (the all, the universe): he refers to it as "the whole heaven or cosmos or, if there is any other name that it especially prefers, by that let us call it—so be its name what it may" (28b). The old name for sky or heaven, οὐρανός, figures in Hesiod's genealogy: broad-bosomed earth first bore starry heaven, equal in size to herself, to cover her on all sides; thereafter she lay with heaven and gave birth to the Titans, the Cyclopes, and other monstrous creatures (*Theogony* 116–53). Later in his first discourse when Timaeus recounts the genealogy of the gods, he refers to this mating of earth and heaven as the beginning from which the entire lineage has sprung (40d–41a). Very often, as the present passage suggests, Timaeus will use οὐρανός synonymously with τὸ παν and κόσμος, though there are passages where, for essential reasons, he lets its sense slip back toward the older usage in which heaven is distinguished from earth.[9] The tradition is that Pythagoras was the first to use κόσμος to designate what the earlier Greeks had called οὐρανός. In Homer the word κόσμος is found in a sense designating the ordered battle-array of an army; from this it came to mean any ordered array, hence, in particular, the ordered array of the stars and planets in the heaven.[10] Just before and just after (27c, 28c) the names

8. *Phaedr.* 250d–e. The full context for these remarks is developed in *Being and Logos,* 153–59.

9. This is noted by Serge Margel, *Le Tombeau du Dieu Artisan* (Paris: Les Éditions de Minuit, 1995), 96.

10. See Taylor, *Commentary on Plato's Timaeus,* 65f.

οὐρανός and κόσμος are proposed, Timaeus calls what these names would designate by the name τὸ πᾶν (the all, the universe), and in the proposal stresses this most inclusive sense by referring not just to the heaven but to the *whole* heaven.

Timaeus poses the question of the cosmos (or heaven or whatever it may be called), the question of its beginning. Or rather, he poses the question of the cosmos as a question of beginning. In his formulation of this question, four variations of the word *beginning* (ἀρχή) occur. He says: "We must investigate the question that has to be investigated in the *beginning* [ἐν ἀρχῇ] in every case—namely, whether it has always been, having no *beginning* [ἀρχή] of generation, or whether it has been generated [γέγονεν], having *begun* from some *beginning* [ἀπ᾽ ἀρχῆς τινὸς ἀρξά-μενος]" (28b—emphasis added). Timaeus answers with a single word: γέγονεν (it has been generated, has come to be). He explains: for it is something visible and tangible, something having body, that is, it is something sensible (αἰσθητόν) apprehended by opinion with sense, and such things are generated. It must, then, have had a cause, a maker. Furthermore, its maker must have fabricated it by looking to the everlasting, to perpetual being; this, says Timaeus, is clear, for the cosmos is the most beautiful of things generated and its maker the best of all causes. That it is beautiful is to say that its maker looked to a selfsame, perpetual paradigm; as indeed he cannot but have done, since he is a good maker, hence one who looks to a genuine paradigm rather than a mere imitation.

With these moves Timaeus thus submits the structure of cosmical production, its distinction between paradigm and image, to the distinction between perpetual being and that which is generated. This ontological determination of ποίησις is decisive: it inscribes the workings of production within the orbit of what will eventually be called the first and the second kinds.

It is precisely at this point, with the determination of ποίησις completed, that Timaeus concludes that the cosmos is, of necessity (ἀνάγκη), an image of something. And it is here, with the schema of ποίησις in place, that he then enunciates the injunction about beginning: "With regard to everything it is most important to begin at the natural beginning" (29b). Is this the point, then, where Timaeus' discourse properly begins? Is this, finally, the beginning? Not yet. Even here, even with the enunciation of the injunction about beginning, his discourse still does not properly begin but rather is deferred for the sake of a brief yet crucial discourse on discourse, on the discourse still to come, on the character of that discourse. In the interval before beginning, Timaeus begins with the question: What kind of discourse is to be produced?

Or rather, he puts in play the reflection of the opening distinction back upon the character of discourse, specifying precisely how it determines the kinds of discourse. The pivot on which the reflection turns is Timaeus' statement that any discourse is akin to that which it is about; literally, it is of the same kind (συγγενής) (29b), so that the character of a kind of discourse, even if not manifest from the discourse itself, can always be determined by reference to that which the discourse is about. Hence, those discourses that tell of what is permanent and stable, of such selfsame paradigms as that to which the artisan god looks in making the cosmos, will themselves be permanent and unchanging; their invincibility will prevent their being forced aside and swept away by other discourses. But discourses about the images of selfsame paradigms will share in their image-character. Such discourses will be of the same kind as the images told of in the discourses: λόγος about an εἰκών will be an εἰκὼς λόγος. One can say *likely discourse,* but only provided one understands *likely* by reference, not to some abstract concept of probability, but to the character of that which the likely discourse is about, its character as a likeness, an image. Like the images of which it speaks, such discourse would be removed from the truth itself, set at a distance from it. Such discourse will be just as impermanent, as changing, as the images of which it speaks. One would also expect it to be multiple, one discourse changing into another or coming to sweep another aside, one discourse developing into another or one coming to interrupt another. So then, corresponding to the two sides of the opening distinction, to what will be called the first and the second kind, there are also two kinds of discourse.

The proportion then stated (being [οὐσία] is to generation as truth is to belief [πίστις]) recalls the elaboration that the central Books of the *Republic* bring to bear upon the distinction with which Timaeus' discourse has opened; and though the proportion appears to situate εἰκὼς λόγος short of truth, associating it with belief, this does not entail that such discourse is simply to be opposed to truth and correctness[11] but only that it is removed from truth in the same way that an image is distanced from its paradigm, but also, therefore, related to it. The very determination of the cosmos as an image prescribes that discourse about it will be εἰκὼς λόγος, which one ought, then, to accept without seeking something beyond it, without construing it as merely a prelude to a discourse on truth itself. Timaeus hints that the attachment of human discourse to images, hence, its character as εἰκὼς λόγος, may not be as dispensable as his reference to the opening distinction may have sug-

---

11. This is emphasized by Witte, who cites several passages in support of a certain association of εἰκὼς λόγος with truth and correctness. In one passage, for example, having referred explicitly to εἰκὼς λόγος, Timaeus then goes on to speak of grasping the truth (ἀλήθεια) concerning the generation of the earth (53d-e). Another passage suggests even a certain equivalence by means of the formula: κατὰ τὸν ὀρθὸν λόγον καὶ κατὰ τὸν εἰκότα (56b). See Bernd Witte, "Der 'Εικὼς Λόγος in Platos *Timaios,*" *Archiv für Geschichte der Philosophie* 47 (1964): 2. Note also the association, more complex and problematic, posed at the threshold of the chorology when Timaeus tells how a certain result said in what is manifestly εἰκὼς λόγος can be *said most correctly* (ὀρθότατα) (51b).

gested: addressing Socrates by name, he recalls the human nature to which discourse is linked ("I who speak and you who judge [what is spoken]"). Then he asks for a certain indulgence: if we prove unable to give discourses that are wholly and in all ways in agreement with themselves, that speak together (like those who speak the same language) (ὁμολογέω), discourses that are carefully finished off (ἀπηκριβωμένος), rounded out, as it were—that we are incapable of such utterly coherent discourse should not arouse Socrates' wonder. Little wonder, then, that the *Timaeus* proves so discontinuous, so indecisive; little wonder that its discourse turns out to be so often—and decisively—interrupted, this discourse that Timaeus advises be accepted and calls, finally, εἰκὼς μῦθος, as he concludes the discourse on discourse. That conclusion is marked as such by Socrates' statement of acceptance, not only his acceptance of what Timaeus has advised, but also his acceptance wondrously (θαυμασίως) of the prelude that Timaeus has presented (29d). The expression of wondrous acceptance, alluding to the begining of philosophy (see *Theaet.* 155d), is the last utterance by Socrates in the dialogue. From this point on, he keeps, as he had promised he would (26e-27a), completely silent: throughout the interval in which the first discourse is interrupted and a new beginning made and then throughout the chorology and all that surrounds it.

ANIMATING THE COSMIC BODY

Having given his wonderful prelude, evoking Socrates' final words of acceptance, Timaeus is ready to begin. Socrates' final words, referring to wonder, have marked the beginning.

Yet in this beginning, as, previously, in the opening scene of the dialogue, as, later, in the chorology, it is a matter of *reception.* Timaeus begins, not by putting something forth, not by proposing a thesis, but rather by accepting something, receiving it (ἀποδεχόμενος). What he receives is a beginning (ἀρχή): he begins, not by making a beginning, but by *receiving* a beginning, receiving it, as he declares, from certain wise men. What does this beginning say? What is said in and as the received beginning? What, in particular, does it say in the beginning? How does it begin? It begins: "Good he was [ἀγαθὸς ἦν]" (29e). Hence, the first word of the beginning, that is, the beginning of the beginning that Timaeus accepts as his way of beginning, is: *good.* If one puts in play Socrates' declaration in the *Republic* that the good is the beginning itself, the beginning of the whole, the beginning of everything (*Rep.* 511b), then one can trace at this point in the *Timaeus* a fourfold compounding of beginning: the *beginning* (the first word) of the *beginning* received as Timaeus' way of *beginning* is the good, which is the *beginning* itself.

Declaring the maker good, the received beginning continues: because

he is good, he has no jealousy (envy, ill-will); thus, in making the all, he
wanted it to be as much like himself as possible, that is, wanted it to be *as
good* as it could be. In effect, this says: he is a good maker and as such
wants to make as good a product as possible. Timaeus tells then of this
production. He tells how the god *took over* all that is visible, or, as may
equally well be said (translating παραλαμβάνω), how the god *received* the
visible. The double sense is appropriate: the visible was there to be taken
up by the god and thus was both taken and received. When the god,
receiving it, came to take it up, it was not at rest but in discordant and disorderly motion. By taking up what he had received, the god brought the
visible from disorder into order (τάξις). As would any good artisan in
coming to form the look and capability of his work. Yet the god, this best
of artisans, fabricated a work that is not only good but also beautiful,
indeed most beautiful (τὸ κάλλιστον). For if the look and capability of a
work are properly formed, if the artisan, looking to a selfsame paradigm,
fabricates the work in such a way that it looks like the paradigm in imitation of which it was to be made, then the work will be the kind of image
that lets its paradigm most shine forth, that is, a beautiful—indeed most
beautiful—image.

A reflection (λογισμός) intervenes—is said by Timaeus to intervene—
as if interrupting and then mediating the specification of the artisan god's
work. In reflecting, the god found that among visible things none of those
lacking νοῦς will be more beautiful than those possessing νοῦς. Timaeus
does not say how the god's reflection brought him to this finding. One
might presume, venturing to reenact such reflection, that the god's finding
derived from reflecting that only a being possessing νοῦς can look to a
selfsame paradigm so as then to produce a good and beautiful image; such
a being would, then, embody the very condition for beautiful things being
brought forth at all. But, without offering any such conditions, Timaeus
moves on to say how the reflection continued, how the god prolonged the
interval for the sake of another finding: νοῦς cannot be present in anything without ψυχή. The results of the reflection are then made to govern
the god's work, to determine it in its specificity: on account of this
reflection, says Timaeus, the god constructed νοῦς within ψυχή and ψυχή
within σῶμα as he fashioned the universe to be the best and most beautiful. Venturing, with due reservations, the traditional translations, one can
say, translating what Timaeus says: the god set intelligence within soul and
soul within body. Explicitly referring to the character of his discourse,
marking it as likely discourse, Timaeus declares—or rather, declares that
one must declare (δεῖ λέγειν)—that the cosmos was, in truth,[12] generated

---

12. This passage is one of the most straightforward instances of association between
εἰκὼς λόγος and truth. See also note 11.

as a living being (ζῷον) endowed with soul and intelligence.[13]

The cosmos is, then, a living being. As such, it is something produced, a work brought forth by means of the cosmic ποίησις of the artisan god. And yet, living beings ordinarily do not come about in this way; they are not fabricated by an artisan but rather are *born*. Here, then, a tension emerges that in the discourse on the cosmos corresponds to that which came into play in Socrates' discourse on the city: the tension between the order of production and that of birth (and, more broadly, of all that is linked to ἔρως). This tension will recur throughout Timaeus' first discourse and indeed beyond it; again and again it will be reconstituted in various forms as a wavering between a discourse of production and a discourse of procreation and birth.[14]

But in the discourse of production to which Timaeus now for the moment adheres, the proper order of questioning is determined: what has to be asked about next is the paradigm that would have governed the god's production of the cosmos. Timaeus pursues this question, though without indicating whether the god too would have pursued it along the course leading to its answer; that is, Timaeus gives no indication whether he is reenacting a reflection that the god would have carried out before then letting its result determine the work, or whether he is merely constructing a discourse leading to a result that to the god would have been immediately manifest, indeed at the very moment the god commenced his work. In any case, it is—at least for Timaeus—a question of which living being would

---

13. Nietzsche's intent to reverse or invert "Platonism" is brought to bear specifically on this identification of the cosmos with a living being: "Let us be on guard against thinking that the world is a living being. Where should it expand? On what should it feed? How could it grow and multiply? We know more or less what the organic is; and we should not reinterpret the exceedingly derivative, late, rare, accidental, which we perceive only on the crust of the earth, and make of it something essential, universal, eternal, which is what those do who call the universe an organism. This nauseates me. . . . Let us be on guard against positing generally and everywhere anything as perfect as the cyclical movements of our neighboring stars; even a glance into the Milky Way raises doubts whether there are not far coarser and more contradictory movements there, as well as stars with eternally linear paths, etc. The astral order in which we live is an exception; this order and the considerable duration that depends on it have again made possible the exception of exceptions: the formation of the organic. The total character of the world, however, is in all eternity chaos . . ." (*Die fröhliche Wissenschaft,* in vol. V/2 of *Werke: Kritische Gesamtausgabe,* ed. G. Colli and M. Montinari [Berlin: de Gruyter, 1973], 145–46 [§109]). It should not go unremarked that the very questions Nietzsche raises in this passage figure prominently in the *Timaeus.* The question of expansion comes into play already in Critias' discourse; later it will return to haunt Timaeus' discourse on the cosmos. Timaeus will also undertake to show that the cosmos is one and hence incapable of multiplying, to say nothing of the way in which the question of doubling a selfsame one will emerge at the center of the dialogue. In one account Timaeus will tell—though not without releasing a bit of comedy—just what the cosmos feeds on, namely, its own excrement.

14. At the most elementary level the tension often involves pairing a form of γεννάω (to beget [of the father], to bear [of the mother]) with other words that refer to production. Some examples: γιγνόμενα καὶ γεννητά (28c); γέγονεν . . . γεννηθέντες (38b); γένεσιν . . . γεννήσας . . . δημιουργὸς πατήρ (41a); ἀπεργάζεσθε . . . γεννᾶτε (41d).

have constituted the paradigm according to which the cosmos was made. It can be taken for granted[15] that the paradigm belongs to perpetual, selfsame being; it is such being as is comprehended by intellection (νόησις) and may accordingly be called, as Timaeus now calls it, intelligible (νοητόν). The question is, then, which of the intelligible living beings (τὰ νοητὰ ζῷα) constitutes the paradigm to which the god would have looked as he came to produce the cosmos. Timaeus' answer is determined by the exigency of comprehension, which is linked to the beauty of the cosmos: not only that the paradigm be one comprehended by intellection but also, indeed primarily, that it comprehend, include within itself, all other living beings, that all other living beings be parts of it, individually and generically (καθ' ἕν καὶ κατὰ γένη).[16] This paradigmatic living being encompasses all intelligible living beings (νοητὰ ζῷα), just as the cosmos contains all other visible living beings.[17] Thus, the cosmos resembles its paradigm not only by virtue of

15. Timaeus has just said, almost exactly as before (see 29b): τούτου δ' ὑπάρχοντος (30c). The most immediate reference is to the conclusion that the cosmos is a living being; but inasmuch as this conclusion involves the declaration that the cosmos is beautiful, the character of the paradigm as intelligible has in effect been also declared, that is, it is established or, considering the initial hypotheticals, can be taken for granted.

16. By the time of Proclus there was already an extended discussion of just how this phrase should be interpreted in this context. Some (e.g., Atticus) contend that ἕν refers to the individual in distinction from the genus, whereas others (e.g., Iamblicus) take the ἕν to refer to the oneness that is proper to every intelligible regardless of the multiplicity of species within a genus (see Proclus' summary in *In Platonis Timaeum Commentaria*, 1:425-47). A. E. Taylor proposes that the phrase means "each νοητὸν ζῷον and each group or 'family' of νοητὰ ζῷα is a member of the αὐτόζῳον"; he insists that "if we attempt any further precision of interpretation, we get into apparently insoluble difficulties" (*Commentary on Plato's Timaeus*, 82). Although the phrase clearly refers to the intelligible living being (the paradigm), it could perhaps also be taken to allude to the difference between inclusion of individuals (in place) and that of species within a genus.

17. The determination of the cosmos as a living being provides the point of departure for a remarkable and insightful essay by Rémi Brague ("The Body of the Speech: A New Hypothesis on the Compositional Structure of Timaeus' Monologue," in *Platonic Investigations*, ed. Dominic J. O'Meara [Washington, D.C.: Catholic University of America Press, 1985], 53-83). Citing the passage from the *Phaedrus* (264c) in which Socrates declares that a discourse should be constructed like a living being (see above, chap. 1, n. 9), Brague proposes that Timaeus' speech, since it is also about a living being, imitates structurally precisely that of which it speaks. Since the living cosmos turns out to be isomorphic to the human being, Brague puts forth the hypothesis that the structure of Timaeus' discourse imitates that of the human being. Thus he shows that Timaeus' first discourse (up to 47e) corresponds to the human head, since it gives an account of the world as governed by νοῦς, which has its seat in the human head, the shape of which imitates that of the universe; and though other bodily parts are mentioned in the first discourse, they are considered solely from the point of view of the head. Brague undertakes to show also that the remainder of Timaeus' discourse corresponds to the trunk of the human body, though in this regard the fit is, as Brague acknowledges, considerably more problematic. He notes that the principal division within this remainder of Timaeus' speech comes at 69a and regards these two subparts as corresponding to the upper trunk (thorax) and the lower trunk, respectively, the two divided by the midriff. This means, then, that the thorax, where the θυμός has its seat, ought to correspond to the part—or subpart—of the discourse that treats of ἀνάγκη and that the lower trunk, even below the liver, should correspond to the conjunction of νοῦς and ἀνάγκη. Yet much that is

being a living being endowed with soul and intelligence but also by virtue of being all-inclusive. It is on precisely this basis that Timaeus can go on to insist that the cosmos is one, that there is only one heaven. Yet, even though both paradigm and image are distinctively all-inclusive, they are inclusive in decisively different ways. The difference has primarily to do with place; that is, what distinguishes the kind of inclusion characteristic of the visible cosmos is that, unlike intelligible inclusion, it holds together in an extended place beings that with respect to one another are in different places within this comprehensive place. It is as if in the transition from intelligible to visible something like place came into play, letting things be set apart as they are gathered into the comprehensive visible cosmos. As the χώρα, which seems like place, will prove always to have come into play in the very opening of the difference.

Timaeus' narrative shifts toward greater specificity, as well as toward a kind of beginning, focusing on the cosmos as it would have been—had it been at all—before being endowed with soul and intelligence. For the moment disregarding these endowments, Timaeus speaks of the cosmos as it would have been—had it been at all—when it was not yet a living being but only a body, only a kind of double, before birth, of the corpse it would become after death, if it were to die. This shift is announced by the first word that Timaeus, having completed the more general account, then goes on to utter: of bodily form (σωματοειδές). The generated, he says, must be of bodily form, visible and tangible. Yet without fire nothing becomes visible; neither can anything become tangible without solidity, nor solid without earth. Thus was the beginning determined: in beginning to compose the body of the universe, the god was making it of fire and earth. But these two could be bound together only by a third. Yet, since it was to be not just a plane surface but solid (and since earth alone was not sufficient for the solidity of the whole, now in the sense of depth, not of resistance to

said in these discourses would suggest, if anything, the opposite: if one grants that (in a passage that Brague cites) "all that comes in to give sustenance to the body is necessary" (75e), then the lower trunk rather than the thorax would seem to correspond to necessity; also the θυμός, located in the thorax, would in the well-known figure from the *Republic* (see 441e) bring about accord between the highest and the lowest (ἐπιθυμία). Brague grants that in the dialogue there are other "logographic necessities" that cannot but interfere with the discourse's imitation of the human body. One instance would perhaps be put in play if one thematized the capital character of the first discourse in relation to the way that same character is exhibited in Socrates' speech, namely, as involving a certain comic disregard for the rest of the body and most notably for all that has to do with ἔρως. One should note also that Brague's insistence on dividing Timaeus' speech into two parts (the second then subdivided) rather than three depends on his hypothesis, so that if one leaves that hypothesis suspended, there will be no reason for not dividing Timaeus' speech into three parts, as it would seem itself to prescribe. Whatever the extent of its possible confirmation, there is no denying that Brague's hypothesis is a powerful one, which, even at points where it seems not to be borne out by the discourse itself, serves nonetheless to reveal connections that would otherwise go unheeded.

touch), an additional middle term, a fourth, was required. Thus binding air and water between the other two in the manner of a proportion, the god constructed the body of the cosmos.

Timaeus describes quite precisely the bonds by which the four are bound together. They are bonds formed by numbers, bonds that imitate the most thoroughly binding bonds between numbers, namely, those formed by a continued geometrical proportion (ἀναλογία). Timaeus defines such a proportion, indicating especially the exceptional binding power of such proportion: "For whenever, of three numbers, the middle one between any two that are cubes or squares is such that, as the first is to it, so is it to the last, and conversely as the last is to the middle, so is the middle to the first, then since the middle becomes first and last and, again, the last and first become middle, in that way all will necessarily come to play the same part toward one another, and by so doing they will all make a unity" (31c–32a). Thus a continued geometrical proportion of three terms, a, b, c, will be such that:

(1) a : b :: b : c

(2) conversely— c : b :: b : a

(3) the middle becomes last and first, and the last and
first become middle— b : c :: a : b

Thus, any one of the three terms can stand as first, last, or middle. In this sense they are interchangeable and thus form a unity, are all one (ἒν πάντα). Yet Timaeus specifies that he is referring to the case of square and cubical numbers (or at least to cases where the two extreme terms are squares or cubes). In the case of squares the proportion would take the form:

$$a^2 : ab :: ab : b^2$$

But whereas one mean suffices to connect squares, it requires (as Euclid proves) two means to connect two cubes in such a geometrical proportion:[18]

$$a^3 : a^2b :: a^2b : ab^2 :: ab^2 : b^3$$

Since the body of the cosmos is solid, such a proportion was established as far as possible between the four:

fire : air :: air : water :: water : earth

Indeed Timaeus declares that the four were thus bound in such unity as is indissoluble except by the god himself. The word by which Timaeus designates

---

18. See Cornford, *Plato's Cosmology*, 45–52; and Sir Thomas Heath, *A History of Greek Mathematics* (New York: Dover, 1981), 1: 84–86, 89–90.

the resulting state of union is φιλία, which no doubt echoes Empedocles[19] but which also may be taken to allude to ἔρως, as if to provoke some suspicion as to whether the body thus composed is indeed that of an erotic being.

This suspicion is borne out in what follows. According to Timaeus' account, the god intentionally used up all the fire, air, water, and earth, so that nothing was left over from which another cosmos could be produced, insuring thus that the cosmos would be one. Also, by leaving nothing outside the body of the cosmos, the god made it immune to aging and illness, which always come upon a body, so Timaeus says, from without (ἔξωθεν). What Timaeus does not quite say is that this is tantamount to making it immune also to death; even before—so it seems—it is endowed with soul so as to become a living being, it is made immortal, or at least indestructible except by the god himself. Timaeus identifies the shape into which the god formed the body of the cosmos: he made it in the shape of a sphere, the shape that is comprehensive of all others and that is similar to itself, selfsame in the sense of having every point equidistant from the center. Thus was the body of the cosmos made in imitation of selfsame being, though as a sphere its selfsameness is a sameness of displacement from one and the same stigmatic locus. Thus will something like place have been operative in the fabrication of the body of the cosmos.

Timaeus continues by telling how and why it was made smooth all around. Since there was nothing outside it to see or hear, it had no need of eyes or ears, no need of openings to the outside. Since there was no air surrounding it, it needed no organ of respiration by which an exchange with the outside would otherwise be made possible. It needed no hands, either for grasping or for repelling anyone, as in battle; neither did it need feet with which otherwise it would venture outside. Instead, making it smooth all around, the god spun it around uniformly in the same place, its movement thus imitating the selfsameness of its intelligible paradigm. Thus the god made it self-sufficient (αὐτάρκης), so much so—and the excess releases now a bit of comedy—that, as he says: nothing went out from it or came into it from anywhere, since there was nothing; it was designed to feed itself on its own waste and to act and be acted upon by itself and within itself. Hence, the body of the cosmos proves to be so self-enclosed that it feeds on its own excrement and affects, feels, only itself. There could hardly be a more perfect cosmic analogue to the Socratic city, most notably, to that self-enclosed, self-sufficient city of artisans that the erotic Glaucon declared a city of sows. The word αὐτάρκης with which Timaeus

---

19. Few other passages put into play in such proximity the Pythagorean and the Empedoclean affinities of the *Timaeus*. One recognizes here the four roots (ῥιζώματα) of Empedocles, as well as that ἀρχή that he calls φιλία. At the same time, number (that is, numerical proportion) also comes to bind the roots together in φιλία. On this double affinity, see A. E. Taylor, *Commentary on Plato's Timaeus*, 88–93.

describes the cosmic body makes the analogy unmistakable: a πόλις αὐτάρκης is a city that supplies its own needs, that wants no imports. Just as the city determined by τέχνη proved, even in its development beyond a simple community of artisans, to be oblivious to ἔρως and to the difference, the incalculable otherness, linked to ἔρως, so the fabricated body of the cosmos is closed upon itself, constructed in such a way that there remains no other; and in Timaeus' description of this body there is absolutely no mention of its genitals, not even a declaration—as with eyes, ears, lungs, mouth, hands, feet, etc.—that it had no need of such organs. As if Timaeus had forgotten that living beings mate and procreate. Indeed, what the body of the cosmos most resembles, among living beings and their parts, is the human head.[20] As Socrates presented the head of a discourse, so has Timaeus now presented a discourse of the head.

But Timaeus calls it a god, a god to be, a god who is to be made by the god who always is. Yet the cosmic body will not have been made a god until it is brought to life, animated, by the god who makes it. Thus, Timaeus tells how the artisan god set soul into body: he stretched soul throughout the whole of the cosmic body and also covered it with soul all around its outside. In this way he made one unique heaven, capable, because of its excellence, of keeping company with itself, needing no other, sufficing to itself as acquaintance and friend, generated thus as a blessed (εὐδαίμων) god.

One might have thought that the soul, brought into the body, would stretch the living being beyond itself, opening it to alterity, drawing it toward others to be consumed, loved, or conversed with, delivering it from the solitude of feeding on its own excrement, of feeling only itself, and of speaking only in monologue, as Timaeus himself is now speaking. Yet, as Timaeus tells the story, the soul came, instead, to be wrapped around the body in such a way as to conceal and enclose it, sealing it off all the more decisively in its self-enclosure. But Timaeus' way of telling the story does not go unremarked: no sooner has Timaeus told of how the soul comes to be in the body than he interrupts the discourse so as to turn it upon itself and declare its errancy. As, at an earlier point, he had taken care to mark distinctly an appropriate transition: in moving from the segment of his discourse in which the cosmos is first characterized as a living being to that segment in which the paradigm of the cosmos is determined, Timaeus doubles the discourse so as to submit it to a prescription. He says: "This being granted [or established: τούτου δ' ὑπάρχοντος], we must declare what comes next in order [ἐφεξῆς]" (30c). Thus Timaeus prescribes that the discourse is to be governed by a certain order, that order is to be observed as the discourse unfolds its story of how the god brought the visible from disorder into order. And yet, as

20. See Brague, "The Body of the Speech," 58.

soon as he finishes telling how the god made the body of the cosmos, Timaeus violates the proper order that the discourse ought to observe: he immediately sets about telling how the god set the soul in the body, *even though* he has said absolutely nothing about how the soul is itself made. Almost as if the soul were ready-made. Or as if it simply came from nowhere. Only after he has told how the soul is set into the body does Timaeus reveal that the soul too, like the body, was fabricated by the god. Only after the discourse has set it into the body does Timaeus go on to tell how the god made the soul; whereas, if the discourse had been properly ordered, he would have told of the fabrication of the soul before venturing his narrative on cosmic embodiment.

This is the disorder, the errancy, that Timaeus declares when he interrupts the discourse that has just set the soul in the body. Or rather, instead of simply making this disorder explicit, he indicates that the discourse is even more disordered than it might have seemed. Since the soul is to rule over the body, it is prior in excellence and birth; it is older than the body, that is, it must have been made first, before the god made the body. Hence, if the discourse were properly ordered, Timaeus would have told first how the soul was made, before then going on to tell of the fabrication of the body and of the joining of the soul to the body. But, instead, Timaeus has told *first* about the fabricating of the body, disordering his discourse from the beginning, from the point at which he began to address the cosmos in its specificity and as it would have been in the beginning. Timaeus has not—and indeed now declares that he has not—begun as he should have, has not begun at the beginning, has not made a proper beginning. To be sure, Timaeus ventures some compensatory moves: he launches an account of how the soul was made, detaching the soul, for purposes of this account, from the body to which his disordered discourse has just joined it, and then, once the account of the soul's fabrication has been completed, he tells, for the *second* time, how the soul and the body are brought together. Yet even these moves cannot compensate entirely for his not having properly begun; they cannot undo his having begun with the fabrication of the body. Despite the compensatory moves, he will nonetheless have begun otherwise than with the beginning, will have begun with what comes later, disordering the discourse, putting it ahead of itself. Eventually Timaeus will break off this discourse and launch a new beginning; then he will, though in a different sense, begin with the beginning or at least in its proximity, providing even a sort of retrospective vindication for having begun with the body, or rather, with the fire, air, water, and earth from which it is composed, even though it will still have been improper, within a discourse on the work of νοῦς, to have begun in this way. Indeed, in the present discourse (the first of Timaeus' three), at the point where it turns upon its own errancy, Timaeus can only appeal to the errancy of human discourse, declaring that it partakes of what is by chance and at random (προστυχόν-

τος τε καὶ εἰκῇ), just as we ourselves do. Exposed to chance and random-
ness, discourse is led astray and caused to wander errantly from the order
otherwise proper to it. As in Timaeus' discourse. Yet eventually, at the
point where Timaeus breaks off his first discourse and launches a new
beginning, he will address his discourse to this errant cause that will already
have led his discourse astray.

Now, as if turning back to an earlier beginning, one preceding the
installation of the soul in the body, if not also the fabrication of the body,
Timaeus tells from what and in what way the god made the soul of the cosmos: "In the middle between the being that is indivisible and is always
according to the same and that which is divisible and is generated in connection with bodies, he blended from both a third form of being [τρίτον . . .
οὐσίας εἶδος], that is, from the nature of the same and of the different; and
in this way he compounded it in the middle between that one of them that
is indivisible and that one that is divisible in bodies. And taking these
three beings, he blended them all into one form, joining by force the
nature of the different with that of the same, despite their being hard to
mix [δύσμικτον]. And mixing them with the being and having made
[ποιησάμενος] one out of three, he next went on to divide the whole into
as many parts as was appropriate, each having come to be (mixed) from
the same, the different, and the being" (35a–b).[21]

This account of the mixings by which the soul was made has been
called "the most perplexing and difficult passage of the whole dialogue."[22]
To be sure, it has been a subject of controversy throughout much of the
history of Platonism. Plutarch reports that even in the early Academy
there was disagreement and debate about it between Xenocrates and his
pupil Crantor, author of the first commentaries on the *Timaeus*. The
significance of the passage is indisputable: the entire discourse on the soul
flows from it and is determined by it. It constitutes a decisive step in the
unfolding of that apparent-yet-questionable distinction that structures the
entirety of Timaeus' first discourse, the twofold distinction between perpetual being and the generated. In view of the high stakes of the passage
and the persistent debate over it, any interpretation to be proposed will
require careful preparation and will gain in precision if not in force by differentiation from certain traditional interpretations. Even then, it cannot
but be hedged with uncertainties and reservations.

Three traditional interpretations bear consideration. The first, which

21. This translation follows the general lines of the version proposed by A. E. Taylor,
though with some variation in the particulars. Following Taylor, the words αὖ πέρι in 35a4
are omitted. Even Taylor seems less than certain whether in 35a5 one should read κατὰ
ταὐτά or κατὰ ταὐτα. From a certain interpretive point of view, the former has the advantage of suggesting, as Taylor notes, that the same and different of 35a4–5 are identical with
the indivisible and divisible of 35a5–6, though the other reading would not preclude this conclusion. See Taylor, *Commentary on Plato's Timaeus*, 107–109.
22. Ibid., 106.

can be extracted from Proclus' extended discussion of the passage, has been more recently proposed by Cornford.[23] This interpretation recognizes, as do most others, two major stages in the blending that produces the soul of the cosmos. Then, focusing on the first stage, the interpretation differentiates between three separate blendings: that of divisible and indivisible forms of being,[24] that of divisible and indivisible sameness, and that of divisible and indivisible difference. Cornford construes the distinction between divisible and indivisible as coinciding with that between perpetual being and the generated,[25] effectively reproducing in modern guise a move found in the *Enneads,* specifically in a text in which Plotinus cites from the very passage in question.[26] Following Proclus, Cornford also relates these blendings, though only loosely, to the passage in the *Sophist* (254b–257a) devoted to the greatest kinds, among which are being, sameness, and difference. The first stage of the blending mixes divisible and indivisible forms of each of these three so as to produce intermediate forms of being, sameness, and difference. At the second stage these three intermediate forms are then blended to form the whole, the one mixture, which will then be cut and shaped into the soul of the cosmos.

This interpretation is not without difficulties, two of which would seem to be decisive. First, it passes over the way in which the passage in its opening phrase connects the same with the indivisible; both belong together on the side of perpetual being. Thus, to suppose a divisible form of sameness is counter to what the passage says. The second difficulty is the complement of the first: by being connected to the generated and to bodies, the divisible is bound to difference. Indeed, it is the very character of difference to be the difference of something from something else, that is, to be dyadic and thus to involve division.

Plutarch's *On the Generation of the Soul in the Timaeus* begins by citing the passage in question and then observing that "to recount at present all the dissensions that these words have occasioned their interpreters is . . . an immense task."[27] Though sparing himself this task, Plutarch does mention two figures the explication of whose interpretations will provide something like a keynote (ἐνδόσιμος).

The first is Xenocrates, head of the Academy from 335 to 314 B.C. According to Plutarch's report, Xenocrates declared that "the being of the

---

23. Proclus, *In Platonis Timaeum Commentaria,* especially 2:137–38; Cornford, *Plato's Cosmology,* 59–66.

24. Cornford's translation of οὐσία as *existence* is a misleading anachronism, for the concept of existence in its intrinsic opposition to essence is decidedly post-Platonic. This is a prime instance of imposing back upon the Platonic texts a language and a conceptuality that first became possible on the basis of what was achieved in and through those texts.

25. In Cornford's anachronistic terminology, the distinction coincides with that between "the real 'being'" and "the 'becoming' of the things of sense" (*Plato's Cosmology,* 62).

26. The words cited are: περὶ τὰ σώματα (*Ennead* IV.2).

27. Plutarch, *On the Generation of the Soul in the Timaeus,* 1012d.

soul is number itself being moved by itself [τῆς ψυχῆς τὴν οὐσίαν ἀριθμὸν αὐτὸν ὑφ' ἑαυτοῦ κινούμενον ἀποφηνάμενος]."[28] Thus, in interpreting the passage in question, Xenocrates focused on the distinction between indivisible and divisible, assimilating this distinction to that between one (the indivisible unit of Greek mathematics) and multiplicity (which results from division, from repeatedly dividing in two) or, more precisely, between the one and the indeterminate dyad (ἕν/ἀόριστος δυάς). What Timaeus is thus taken to be describing in the passage in question is the derivation of numbers, the generation of them by the blending of the one with the indeterminate dyad, each ἀριθμός being, according to Greek mathematics, a number of ones. Yet the soul is not taken merely as number but as self-moving number, and this is why a second blending is required: the second blending mixes with number the ἀρχαί of rest and motion, namely, sameness and difference.

Over against Xenocrates' interpretation it would seem sufficient to cite Plutarch's own critical remark: "It is not the same, I think, to say that the soul is put together according to number and to say that its very being is number."[29]

According to Plutarch, a very different interpretation was put forth by Xenocrates' pupil, Crantor of Soli. In general, Crantor took the soul to be a mixture of the intelligible and the opinable-sensible nature. More specifically, he supposed the soul's peculiar function to consist in discriminating or judging (κρίνειν) regarding intelligibles and sensibles as well as regarding the samenesses and differences occurring in relation to these. Assuming that like is known by like,[30] he concludes that, in order that the soul may know—that is, judge—all, it has been blended together out of all, that is, from the intelligible and bodily and from sameness and difference.

In view of this interpretation let it suffice to remark that, though the intelligible is (at least in Plutarch's report) characterized as being according to the same (κατὰ ταὐτά), the intelligible and sameness are deployed as though they were simply two distinct moments that subsequently are mixed together in the formation of the blend. As in the other two interpretations, the mutual implication between the various oppositions goes unheeded. If, on the other hand, one acknowledges that the indivisible (one) *and* perpetual, selfsame being *and* sameness are bound together in their very sense, as are likewise their symmetrical opposites (the divisible *and* the generated *and* difference), then one will conclude that a mixing of one pair of opposites cannot but also mix the other pairs. In other words,

28. Ibid.
29. Ibid., 1013c–d.
30. This assumption is not explicitly stated by Plutarch. See Cherniss' note *e* to ibid., 1013a.

there are not multiple, parallel blendings in this sense (that is, of being, of sameness, and of difference); rather, these are only multiple facets of a single blending, the first of two stages in the composition of the soul of the cosmos.

Another interpretation may, then—with due reservations—be ventured. Its general schema is similar to that proposed by A. E. Taylor and, within a very different interpretive horizon, by Margel,[31] though there are differences in emphasis, in some specifics, and especially in the consequences that are drawn out. It is also similar to the interpretive schema proposed by the young Nietzsche in his Basel lectures on Plato.[32]

There are two stages in the blending that produces what will become the soul of the cosmos; these two stages, these two blendings, correspond to the two parts of the passage (the second part beginning with the words: "And taking these . . ."). In telling of the first blending, Timaeus in effect repeats the counting (1, 2, 3) with which the dialogue began. But he repeats it now as a counting of being or of kinds: he counts out the two kinds of being from which the god blended a third kind. First, there is perpetual being, which is indivisible and selfsame. Second, there is the generated, which is divisible and, as connected with bodies, incessantly differs from itself. From these two and in the middle between them, the god blended a third form of being (τρίτον . . . οὐσίας εἶδος). In a sense this forming of a third kind violates the twofold that governs the determination of ποίησις and that indeed has governed Timaeus' discourse on the production of the cosmos. And yet, since the third kind—*this* third kind— is merely blended from the other two and lies in the middle (ἐν μέσῳ), the twofold remains intact.

31. "Thus the operation the Demiurge is pictured as performing is clear enough. He first takes two ingredients A and B and by blending them produces an 'intermediate' C. He then makes a single uniform whole by blending A, B, and C and finally he divides that whole into a number of 'portions'" (A. E. Taylor, *Commentary on Plato's Timaeus,* 109). See Margel, *Le Tombeau du Dieu Artisan,* 82.

32. In the schematic representation in which Nietzsche casts his interpretation, the major distinction is between the two blendings. The first he characterizes as a blending of two elements so as to form a τρίτον οὐσίας εἶδος between these two; the second blending he describes as a blending of these two elements with the third that resulted from the first blending (Friedrich Nietzsche, "Einleitung in das Studium der platonischen Dialoge," in vol. II/4 of *Werke: Kritische Gesamtausgabe,* ed. Fritz Bornmann and Mario Carpitella [Colli-Montinari edition] [Berlin: Walter de Gruyter, 1995], 71). At the very end of his lectures, Nietzsche returns to this theme and presents the schema again in the following simplified form (ibid., 188):

Erste Mischung: ταὐτὸν θάτερον
                        \   /
                    τρίτον οὐσίας εἶδος

Zweite Mischung: ταὐτὸν ἡ οὐσία θάτερον
                        \ | /
                          Weltseele

Then, in telling of the second stage, the second blending, Timaeus again repeats the counting (1, 2, 3). Having told how the god blended the first and the second so as to form the third, Timaeus now tells of another blending in which these three were blended so as to form the mixture from which the soul of the cosmos is to be made: the god took the first kind (perpetual being, indivisible and selfsame), the second kind (the generated, divisible and self-differing), and the third kind that has been blended from the other two. "Taking these three beings," he blended them, mixing the nature of the same (the nature that is selfsame, the first kind) and the nature of the different (the second kind) with the being yielded by the previous blending (the third kind, in the middle).[33] Thus he made one out of three. As, in counting, 1, 2, 3, one gathers the three ones into the counting number (ἀριθμός), into the number 3.

There is a consequence to be drawn from this double counting of being, these countings by which Timaeus tells of the blendings in a way that reenacts them in discourse while also repeating the counting with which the *Timaeus* began. The consequence is decisive for the remainder of the dialogue, above all, for the chorology.

This consequence can be discerned in regard to each of the blendings but perhaps most readily in the second. In the second blending the god puts selfsame being, along with the other two kinds, into the soul of the cosmos, into the mixture that the god will then cut and shape into the cosmic soul. In this way selfsame being becomes part of the visible cosmos, one of the three components in the mixture. Timaeus is explicit that the soul, though itself invisible, belongs to the visible order, to the order of things generated: it is, he says, "the best of things generated" (37a). Thus it is indisputable: in being mixed into the soul mixture, selfsame being is incorporated into the visible cosmos. And yet, according to the opening distinction, selfsame being is set *over against* the visible, providing the intelligible paradigm on which the god set his gaze in making the cosmos. But it would seem, on the other hand, that the god's blending of the mixture has the effect of collapsing the distinction in such a way that nothing would remain outside the visible cosmos, not even the paradigm to which the god was said to look in making the cosmos. This would be the case *unless,* in being set into the visible cosmos, selfsame being also somehow remained over against it. The possibility of such a remainder would require that selfsame being be capable of *duplication,* that in being set into

33. For this interpretation of the second blending, two suppositions are essential. The first has been, to some degree at least, justified above: it is the supposition of mutual implication between the three pairs of opposites. This supposition allows one to interpret the expression "joining . . . the nature of the different with that of the same" as designating a mixing of the first kind with the second kind. The second essential supposition determines the reading of the expression "And mixing them with the being [μετὰ τῆς οὐσίας]": the supposition is, as A. E. Taylor proposes, that "τῆς οὐσίας = the οὐσία which has already been described as itself a blend of the other two factors" (*Commentary on Plato's Timaeus,* 109).

the cosmos it effectively *doubles itself,* remaining also over against the visible in such a way as to preserve the distinction.

The same consequence can be drawn in reference to the first blending. In this case selfsame being is blended with the generated so as to form a third kind; it is blended into the third kind. Yet it must also remain distinct from the third kind in order to mark the very distinction with respect to which the third is third, is in the middle; and it must remain distinct in order to be itself at the disposal of the god when he carries out the second blending.

In general, then, any blending of selfsame being will require *duplication of being* if the distinction is not to be collapsed and the very production of the cosmic soul disrupted. For there is no question but that the paradigm is to remain effective in the subsequent phases, for example, when the god comes to produce time in order to make the cosmos more like its paradigm. It must, therefore, be possible for selfsame being both to be set into the blend (indeed twice) and to remain as such outside the blend, outside the visible cosmos. Selfsame being must be capable of duplication, of being doubled within the visible, of having there its double.

And yet, though duplication of being must be possible, in another respect it is impossible. If being were doubled, then it would be two and divided rather than one and indivisible; and then it would be other than itself, different from itself, rather than selfsame. A kind of double bind (in a double sense) would seem inevitable: in order to preserve the distinction between selfsame being and the generated, there must be duplication of being; and yet, duplication of being has the effect of violating the very sense of selfsame being, its determination as such, thus eroding the very distinction that was to be preserved. Nonetheless, in Timaeus' account of the cosmic soul and indeed throughout the remainder of his first discourse, this consequence remains unformulated and out of play. It will come to exert its force only when, in his second, newly begun discourse, Timaeus introduces another counting of being, a different way of counting 1, 2, 3, a different way of counting to 3. In this other counting of being the third will prove to be, not in the middle between the two terms of the opening, twofold distinction, but rather—in the most decisive sense—*outside* the twofold in a manner that disrupts it abysmally.

Timaeus' account of what the god did next, after blending the soul of the cosmos, is itself blended into his account of the blending. Between two restatements concerning the blending, Timaeus inserts a general indication of what the god went on to form from the soul mixture that had been blended: ". . . and having made one out of three, he next went on to divide the whole into as many parts as was appropriate, each having come to be (mixed) from the same, the different, and the being" (35b). Timaeus describes with arithmetic precision how the god portioned out the whole, how he took from the mixture various arithmetically determined portions and then arranged them linearly in orderly, that is, harmonic, relations. In portioning out the mixture so as to form a long, harmonically articulated band, the god proceeded in what Timaeus articulates as three stages.

First, he took portions corresponding to squares and cubes in the odd and the even series of numbers. This double progression has traditionally been represented by a diagram in the form of a lambda:[34]

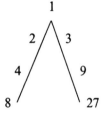

If arranged linearly, these two series generate the series:

$$1 \quad 2 \quad 3 \quad 4 \quad 8 \quad 9 \quad 27$$

At the second stage the god took further portions from the mixture so as to fill in the intervals. Specifically, he placed within each interval (a,b) two means (m):

(1) the harmonic mean, which corresponds to the musical interval of the fourth:

$$\frac{m-a}{a} = \frac{b-m}{b}$$

(2) The arithmetic mean, which corresponds to the musical interval of the fifth:

$$m - a = b - m$$

Inserting these means in the two series (odd and even) produces the following two series:

$$1 \quad 4/3 \quad 3/2 \quad 2 \quad 8/3 \quad 3 \quad 4 \quad 16/3 \quad 6 \quad 8$$

$$1 \quad 3/2 \quad 2 \quad 3 \quad 9/2 \quad 6 \quad 9 \quad 27/2 \quad 18 \quad 27$$

Omitting those that occur in both series and combining the two series:

$$1 \quad 4/3 \quad 3/2 \quad 2 \quad 8/3 \quad 3 \quad 4 \quad 9/2 \quad 16/3 \quad 6 \quad 8 \quad 9 \quad 27/2 \quad 18 \quad 27$$

The third stage involved filling the intervals that resulted from the

___

34. The tradition reportedly goes back to Crantor, who is said to have used this representation in his commentaries on the *Timaeus* (see A. E. Taylor, *Commentary on Plato's Timaeus,* 137).

insertion of the means, intervals of 3/2, 4/3, and 9/8. Timaeus explains, specifically, that wherever there was an interval of 4/3 (for example, between 4/3 and 1, between 2 and 3/2, between 4 and 3), the god filled it with 9/8 intervals. Thus, in the interval between 3 and 4 he inserted:

$$3 \times 9/8 = 27/8 \quad \text{and} \quad 3 \times 9/8 \times 9/8 = 243/64$$

Still another could not have been inserted, since:

$$243/64 \times 9/8 = 2187/512 > 4$$

As Timaeus points out, there was, then, a remainder, since the two intervals of 9/8 did not completely fill the interval between 3 and 4. This remainder is expressed by the ratio:

$$4/1 : 243/64 = 256/243$$

Timaeus notes that at this point the god had used up all the mixture from which he had been taking all these portions.[35]

Timaeus tells how the god took the harmoniously articulated band and formed it into the cosmic soul. First of all, he split it lengthwise. Then, joining the two bands at a point, he bent each of them around to the opposite point so as to form them into two intersecting circles. Each he set revolving uniformly (κατὰ ταὐτὰ καὶ ἐν ταὐτῷ); one band he made inner, the other outer. The outer revolution he called that of the same, the inner that of the different. The revolution of the same was made to go toward the right and to be horizontal; that of the different was made to go toward the left and was tilted so as to be at an oblique angle with the outer band. The inner revolution, that of the different, the god split in six places so as to form seven unequal circles, arranging these according to the double and triple intervals. Three of these were made to revolve at equal speeds, the other four at speeds equal neither to the other three nor to each other.

The revolution of the same corresponds to the sidereal equator. Thus, it represents the movement of the fixed stars, though it is a band or ring and not the sphere as a whole in which the stars are set. Timaeus mentions that to this revolution the god gave supremacy, that is, this revolution is such as to carry around everything in the cosmos. The revolution of the different, split into seven revolutions around the common center

---

35. See Cornford's account of the mathematical details of this section of the dialogue. In the course of that account, Cornford insists that "these considerations are concerned with theories about the nature of number and with the functions of the soul as a bond holding the world's body together; they have nothing to do with music" (*Plato's Cosmology,* 68). While he is no doubt correct that the concern here is not solely with musical theory, much less with music in a more practical sense, the enormous significance that will be ascribed to music at the very end of Timaeus' first discourse (47c–d) precludes dissociating the present passage entirely from its manifest reference to music.

and arranged according to the squares and cubes in the series of odd and of even numbers (thus: 1, 2, 3, 4, 8, 9, 27), represents the movement of the planets, including the sun and the moon, or rather, the second component of such movement (along with that of the same).[36] In all cases the circles in the cosmic soul represent only the motion or orbits of the heavenly bodies, *not* those bodies themselves, which only later will be placed in the orbits. Very shortly after his description of these circular bands that constitute the cosmic soul, Timaeus declares explicitly that, though the soul has been generated, it is invisible (36e). Thus, all the circular bands and their revolutions remain entirely unseen, invisible, until the god takes the decisive step of setting the heavenly bodies in these revolutions, in these orbits. Only then does it become possible to behold the starry heaven.

Timaeus marks the completion of the making of the soul: "And when, to the mind of its maker, the making of the soul had been completed, after that he fabricated within it all that is bodily, and, uniting them center to center, he fitted them together" (36d-e). Thus, for the *second* time in the discourse, the god sets soul and body together, center to center, weaving the invisible soul throughout the visible body of the heavens and, as previously, enveloping the heavens by wrapping the soul around its outside. Now it is that the discourse, setting the soul into the body for the second time, can declare the soul's proper beginning: the soul, "itself turning within itself, began a divine beginning of unceasing and mindful [ἔμφρων] life for all time" (36e). One could say that at this point—where it marks the beginning begun by the soul—Timaeus' discourse has in a certain respect caught up with itself, even though its arrival at this point cannot entirely compensate for his not having begun at the beginning. For the discussion has come back around to the point that previously was introduced out of order, in advance of its proper occurrence in the process of the god's fabrications. Now, as the god brings soul and body together for the second time, the discourse thus proves to have circled around to the same point; and, at the very moment when it has come to circle around to the selfsame point, Timaeus speaks of *time* (χρόνος), declaring that the life of the soul, thus properly begun, is a life for all time. In this movement the discourse enacts the very circling around to the same that will constitute the primary figure in the discussion of time that is almost ready to commence.

It is to the mind of its maker that the completion of the soul is mani-

---

36. According to Cornford, the three that revolve at the same speed are the sun, Venus, and Mercury. He observes too that the distances between these seven bands correspond in an unspecified way to the series 1, 2, 3, 4, 8, 9, 27. He continues: "The simplest view is that these figures measure the radii of the successive orbits: the radius of the Moon's orbit = 1, that of the Sun's = 2, and so on." Cornford also argues that there must be a third component determining the motion of some of the planets and that it is left unexplained (ibid., 72–93).

fest. The phrase κατὰ νοῦν can mean *to his mind* or *in his view*, and no doubt this signification is operative in the present passage; like any able artisan, the artisan god can discern the point at which his artifact is finished and thus is ready to be released from the productive process, beginning thus its subsistence as something produced. Yet the occurrence of this phrase at just this point—as marking this point—suggests, too, that in being brought to its completion the soul has been made in accord with νοῦς. Near the beginning of his discourse Timaeus declared that the production of the cosmos involves setting νοῦς into the soul and the soul into the body (29b). Now Timaeus has told—indeed one time too many—how the soul was set into the body. And, though he has stopped short of an explicit declaration, he has also indicated how in effect the god has set νοῦς into the soul. The god has done so in his very way of making the soul, and not only (as with any able artisan) by fabricating it in the image of an intelligible paradigm. He has also made it κατὰ νοῦν by portioning and shaping it according to purely noetic measures and relations, specifically, by the proportionality of the portioning and by the orderly arrangement and movement of the circles.

Timaeus' narrative has reached the point where the soul has been completed, embodied, and released into its beginning. At this point Timaeus mentions the proportionalities and circularities by which νοῦς has effectively been set into the soul. But now he mentions these as two of the three factors that make it possible for the soul to carry on discourse (λόγος). One is presumably to understand that the soul's being proportionally divided and bound together and its revolving upon itself prepare, respectively, the basis within the soul for the articulation that belongs to discourse and for the circling between saying and that about which something is said.

The third factor is mentioned first by Timaeus, and its role in making discourse possible is the most conspicuous in the immediately following discourse on the beginning of discourse. This other factor lies in the very composition of the soul, that it is compounded from the natures of the same and the different and from being (οὐσία), that it includes these three parts. Following the interpretation proposed of the passage on the composition of the soul, these three would consist of the nature of the same and of the different, each taken with all that is implicated in its very sense, and that third form of being (οὐσία) blended from them. These are the three that are then, in turn, blended, the god making one out of three, thereby composing the soul, which has then only to be portioned, shaped, and set in motion by the god.

Timaeus declares that when the soul touches something, whether it be something whose being is dispersed (σκεδαστός) or something whose being is indivisible, the soul is moved all through itself. Thus he traces at the very threshold of discourse the circularity that discourse will, from its inception, reenact. Being moved throughout itself, the soul says (λέγει) in what respect and how and in what sense and when it comes about that anything is either the same or different with respect to something, whether among generated things or among those that are ever selfsame (37a–b).[37] In this discourse (λόγος) the soul says the sameness and difference of various beings. Already with Crantor, it seems, this passage comes to be linked to an alleged general principle according to which like knows like.[38] And yet, it would be surprising if both this passage and by implication the earlier one on the composition of the soul were such as simply to presuppose such a general principle, even assuming that it is certain what would be meant by *generality* and *principle* in the context of the *Timaeus*, as if γένος—hence generality—and ἀρχή—hence *principio, principle*—were not utterly in question in this dialogue. Indeed, if *principle* is taken as beginning, then one could say that nothing is more thoroughly put in question in the *Timaeus* than presupposing a principle, that is, not beginning at the beginning.

Having within itself the natures of the same and the different as well as (a third form of) being, the soul can touch and be moved by things so as then to say the sameness and difference of those things. What is decisive in this inception of discourse is not the operation of some abstract cognitive affinity between like and like but rather the peculiar circularity that belongs both to discourse itself and to the comportment that, anterior to discourse, is assumed by it. This circularity is not unlike that which the dialogues sometimes address in more or less mythic fashion as recollection or remembrance (ἀνάμνησις). In touching beings that are the same as or different from other beings, the soul can be moved because these beings, in their samenesses and differences, draw out the being, sameness, and difference that lie within the soul; as by seeing two equal sticks one is led to recollect equality itself, which lay already within the soul. In touching things the soul can be moved because it is itself touched in turn, touched in such a way that something is drawn out of it. But what is, in the end, drawn out of the soul is not just being, sameness, and difference but rather a discourse in which these three are woven together, a discourse of which the soul is capable precisely because of the proportionalities and circularities that belong to it. And as the recollection of equality itself allows one to apprehend those things that are truly

---

37. The constructions in this passage present some difficulties, as noted by Cornford, *Plato's Cosmology,* 94 n. 4. See also A. E. Taylor, *Commentary on Plato's Timaeus,* 177f.

38. According to Plutarch, "Crantor and his followers . . . say that the soul, in order that it may know all, has been blended out of all" (*On the Generation of the Soul in the Timaeus,* 1013a). Aristotle, too, discussing the *Timaeus,* says that Plato holds "that like can only be known by like" (*On the Soul,* 404b). Cornford reaffirms this principle. He mentions that Albinus in his *Didascalicus* starts his account of the soul (of its composition according to the *Timaeus*) with "the principle 'Like knows like'" (Cornford, *Plato's Cosmology,* 64f. [see especially n. 3]).

equal, so does discourse, drawn out from the soul, have the power of saying truthfully (ἀληθής), hence disclosing, the samenesses and differences of beings.[39]

As the soul, though generated, is invisible, so is the discourse of the soul inaudible: it is a saying without voice (φθόγγος), without sound (ἠχή). Timaeus gives not the slightest indication that the soul's speech engages the body of the cosmos, which in any case lacks both the hearing and the respiration that voiced speech would entail (see 33c). The soul's speech is without body; it is a speech unburdened by somatic production and the audible products thereof, a speech less remote from what it says, less distant from what is said in the speech.[40] Or, more precisely, it is a speech that, unburdened by anything somatic, can say what is to be said; it is a speech in which what is said would come as near as possible (within the sphere of the generated) to that which is to be said, namely, the intelligible εἴδη, the noetic as such.

Timaeus hints at this proximity in his way of describing how this speech is carried out. When that about which something is said is the sensible (τὸ αἰσθητόν), then for such dispersed being it is the circle of the different that is engaged, that carries out the unvoiced speech, that proclaims it throughout the soul. But when that about which something is said is such that its being is indivisible, then it is the circle of the same that is engaged and that carries out the unvoiced declaration. What hints at the proximity is the word by which Timaeus at this point designates what otherwise is called indivisible or selfsame being: now he calls it the λογιστικόν, thus slyly substituting the designation of what is said for the designation τὸ νοητόν, which one would have expected in parallel with τὸ αἰσθητόν.[41]

Something issues from speech. Timaeus says that when the circle of the different proclaims what it says throughout the entire soul then opinions (δόξαι) and beliefs (πίστεις) are generated; more precisely, the circle,

---

39. Without attempting here to reconstitute the context in which the example of the equal sticks comes under discussion in the *Phaedo* (74a–75b), let it be noted merely that, as with the discussion of discourse in the *Timaeus*, the context is that of a discussion of the soul. The relevant circularity is perhaps nowhere more conspicuous than in this discussion of equality. On the one hand, says Socrates (in the interrogative form), it is in seeing such things as equal sticks that we come to a knowledge of equality itself (74b). But, on the other hand, we must have had knowledge of equality before the time when we first saw equal things and thought, "All these things are aiming to be like equality but fall short"; that is, we can apprehend the sticks as equal only if we possess already a knowledge of equality (75a). How little it is a matter of mere affinity between like and like is indicated by Socrates' remark at the beginning of this discussion: "Thus all these [examples] show that recollection comes from like things *and also from unlike things*" (74a—emphasis added).

40. Despite the very different contexts, this passage invites comparison with a passage in the *Theaetetus* in which Socrates describes thinking (διανοεῖσθαι) as "discourse [λόγος] that the soul sets forth to itself . . . , not by the voice [φωνῇ] but in silence [σιγῇ] with itself" (189e–190a).

41. Proclus observes that here λογιστικόν means, not the one who thinks or speaks, but that which is said or thought (αὐτὸ τὸ νοητόν) (*In Platonis Timaeum Commentaria*, 2:312).

moving aright (ὀρθός), generates through its speech opinions and beliefs that are firm and true. On the other hand, when the circle of the same, turning smoothly, declares what it says, then νοῦς and knowledge (ἐπιστήμη) result of necessity. Thus, the discourse of the cosmic soul does not express opinions or knowledge anterior to it but rather gives rise to them. First of all, the soul touches and is moved, then it speaks, and then from its speech opinions, knowledge, etc. result. Even νοῦς is such a result—that is, in and through discourse νοῦς as set into the soul is drawn out. The discourse of the soul makes manifest the νοῦς set into the soul.

It is as if in its discourse the soul, which has just undergone embodiment, were already unburdened, as if precisely in speech it could escape its entanglement with the body and take up its proper movement of ascent. And yet, in what Timaeus says, there is a hint that this ascent will not be unconditional or untroubled: for even in that proximity to the purely noetic in which the circle of the same would carry out its discourse, the νοῦς and knowledge that issue from this discourse are said to result from necessity (ἐξ ἀνάγκης). Even in the ascensional draft of νοῦς, in this work or deed of νοῦς, necessity will have been covertly implicated.

THE STARRY HEAVEN

A time of delight ensues. It is a time in which, moreover, a thought comes over the god, the thought of making his already delightful product an even better replica of its model. It is a time in which, too, like any good artisan, he goes on to produce what he has foreseen. In and through this production, time itself comes to be generated.

Yet, it is the figure, not of production, but of procreation that—initially at least—governs Timaeus' discourse on this time: when the father who had begotten it saw it in motion and alive (for it is a living being in whose soul the various circles have been set revolving), he was delighted with it. In particular, he was struck with admiration when he beheld it as a sanctuary (ἄγαλμα) generated for the everlasting (ἀίδιος) gods. The word that comes here to describe the cosmos, the word ἄγαλμα, can mean simply a thing of delight, for instance, a gift pleasing to the gods or a statue in honor of a god, hence, by extension, an image, though one of a special sort, an image embodying the god himself, an image in which the god would be present. But other senses resonate even more profoundly with Timaeus' discourse: that the word can designate the skull of an animal serves as a reminder that this living being, the cosmos, has the shape of a head (without trunk and limbs),[42] mirroring thus the heady character of the discourse itself. Most significantly, the word conveys the sense of sanctuary, of a sanctuary for

---

42. Rémi Brague, *Du Temps chez Platon et Aristote* (Paris: Presses Universitaires de France, 1982), 50.

the gods.[43] Precisely in the production that the god is about to initiate, he will bring forth everlasting gods and set them in this sanctuary that he has prepared for them. Only then will it become an image, though not of these gods but of something superior to them.

Timaeus continues: And being well-pleased, he thought of making it more like its paradigm. More precisely, the thought came over him, occurred to him (ἐπινοέω), in a sort of reflection through which a certain design unfolds before him.[44] Yet that design cannot but be limited, for the paradigm, the nature of living being, is eternal (αἰώνιος), whereas this character cannot be conferred completely on whatever is generated. It is this limited design, one suited to the cosmos as something generated, that now unfolds, first as a thought that comes over the god, and then as a productive—or procreative—deed. This unfolding is expressed in a celebrated passage that has almost always seemed so secure as to allow one to detach from it, with complete impunity, a formula definitively stating what Plato took to be the nature of time. Only recently has its aura of self-evidence been disturbed, largely through the work of Rémi Brague, so as again to open the passage to reinterpretation and to put in question the traditional formula that, almost from the beginning, has been extracted from it.

The following translation is set within this new opening, which puts in question the allegedly Platonic definition of time as the moving image of eternity: "The thought occurred to him of making a moving image of eternity; and in ordering the heaven he makes the heaven as an image of the eternity that abides in unity, an image moving according to eternal number, that which we call time" (37d).

Brague has shown that the traditional formula by which time is the moving image of eternity becomes current much later than might be supposed. In the earlier testimonies, those prior to Middle Platonism, it is not to be found; in particular, it is not cited by any of Plato's direct or indirect students, nor does it enter at all into the theories put forth by them. On the contrary, one finds time being characterized as the movement of the sun or of the universe as such. Even with Philo and Plutarch the doxographic formula is not yet in place. Only with Plotinus does the traditional definition come to be neatly formulated as expressing the Platonic view of time. Thus, it is only in the epoch of Middle Platonism that the traditional formula comes to be constituted as such.[45]

Several features of the passage itself make one hesitant to replace it

---

43. Margel translates ἄγαλμα as *sanctuaire* (*Le Tombeau du Dieu Artisan*, 92). Cornford translates it as *shrine* and notes that at this point the everlasting gods "have still to take their place in this vacant shrine" (*Plato's Cosmology*, 101). Brague observes: "The universe is the *sanctuary* [sanctuaire], and not the image, of the eternal gods" (*Du Temps chez Platon et Aristote*, 50).

44. Margel contrasts ἐπινοέω with νοέω. Whereas the latter refers to the lucid comprehension that has its object distinctly in view and that, more specifically, is in direct contact with the intelligible content it apprehends, ἐπινοέω expresses "*ce qui vient à* l'esprit; c'est ce qui lui arrive *après coup*, d'où la préposition ἐπι" (*Le Tombeau du Dieu Artisan*, 90).

45. Brague, *Du Temps chez Platon et Aristote*, 11–27.

with the traditional formula. To be sure, the initial clause invokes a moving image of eternity, though without yet mentioning time, leaving open the question whether this moving image of eternity is to be identified as time. The moving image of eternity is introduced as the object of the god's thought, of the thought that comes over him and unfolds a certain design before him. The thought is oriented to production: it is the thought of making a moving image of eternity.

What is to be understood here by the word αἰών? Is one compelled to translate it, without further ado, as *eternity?* The word can designate one's age or a lifetime. It can also signify a period of time of indefinite length, hence an age or a generation, and from this sense it can be extended to mean something like what one might understand as eternity, though normally these significations obtain only in cases where the noun is preceded by a preposition.[46] There are two adjectival forms corresponding to the noun: the common form ἀΐδιος, which has just been used to characterize the nature of living being, that is, the paradigm, and αἰώνιος, which is used in the celebrated passage and which does not appear prior to Plato. The precise sense of the latter is not sufficiently clear as such to necessitate translating it as *eternal.* The most appropriate way of determining the sense of these words is by adhering rigorously to the indication that the passage itself provides: according to what the passage says, it is a matter of the αἰών that "abides in unity [μένοντος . . . ἐν ἑνί]." In other words, αἰών is determined as an abiding in unity, as remaining within oneness, as something's remaining one and the same with itself, its being perpetually selfsame. If one agrees to retain the traditional translation of αἰών as *eternity,* one will need to insist that the word means—and only means—perpetual selfsameness. It is this sense alone that links the word to the noetic or intelligible. Most emphatically, one will need to keep the sense of αἰών distinct from that which *aeternitas* comes to have, for instance, with Augustine, that of a present that never passes, of eternal presence.[47]

The passage refers to two activities on the part of the artisan god: an *ordering,* a setting in order (διακοσμέω), and a *making* (ποιέω). The traditional construal takes these two activities to be distinct and to have distinct objects, even though they occur together, at the same time (ἅμα): what is set in order is the heaven, and what is made is the image of eternity, that is, time. But recent research has shown that a more natural construal of this portion of the passage would be: in ordering he makes the heaven.[48]

46. Ibid., 29.

47. Augustine writes: "As for the present, if it were always present and never moved on to become past, it would not be time but eternity" (*Confessions* XI.14). As he proceeds to determine time as *distentio animi,* reaffirming a transition, already effected in Middle Platonism, from the cosmological to the psychological order, Augustine engages and rejects the view of time that affiliates it with the heaven: "I once heard a learned man say that time is nothing but the movement of the sun and the moon and the stars, but I did not agree" (ibid. XI.23).

48. "The ancient readers . . . have chosen a construction less natural in order to be able to understand what they already supposed the text ought to contain. This construction sup-

Not only does this construal tend to break down the mutual distinctness of the two activities, but also it indicates that what the god makes is the heaven and not some image distinct from the heaven, not a distinct image that would then be identified as time. The word *image* is not, then, the direct object of the making, but rather it stands in apposition with *heaven,* that is, it explicates the character of the heaven as made by the god. One can go even further and construe the *heaven* as the object not only of the making but also of the ordering; the two activities would, then, prove to have the same object.[49] Indeed, the adverb ἅμα *(at once, at the same time)* suggests that the god's ordering of the heaven is the very same deed as that by which he makes the heaven as an image of eternity.

What, then, is the heaven that, almost as an afterthought, the god orders and makes? In a sense he has already fabricated the entire cosmos, shaping its body, fashioning its soul, and setting soul into body. Is the heaven anything other than the cosmos? To be sure, at the beginning of his discourse Timaeus identifies the heaven (οὐρανός) with the cosmos (κόσμος), that is, with the whole of the sensible universe (28b). Yet, earlier, in Critias' discourse (22d, 23d), the word οὐρανός clearly has its ordinary meaning: the heavenly vault, the sky, the heaven as distinct from the earth, hence not including the earth. It is this restriction that Timaeus removes when he identifies the heaven with the cosmos. Nonetheless, there are several passages later in Timaeus' first discourse where the word is again used in the restricted sense (39d, 47a–b). Also in the passage on time, if less manifestly, οὐρανός has primarily the restricted sense: it designates the sky considered especially as the region in which the movements of the heavenly bodies occur, the starry heaven.

This, then, is what the god makes at this stage: the starry heaven. In this production he takes over what has already been set in place: the body

poses that twice the direct object is placed after the verb that governs it, and separated from it, in the first case, by one word: διακοσμῶν ἅμα οὐρανόν, and by *eight* words in the second case: ποιεῖ μένοντος αἰῶνος ἐν ἑνὶ κατ' ἀριθμὸν ἰοῦσαν αἰώνιον εἰκόνα (37d6). It is known that in the epoch of Plato the normal order of a Greek sentence is: subject-object-predicate (verb). . . . And it is known that in Plato and the orators the order object-predicate has a significant preponderance. . . . On the other hand, the manner in which the beginning of the sentence is always articulated supposes the construction διακοσμῶν ἅμα οὐρανόν (present participle/adverb/object). This construction does exist, but it is rare. . . . In Plato, at least as far as we know, it is never found. On the other hand, there exists another construction, more frequent (we know of eight examples of it), in which the adverb 'at the same time' *follows* a present participle used absolutely. . . . Nothing forbids, then, thinking that this is the construction used in our sentence. Then it would have to be understood, for example, in this way: 'And, in carrying out his ordering activity, he made. . . .' Such a construction, besides the fact that it exists elsewhere in Plato, has the advantage of freeing the word 'heaven' and of allowing it to be attached no longer to the verb that precedes it, but, as is natural, to that which follows it. What the demiurge makes is the heaven and no longer the image that we call time" (Brague, *Du Temps chez Platon et Aristote,* 44–46).

49. Ibid., 47.

of the cosmos, especially its fiery part, which belongs to the upper region, and the soul of the cosmos with its still invisible circles that have been set revolving. To make the starry heaven, the god has then only to form the heavenly bodies, to set them in the orbits already determined by the circles in the cosmic soul, and to set them moving in these orderly movements. Thus it is that in one and the same act the god both makes the heaven and sets it in order. It is the ordered movement that is decisive: that Timaeus also lets the sense of οὐρανός expand so as to coincide with that of κόσμος is precisely a way of saying what the very word κόσμος already says: what makes the cosmos a cosmos is that its movements are ordered.

The moving image that the god makes is nothing other than the starry heaven, the stars (including also the sun, the moon, and the planets) in their ordered movement. By setting the stars in the various orbits determined by the revolutions in the cosmic soul, the god makes a visible image of the ordered revolutions in the soul; by making those revolutions visible, he, in turn, makes a moving, visible image of the noetic order that has been set into the soul. But, as noetic, as intelligible, that order is itself perpetually selfsame. In making the starry heaven, the god makes a moving image of eternity, of the eternity that abides in unity. The movement of this moving image is ordered, and as such it is a movement according to number.

In the traditional translation the passage also characterizes the image, which moves according to number, as an *eternal* image (using the adjectival form αἰώνιος, corresponding to αἰών). This characterization by which there would be an eternal image of eternity, by which, therefore, eternity would not be restricted to the side of the noetic, has troubled commentators and translators.[50] One might attempt to resolve the difficulty by noting that the stars are soon to be identified as heavenly gods and characterized as everlasting, their perpetuity being assured by the artisan god. But in this characterization the adjective used is ἀΐδιος (40b), not αἰώνιος as in the passage on time, whereas one would expect the explicit difference between the noetic and the heavenly gods to be expressed by a consistent distinction between the two adjectival forms, in which case αἰώνιος would be restricted to the noetic. Since this is not the case, granted the traditional construal of the sentence, the better approach is, it seems, that proposed—as a hypothesis—by Brague: one could construe the sentence in such a way as to attach the adjective *eternal* (αἰώνιος), not to *image* (εἰκών), but to *number* (ἀριθμός). Then one would translate (as above):

---

50. Cornford, for example, calls attention to this feature and in his translation relies upon a distinction that the text alone does not warrant: introducing a distinction between *everlasting* and *eternal*, a distinction that does not exist in the Greek text, he construes the sentence in such a way that image is an "everlasting image," whereas that of which it is an image is "eternity" (*Plato's Cosmology*, 98 [especially n. 1]).

"an image moving according to eternal number"—thus taking as eternal, not the image, but the number by which this image (the starry heaven) is governed in its movement.[51] Unlike the perpetuity of the starry heaven, of the heavenly gods, which must be guaranteed by the artisan god, the eternality of number is intrinsic and noetic in its constitution.

Regardless of how one deals with this difficulty, the sense of the passage remains intact. It says initially: the artisan god makes/orders the starry heaven by fashioning the stars and setting them in motion in the orbits already determined for them by the revolving circles in the cosmic soul. The passage continues with an appositive, the first appositive: thus he makes the heaven as an image of the eternity that abides in unity, an image moving according to number. Then it concludes by naming, finally, time, introducing it as a second appositive: that which we call time.

But what, then, is time? Granted the appositional structure of the passage, one can say: time is the same as the image, which is the same as the starry heaven. Thus, one can say, as does the traditional formula, that time is a moving image of eternity—but only on the condition that one also say that time is the same as the starry heaven. As the image of eternity, time is nothing other than the starry heaven. In the definition that Brague proposes: time "is the movement of the heaven as governed by number." Or, echoing Timaeus himself: the starry heaven is "that which we call time." Nothing would prevent accentuating the *we,* the *we call,* so as to regard *time* as the name that mortals give to that which in a more proper speech, a language of the gods, would be named *heaven-moving-according-to-number.*[52]

Yet how, more precisely, is the apposition to be understood? How is it that time—at least what we call by the name *time*—is the same as the starry heaven? For, even as one affirms their sameness, a differentiation—marked by the two names—will have been at work.

Timaeus says that time was generated along with the heaven (μετ' οὐρανοῦ), that time and the heaven were generated simultaneously, at the same time (ἅμα), so that if ever they were to undergo dissolution, they would be dissolved at the same time (38b). Yet this togetherness cannot be a simple simultaneity: the ἅμα must designate a togetherness irreducible to temporal simultaneity, since what is here marked, the very generation of time, is the event with which simultaneity first becomes possible. It is like the *before* (πρό) that Timaeus will use later in speaking of the state of things "before the generation of the heaven" (48b); since this state would also precede the generation of time itself, its precedence is irreducible to mere temporal antecedence.

Yet, even before Timaeus speaks so explicitly of this togetherness as such, indeed immediately following the celebrated passage, he tells how

---

51. Brague, *Du Temps chez Platon et Aristote,* 65f.
52. Ibid., 61–63.

the god made time along with the heaven. In his account of this double fabrication, too, the word ἅμα marks the togetherness, the sameness: "For there were no days and nights and months and years before the generation of the heaven; but he contrived that they should come to be at the same time [ἅμα] that the heaven was composed. All these are parts of time [μέρη χρόνου]" (37d–e). Thus, in making the heaven, the god made, at the same time, the parts of time, that is, days, nights, months, years. But, as Timaeus goes on to explain, in order to make these parts of time—and hence, presumably, the whole of time—the god had to make the heavenly bodies whose movements measure out and make visible these parts of time: "In order that time be generated, the sun and moon and five other stars—wanderers [πλανητά], as they are called—were generated for the determination and guarding of the numbers of time. And when the god had made the bodies of each of them, he placed them in the orbits along which the revolution of the different was moving, seven orbits for the seven bodies" (38c–d). The revolutions of these seven bodies together with that of the fixed stars turning in the circle of the same measure out the parts of time. This is why Timaeus calls the stars the instruments of times (ὄργανα χρόνων) (41e) and the instruments of time (ὄργανα χρόνου) (42d). The revolution of the fixed stars generates day and night, the revolution of the moon measures out months, and that of the sun determines year. Timaeus notes that the revolutions of the other heavenly bodies also measure out parts of time, though men have not discovered them and thus have no names for them. Timaeus mentions a kind of whole of time, the complete number of time (ὁ τέλεος ἀριθμὸς χρόνου) or complete year, which would have elapsed when all the heavenly bodies come back to the same position, when all the revolutions finish together.

Yet, still, what is time? Timaeus answers this question directly in the passage in which he refers to those revolutions of which men are unaware, those parts of time for which they have no names. He says: "They do not know that the wanderings [πλάναι] of these bodies is time" (39d). What decisively determines time—these wanderings—as the moving image of eternity is not just that the measuring out of time exemplifies certain arithmetic orders that are themselves noetic. Rather, what is decisive is, as Timaeus openly declares, that time "imitates eternity and circles around according to number" (38a). Time involves circling around to the same, as the sun circles around the earth each day but also, more decisively, as it returns annually, in its circling, to identically the same circle (so that what the sun preeminently measures out is the year). Whereas the eternal is perpetually the same and eternity (αἰών) is precisely this remaining always selfsame, the heavenly bodies always *circle back to the same,* and time is precisely these circlings, these wanderings.

This is what time is. Or this is the closest the *Timaeus* comes to an answer to the question: What is time? If this answer seems still insufficient, merely identifying time with the stellar wanderings from which, nonetheless, one would also somehow have to distinguish it, this insufficiency may be taken to indicate the insufficiency, even the inappropriateness, of the question. For in asking "What is time?" one asks about the proper of time without asking also whether time is such as to have a proper, an itself. Or, translating back into Greek, the question "What is time?" presupposes that time is such as to have a *what*, an εἶδος. Does time have an εἶδος, as a stone may be said to have an εἶδος, a look, that shines through it, in it, from it, when, for instance, it shows itself protruding from the earth into brilliant sunlight? Or does the name *time* not serve to say how the starry heaven is an image, not just of some εἶδος or other, but of the eternity, the perpetual selfsameness, that belongs to every εἶδος as such? Does the name *time* not then say how the starry heaven is, in precisely this sense, the image of all images: that it is such by means of the visible circlings that measure out the parts of time, even if never time itself? Like the name χώρα, the name *time* (χρόνος) would say something about the possibility of images rather than designating an εἶδος of which certain things would be images.

Timaeus continues: in order that there be a bright, brilliant measure (μέτρον ἐναργές), in order that the heavenly measure, the measuring out of the parts of time, be visible, the god kindled a light in the second orbit from the earth, that which we now call the *sun,* to shine throughout the entire heaven. Thus, the god not only sets νοῦς into the cosmos, fashioning there exemplifications and imitations of the noetic, but also, as it is set there in the midst of visible things, it is *lighted up,* made bright, so that it can be beheld by those living beings within the cosmos who themselves possess νοῦς. Timaeus says: the god kindled a light "that all living beings to whom it was fit might partake of number, learning it from the revolution of the same and like" (39b). Within the cosmos there is not only the noetic (as, most notably, intelligible order) but also, through its manifestness, an evocation of the exercise of νοῦς.

In order for the cosmos to be like its paradigm, it must, as a living being, contain the full range of living beings that νοῦς can discern in the paradigm of living being; it must be made to contain all four kinds to be discerned in the noetic model, not only the heavenly kind of gods, but also those beings that traverse the air, those that inhabit the water, and those that go about and live on dry land (corresponding thus to fire, air, water, and earth). The first kind, the divine kind, the artisan god made for the most part from fire, so that they might be as bright as possible. He made them spherical, that is, determined by sameness and, hence, in the image of selfsame being; and he made them revolve uniformly while circling in one of the great circles. These "divine and everlasting [ἀΐδιος] living beings" are the stars and planets (40b).

Timaeus says that the god also made the earth as the guardian and crafter (δημιουργός) of day and night, also as the first and eldest of the gods generated in the heaven. At this point the sense of *heaven* (οὐρανός) clearly expands: now it designates not only the starry heaven above but also the earth below. But it is not evident how the earth can be said to be older than the other heavenly gods such as the sun, moon, and planets, which are also required for guarding and crafting time. It would seem that all these guardians and crafters of time would have been made at the same time, at the same time as time. If, on the other hand, the earth is somehow older, then the discourse will again have proved (as with the body and soul of the cosmos) to be disordered: if the earth is older, it should have been told of first, at least if one is to adhere to the injunction that one is to begin at the beginning. If the earth is older, then it must precede the making of the starry heaven (with a precedence irreducible to temporal antecedence); it must have been *before* the generation of the heaven, and it will have turned out that Timaeus' discourse on the starry heaven comes to an end by turning back to an earlier beginning. This palintropic turn would thus anticipate the turn of the same kind that will be made in the transition from Timaeus' first to his second discourse, which begins—and says that it begins—with a turn back to the state of things "before the generation of the heaven" (48b). Thus it would seem not entirely fortuitous that the earth is called the *nurse* (τροφός) (40b), a name that, much later in the *Timaeus* (88d), will be brought to bear on the χώρα.

On the other hand, there is indeed a discourse in which the earth is said to be the oldest, preceded only by χάος, namely, Hesiod's *Theogony:* "First of all chaos came into being, but next wide-bosomed earth, the ever-sure foundation of all. . . . And earth first bore starry heaven, equal to herself, to cover her on every side and to be an ever-sure abiding place for the blessed gods" (116–17, 124–26). In effect, then, Timaeus' discourse, in its insistence on the precedence of the earth, links up with the traditional μῦθος. And just at this point where it touches on the traditional stories of the gods, Timaeus marks a certain conclusion: "But let this suffice for us, and let our talk [εἰρημένα—thus he avoids both λόγος and μῦθος] about the nature of the visible and generated gods have an end" (40d).

GODS AND MORTALS

Yet there are other gods, other than the visible and generated gods who perform their choral dance (χορεία) in the starry heaven. It is of these other gods that the poets sing. It is of these other gods that Hesiod tells, of their parentage and their birth. And it is of these gods that Timaeus now begins to speak, now that his discourse on the earth has touched on the traditional μῦθοι. Indeed he calls them "the other gods," marking the difference by using the name δαίμων instead of θεός.

With apparent irony he says that discovering their genesis is too great a task, that we must trust those who have made declarations about these other gods. Timaeus observes that those who have made such declarations are, as they themselves affirm, the descendants (ἔκγονοι), the children, of the gods. The irony becomes unmistakable as he continues: even though what these descendants say lacks demonstration (ἀπόδειξις), we must believe them because they are telling of family matters, of things that are οἰκεῖος, that have to do with the home, the household, one's own family. The difference is evident: these other gods and their descendants who tell of them have to do with the order of the household, of family, of descent, of lineage, whereas the heavenly kind of gods are made by the divine artisan, hence arise from the order of production.

Following—or pretending to follow—what their descendants declare, Timaeus proceeds to recite a genealogy of these other gods. He offers a kind of imitation of the Hesiodic theogony: it begins with Earth and Heaven and traces the generations up through Zeus and Hera, referring then also in general to their descendants, including, by implication, those who declare such genealogies. What is most curious is that in this story of the seemingly continuous succession of generations there is an error, a discontinuity. It is said that from Oceanus and Tethys were born Phorcus, Cronos, and Rhea, among others. However, according to Hesiod, Phorcus was not born of Oceanus and Tethys but rather was the offspring of the sea-god Nereus and Earth.[53] Furthermore, he mated with his sister Ceto (whose name suggests sea-monster [κῆτος]) and fathered monsters such as the Gorgons and, in particular, Medusa.[54] In general, Phorcus was regarded as the father or leader of sea-monsters.[55] Thus, in the genealogy that Timaeus presents, something strange, indeed monstrous, turns up: in the otherwise continuous succession of generations, there is an unannounced moment of monstrosity. The genealogy has the effect of reinscribing the question of procreation, birth, ἔρως, of reinscribing it in the form—or in the deformation—in which it broke out in and around the Socratic discourse on the city. Over against the traditional stories alleged to be the proper legacies of the descendants, over against the stories of a continuous and predictable succession of generations, Timaeus' genealogy is one in which the order of generation and birth is burdened with discontinuity and unpredictability.

This entire portion of the *Timaeus* is manifestly woven between the poles of the opposition between the order of production and that of ἔρως, of procreation, birth, generation, most generally, of φύσις. Thus there are the heavenly kind of gods, who are produced by the divine artisan, and the other gods, who are told of in stories of their parentage and birth. Curiously, in the speech that the artisan god himself is about to address to all the gods, he names himself in a way that is indicative of both orders: he

53. Hesiod, *Theogony*, 237–39.
54. Ibid., 270ff.
55. *Oxford Classical Dictionary*, s.v. "Phorcys."

calls himself both artisan (δημιουργός) and father (πατήρ) (41a). And a little later, at the very threshold of birth, just before the heavenly gods form the mortal bodies and bind in them the souls of the other kinds of living beings, Timaeus refers to the artisan god as father and to the heavenly kind of gods (the stars) as his children (42e). The implication is that, even though the god is preeminently an artisan who makes the cosmos, he cannot carry out this production without also coming into relation with the other order, that of procreation and birth, which is also the order of the generations and the disorder of monstrosity.

Immediately following the genealogy, the discourse doubles up into a discourse on a discourse, a speech within the speech: Timaeus tells about what the artisan god told all the gods in an address delivered to them. It is as if, once all had come to be born, they were assembled before the divine artisan. He speaks to them of birth and death. He makes a promise to them and refers to his will as surety that the promise will be kept. Specifically, he tells the gods—both kinds are there, listening—that because they are born or generated, their bonds are not indissoluble; they are not immortal. This declaration, were it to go unqualified, would border on outrage, at least for the traditional gods, who share the principal epithet *immortal* (ἀθάνατος). But the artisan god goes on to offer his promise, the promise that, by his will (βούλησις), he will separate birth from death, divide natality from mortality, shelter them from having to die by virtue of having been born. Although their natality exposes them to death, he assures them that they will not incur the doom (μοῖρα) of death; for, he says, his will will bind each of them together indissolubly, more securely than the bonds by which they were bound together at birth.[56] Such is the promise he gives—before then instructing the gods that they are to receive from him the immortal souls of the other kinds of living beings, which they are then to bind into mortal bodies that they will fabricate, imitating the god's fabrication of themselves. Here his speech ends—that is, it gives way to the deed of attending to birth, to the birth of the other kinds of living beings.

Timaeus describes the manner in which the god set about this deed: from the mixing bowl used previously he took the residue of the soul mixture and divided it into souls equal in number to the stars; then he assigned each to a star and, setting each of them in a chariot, he showed

---

56. For Margel's interpretation of the *Timaeus* as a whole, this promise has enormous significance. A brief excerpt: "Lacking the power to assure to the world a genetic autonomy of conservation, the demiurge will now engage his speech; he *will promise* the world that he will never break the bonds that order it mimetically with reference to the ideality of the model. This last gesture, this gesture of *promise* developed from 41b, will constitute both a salutary act and the most radical idleness [*désoeuvrement*] of the demiurge" (*Le Tombeau du Dieu Artisan,* 56). On the other hand, one might suppose that an even more radical idleness comes over the god at the beginning of the second discourse, an idleness so radical that the god is completely absent from the scene.

them the nature of the universe (τὴν τοῦ παντὸς φύσιν) (41d-e).[57] Then, again, the discourse doubles up, though now indirectly: Timaeus reports what the god said to the new souls in declaring to them the laws of destiny, the laws concerning what is allotted, what one receives as one's portion. The god declares—Timaeus says that he declared—that what they receive depends entirely on whether they master the violent affections, the disorder, to which they will be exposed when, of necessity (ἐξ ἀνάγκης), they are set into their bodies, that is, born. Then, once again, the discourse shifts: whereas Timaeus has just been telling what the god foretells about birth, now Timaeus tells directly of that birth. He tells how the children of the artisan god put together bodies from portions of fire, air, water, and earth borrowed from the cosmos and how they then bound the revolutions of the soul within these bodies, as within a "mighty river" (43b), in the midst of disorder.

In these discourses on the disorder to which mortals are exposed at birth, there seems to be a certain disorder. Having told of the disorderly movements in the newly born, Timaeus then draws a contrast between those whose inner revolutions come to be correctly ordered and those in whose souls the movements remain disorderly. The disorder in the discourse has to do with these disorderly ones, with those whose souls remain disorderly. Timaeus says of them: they "return unperfected and unmindful [ἀνόητος] to Hades" (44c). Yet, as soon as he says this, he interrupts the discourse and says: "These things, however, come about later." He does not say why. Yet, by drawing attention to this apparent disorder, he hints at another, prompts one to notice it: for there is a disorder between this account (by which the disorderly souls return to Hades) and another account, a bit earlier. In the earlier account (42a-b) reference is made to sexual difference, to the superiority of the male sex, and then, among the laws of destiny being shown to the new souls, the following is mentioned: that those who fail to master their disorder "will be changed into woman's nature at the second birth" (42b; see also 91a). What, then, is the fate of those who remain disorderly? Do they return (unperfected and unknowing) to Hades or do they get reborn as women? Or do they return to Hades and then get reborn in female bodies? In this case would it not have been more in order for Timaeus to tell *first* of the return to Hades *and then* of rebirth in the body of a woman—even granting the difference of level between the two discourses, the first reporting the laws of destiny declared to the new souls, the other narrating the course of that destiny and getting

---

57. The passage invites comparison with the passage in the *Phaedrus* where Socrates introduces the image of a chariot, likening the soul "to the union of powers in a team of winged steeds and their charioteer" (246a). Especially pertinent is the description that Socrates gives of the banquet in which the chariots pass in procession up through the heaven until they come to feast on the vision of being itself (246e-247e). See my extended discussion of this passage in *Being and Logos,* 140-53.

to that extent ahead of itself, provoking, so it seems, the interruption in the discourse? In any case, the discourse does not, as a well-ordered discourse presumably should, express the relation between these two destinies. Are they simply to be conjoined extrinsically? Or is there some intrinsic connection between returning in a disorderly condition to Hades and being reborn into the body of a woman? What do female bodies have to do with the shades of Hades?

After a brief discussion of the human body, including the comedy of the head trying to make its way over the heights and out of the hollows, including also a discussion of vision, Timaeus concludes by speaking of the greatest good of vision and of hearing. He says that it is the vision of the heaven, of day and night and months and circling years, that has endowed us with number and with the thought of time, as well as furnishing us the means of inquiring about the nature of the universe. From these has come philosophy itself. As Timaeus remarks, man has been enabled thus to give such accounts as he himself has just been giving; hence, at this point the discourse comes to expose its own precondition.

But what is the good of attending to things in the heaven rather than, for instance, human actions in the city? The good, the greatest good, of vision is that by beholding the noetic revolutions in the heaven we might then make the revolutions within ourselves imitate those celestial revolutions. It is a matter of mimesis between the human soul and the cosmos, of imitating within oneself the order beheld in the heaven above, of making the order within be like that of the starry heaven above. Timaeus adds that hearing serves the same good in relation to speech (λόγος) and in relation to music the harmony of which can serve to restore the harmony in the soul. Thus Timaeus comes around to speaking of music in what is virtually a song in celebration of celestial mimesis. His first discourse concludes with this song, celebrating the mimesis in which one would look to the heavens and produce in one's soul an image of the orderly revolutions seen above. In such mimesis one would also be imitating the artisan god: just as he looks to the noetic paradigm so as to produce in the cosmos an image of it, imaging it preeminently by the orderly movement of the starry heaven, so through the vision of that orderly movement above one would produce an image of it in one's soul.

As this song is heard, there is only the slightest dissonance. The dissonance comes from the brief mention, just before the song broke out, of something else that is involved in the divine and human production oriented to the intelligible paradigm, something very different, something scarcely noticed. Timaeus has just been discussing vision. His discourse pictures the eyelids closing in sleep and evokes the images (φαντάσματα) formed in dreams. Thus he is led to speak more generally about images. And though he observes that it is not difficult (χαλεπόν) to understand the making or formation of images (εἰδωλοποιία) in mirrors and other surfaces (46a), the discussion into which Timaeus is led through the question of image-making will prove to have imaged from afar the problem of image-making as it will arise in the second discourse, the problem of the very possibility of images, a problem that, to say the least, will prove difficult.

In discussing the formation of images in mirrors and other surfaces, Timaeus begins to speak of another kind of cause, causes that are auxiliary, accessory, secondary (ξυναιτία), causes that operate along with the primary, paradigmatic causes. He mentions cooling and heating, solidifying and dissolving; and in his account of vision he has just described how the fire of vision coalesces with the fire arising from the visible thing. Such causes, he says, are incapable of having νοῦς: only a soul can have νοῦς, not such visible bodies as "fire and water and earth and air" (46d). Thus, on the one hand, the primary causality has set νοῦς into the soul and the soul into the body, thus embodying νοῦς in the cosmos as intelligible order and as the time that images the eternity of the noetic. But there is also operative an auxiliary causality that has no connection with νοῦς. And even the greatest good made possible by the embodiment of νοῦς, namely, the vision of the orderly movement of the starry heaven—even this requires the operation of this other kind of cause, this anoetic causality.

This dissonance of the anoetic, resounding in the very moment of the upward vision with which Timaeus' first discourse ends, announces that this end is more properly an interruption. It announces also, in the names *fire, water, earth,* and *air,* that to which Timaeus will of necessity turn back in launching his second discourse. Yet even before he turns to what these names would—but in the end cannot—name, he calls the other causality, the anoetic causality, by a name that has by no means been absent in the first discourse but that comes into its own only at the moment when Timaeus launches another, a second discourse: the name *necessity* (ἀνάγκη).

3

The Χώρα

ANOTHER BEGINNING

Interruption appears doubly at this juncture. It enters doubly into the discourse, dividing the discourse at the very moment that it becomes the theme of the discourse. For the discourse is interrupted in order to be redirected toward that which can and indeed does interrupt the very workings of νοῦς to which Timaeus' discourse has in large part been addressed up to this point of interruption. Timaeus marks the interruption, the juncture: whereas the foregoing speech, except for a small part, has set forth the works crafted by νοῦς, now a discourse is to be furnished on what is generated by necessity (ἀνάγκη). For, he continues, the generation of the cosmos came about as a mixture from the combination (σύστασις) of νοῦς and ἀνάγκη. It was for the most part a matter of νοῦς ruling over, governing, ἀνάγκη, persuading it. Thus it was that the universe (τὸ πᾶν) was made in the beginning (κατ' ἀρχάς), namely, in such a way that the greatest part of the things generated were led toward what is best. Timaeus concludes that if it is to be told how the universe was thus generated, then the errant form of cause (τὸ τῆς πλανωμένης εἶδος αἰτίας) must also be brought in (47e–48a).

In referring to what was produced, crafted, by νοῦς, Timaeus uses a form of δημιουργέω: to make, craft, produce by way of τέχνη, through ποίησις. The word makes it explicit that Timaeus is speaking of the cosmic ποίησις carried out by the artisan god, who has repeatedly been called δημιουργός. But why does Timaeus describe the products as works crafted by νοῦς? Again it is the structure of ποίησις that is being adumbrated: ποίησις depends on looking to an intelligible paradigm, which is accessible only to intellectual or noetic vision, that is, to νοῦς. Indeed, what forms the very center of the structure of ποίησις is this noetic vision of the paradigm, as an image of which the product is then brought forth. Moreover, as overseen by νοῦς, the crafting of the cosmos not only produces an image of the paradigm but also, in a distinctive way, installs νοῦς in the cosmic soul and thus in the cosmos as such. By his reference to such production as a crafting by νοῦς, Timaeus emphasizes the centeredness of the making in noetic vision while also alluding to the installation of νοῦς in the cosmos.

But what is this other kind of cause that Timaeus now finds it necessary to introduce? At the end of the first discourse its sense was determined almost entirely by its opposition to the noetic kind of cause, and it entered as hardly more than a dissonance haunting Timaeus' song in celebration of celestial mimesis. But what is this necessity that it is necessary to introduce, this necessity that compels its very entrance into the discourse? What is this errant form of cause—assuming for the moment something that will eventually prove highly questionable, namely, that ἀνάγκη can be made to submit to the question "τί ἐστι . . . ?", that one can fittingly interrogate ἀνάγκη by asking about its *what?* Contrasting ἀνάγκη with the operation of νοῦς that forms the central structure of cosmic ποίησις, Timaeus speaks, not of what is produced by ἀνάγκη, but rather of what is generated. A clue to the appropriate sense is provided by a passage in the *Laws* in which ἀνάγκη is linked with *chance:* as the Athenian is discussing fire, water, earth, and air (precisely that which Timaeus is about to discuss), he observes that the way they move and interact is according to chance from necessity (κατὰ τύχην ἐξ ἀνάγκης), as opposed to things that are determined by τέχνη (*Laws* 889c).[1] Thus, if one is to translate ἀνάγκη as *necessity,* it must be insisted that this necessity is not the necessity of law, that it is not that form of necessity to which one would refer in describing something as bound by law. It is rather a necessity that would operate outside the law, that would even determine this very outside; this necessity would be an outlaw eluding the noetic supervision that determines the lawfulness of ποίησις, resisting the rule of νοῦς even if responsive to its persuasion.[2] This necessity is also called the *errant* form of cause. The verb πλανάω means: to lead astray, mislead, lead into error. In the passive and middle forms it means: to wander, roam about,

---

1. In this passage chance is conjoined not only with necessity but also with nature (φύσις). Indeed the Athenian declares, first of all, that fire, water, earth, and air are said to be by nature and chance, and not by τέχνη. Then he adds, as if in apposition, the description of them as moving and interacting according to chance from necessity.

2. A. E. Taylor stresses that ἀνάγκη is not "scientific necessity" or "the reign of law," since it is "the πλανωμένη αἰτία, the 'rambling' or 'aimless' or 'irresponsible' cause." He says: "Thus it is not the 'necessary' but the 'contingent,' the things for which we do not see any sufficient reason." However, he regards this contingency as resulting only from the limitation of human knowledge: "If we could ever have complete knowledge, we should find that ἀνάγκη had vanished from our account of the world" (*Commentary on Plato's Timaeus,* 300f.). While agreeing with Taylor that ἀνάγκη is to be distinguished from law, Cornford recognizes how far the *Timaeus* is from declaring ἀνάγκη to be merely a residuum of unexplained facts to be reduced to nothing once complete knowledge is attained. Cornford cites a

stray. It can mean even: to err—a πλάνη can be an erring or an error. The πλάνητες are wanderers, especially those that wander in the heaven, the planets. In translating the participial form (πλανωμένη) as *errant,* the word is to be heard in the double sense of *wandering* (hence, as involving indeterminacy, as outside—or at least resistant to—the supervisory governance by a paradigm) and of *erring* (in the sense not so much of committing an error but rather of that which makes error in the usual sense possible, as, for instance, being deceived about something can lead one to make an error in dealing with it).[3]

Thus was the cosmos generated in the beginning: from the combination of νοῦς and ἀνάγκη—or rather, giving the word σύστασις its full force, from a *standing together* of νοῦς and ἀνάγκη, not only in the sense of their meeting, their being joined together in a kind of union, but also in a sense involving hostility, as when two soldiers stand together face to face in battle, in close combat with one another.

Timaeus continues: "Thus going back to this and taking up another beginning (ἑτέραν ἀρχήν) that is suitable to these same matters, now again we must begin from the beginning regarding these things, as we did formerly regarding those" (48a-b). Thus, another beginning is to be made, an other beginning, a different beginning, different from the beginning with which Timaeus began his first discourse. Now the beginning will not be made by posing—even if as a question and an opinion—the distinction between that which perpetually is and that which is generated. Nor will Timaeus begin now by telling how the god took over the chaotic whole of the visible so as to set it in order. For merely to tell about how this was *taken over* is not yet to begin at the beginning.

A different beginning is now required, was indeed already required from the beginning if the injunction to begin at the beginning was to be heeded. Now Timaeus gestures in the direction of the palintropic move required: "We must bring into view the nature itself of fire, water, air, and earth before the generation of the heaven and what befell them. For as of

---

formulation by Grote: "This word (necessity) . . . is now usually understood as denoting what is fixed, permanent, unalterable, knowable beforehand. In the Platonic *Timaeus* it means the very reverse: the indeterminate, the inconstant, the anomalous, that which can be neither understood nor predicted." Against Taylor, Cornford insists "that the body of the universe is not reduced by Plato to mere extension, but contains motions and active powers which are not instituted by the divine Reason [thus Cornford ventures to translate νοῦς] and are perpetually producing undesirable effects" (*Plato's Cosmology,* 171-76).

3. In the *Laws* a certain semantic affinity is posed between errancy (as wandering) and the word (if it be a word) χώρα, which will finally name that to which the discourse on ἀνάγκη will lead. But in the *Laws* this affinity is posed at a level that, in relation to that of the *Timaeus* and especially of Timaeus' second discourse, can hardly be more than prephilosophical. The subject is the krupteia ("secret service"), which is said to afford wonderfully severe training in endurance, as those involved go barefoot in winter and "wander [πλανωμένων] throughout the whole countryside [χώρα] both by night and by day" (*Laws* 633c).

now no one has ever disclosed their generation, but we speak as if men knew what fire is and each of these and take them as beginnings, as elements of the universe [στοιχεῖα τοῦ παντός]" (48b). Yet, having thus spoken of fire, air, water, and earth as elements, Timaeus immediately withdraws the designation: these are not to be likened to syllables, that is, they are not to be regarded as constituting within φύσις something like the units that syllables constitute within λόγος. In play here is the original sense of στοιχεῖον as syllable (as unit or "element" of discourse) and the question of the appropriateness of extending that sense from the sphere of λόγος to that of φύσις, an extension first ventured in Plato's *Theaetetus*.[4] One suspects that Timaeus' reservation, his declaration of the inappropriateness of the extension, has to do with what Timaeus is to say about the relation between λόγος and φύσις, specifically, about what happens when, in λόγος, the attempt is made to grasp the nature of fire, air, water, and earth, to grasp these as originary "elements" of φύσις. To say nothing—yet—about the inappropriateness even of the designations *fire, air, water, earth.*

In this passage Timaeus identifies that small part of his first discourse that, as he said, did not pertain to the work of νοῦς. This part occurred at the point where Timaeus began describing the god's production of the body of the cosmos, specifically, at the point where the god is said to have taken fire, air, water, and earth and to have bound them together to form the body of the cosmos. It is precisely in reference to this small part of his first discourse that Timaeus now observes that we speak as if it were known what fire is, as well as the others, taking these four as beginnings. But they are themselves generated, and their generation, even if never yet disclosed, will certainly have deprived them of the status of beginnings. Timaeus' first discourse proves, then, not to have begun at the beginning: by beginning at that point where the god took fire and the others and set about making the cosmic body, the discourse got ahead of itself; it proves to have been ahead of itself from the beginning. Now it is incumbent upon Timaeus to make a different beginning, one that would begin at the beginning. Now what is required is a palintropic move: Timaeus must let the alleged beginning collapse into an earlier beginning, that is, he must turn back to what was passed over by the first discourse. By turning back to the prior generation of fire and the others, his discourse will attempt now to catch up with itself.

Such a turn—indeed, even its mere prospect—cannot but seem so extremely archaic as to threaten the very discourse in which it would be announced. For Timaeus has declared unequivocally that it was in making the heaven that the god made time, that time and the heaven were made at the same time (ἅμα). Thus, in turning back to consider fire and the others

---

4. *Theaet.* 201e. See Cornford, *Plato's Cosmology,* 161 n. 1.

as they were "before the birth of the heaven [πρὸ τῆς οὐρανοῦ γενέσεως],"
Timaeus is turning back to a kind of time before time as such, to a kind of
time when there was not yet time itself. Even to announce the move as a
turn back to the nature of fire and the others *before* the generation of the
heaven requires displacing the *before* (πρό) to an order of precedence that
is not simply that of time, reinscribing it in an order like that in which the
at the same time (ἅμα) must operate in the declaration that time and the
heaven were made at the same time. The discourse cannot but be twisted
and made to sound in different registers as soon as it is directed to a kind
of time *before* time, to a time *when* there is *not yet* time. And yet, to the
extent that one rigorously adheres to the identification of time with the
starry heaven, there will have been no time, no kind of time, before the god
set the heavenly bodies moving in their orbits so as to produce the starry
heaven as a moving image of eternity. The turn back will thus be a turn
out of time, not from time to eternity, but to the cosmos in a condition in
which neither time nor eternity has any pertinence.[5]

Whether it is regarded as belonging to a time before time or to no time
at all, this other beginning, this more archaic beginning, must be
addressed in the new beginning that Timaeus now makes, the new beginning in which now he would—as the injunction requires—begin at the
beginning. Yet, even if he succeeds, even if his discourse now begins at the
beginning, it may turn out not *simply* to begin with that beginning, as if
the beginning were a point at which the discourse could arrive and from
which it would then proceed. The otherness of this beginning, in particular, its character as errant and its prospect as being like a soldier face to
face in battle with νοῦς, can hardly not provoke suspicion that nothing
here will be simple or linear, that the discourse will be compelled—by
necessity itself—to engage in a more complex, if not aporetic, movement
with respect to the beginning.

In broader perspective the break in the discourse can be regarded as
provoked by something falling completely outside the scope of the discourse up to this point, namely, what Timaeus provisionally identifies as

---

5. Brague calls the cosmos in this condition *the sensible:* "In the *Timaeus* the sensible is
not *as such* in time. . . . It is in time only to the extent that it is ordered into a universe *(oura-
nos)*. . . . As to the sensible, if it is not as such in time, it is important to note that neither is it
in eternity. It is totally outside the domain within which the difference between time and eternity is pertinent" (*Du Temps chez Platon et Aristoteles,* 54). On the other hand, it should be
observed that this pretemporal condition would occur in several different phases, not all of
which can with equal appropriateness be designated as *the sensible.* Thus, there is the cosmos
in that phase in which its body and soul have been produced and joined center to center; this
phase, in which perpetual being and its order have already been mixed into the cosmos (so
that it is not just sensible), immediately precedes the making of the starry heaven and hence
time. From this phase one could distinguish another in which there is (as at the beginning of
Timaeus' discourse on the body of the cosmos) only fire, air, water, and earth. But what is
decisive for the second discourse is that even these four have come to be from a condition in
which, as Timaeus will eventually say (53b), they were only traces of themselves.

the generation of fire, air, water, and earth. The break is made precisely in order to launch another discourse, a different one capable of being extended to that which remained outside Timaeus' first discourse. The break thus serves in effect to mark a limit, specifically, a limit of the first discourse and a limit of the cosmic ποίησις to which that discourse is rigorously oriented. The limit has to do with material: whatever is made is made *from* something. Whatever is produced by τέχνη presupposes, either directly or indirectly, something that is by nature. This is the same limit that was marked in Socrates' discourse on the city: in the city material is needed for the practice of the various τέχναι, material that must come eventually from outside the order of τέχνη. Indeed this need for material is what leads to the polemic expansion of the city once the unnecessary desires are released within it; it is precisely such expansion that brings about the disruption of the simplest city, of the arcadian union of artisans.

Marking this limit with regard to the artisan god's cosmic ποίησις will also prove disruptive. In marking this limit, Timaeus marks the limit of the twofold distinction that from the outset determined the structure of ποίησις and thus governed the entire discourse on the production of the cosmos. In marking the limit of this twofold, Timaeus disrupts the framework that has rigorously controlled his entire first discourse from the moment that discourse began by posing this twofold. He disrupts the operation of that twofold framework, demonstrates its insufficiency, and thereby he prepares the way for the most decisive move of the entire dialogue: in place of the twofold of paradigm and image, Timaeus is about to declare that there are three kinds. The initial part of the second discourse (up to 53c) revolves around several countings of these three kinds. The discourse ordered and punctuated by these countings is the deepest, most archaic, most abysmal part of the entire dialogue. It is a kind of beginning of the entire discourse delivered by Timaeus, a beginning for that discourse, indeed for the entire dialogue, since the order established by Critias sets the Timaean cosmology at the beginning. This most archaic phase of Timaeus' discourse is a kind of beginning set into the dialogue, not far from the center, as though it were both a withdrawing or self-effacing beginning and a slightly displaced center, a beginning in which the dialogue would almost be centered. But, in turn, all that proves troublesome in this discourse is compounded almost without measure in the passage in which the entire discourse on the three kinds is gathered up, the passage in which the third kind comes to be called χώρα, the passage, the discourse, that I shall call the chorology.

Before Timaeus begins, before he begins again, though differently, now from the beginning, at the beginning, he inserts—before beginning— a brief discourse on discourse, just as he did prior to the beginning of the first discourse proper. Now he declares: "We will not now speak about the beginning of all things—or their beginnings, or whatever else might seem appropriate" (48c). Posing thus a possible pluralizing of beginning, Timaeus underlines his very indecisiveness regarding the mode of discourse appropriate to the beginning: even in declaring that he will not—for now at least—speak about it, he is indecisive about what name to call it, about the appropriate form of the name (singular or plural or . . .). But why is he not now going to speak about it? Why not begin at the beginning by saying that beginning? "Because," says Timaeus, "there is difficulty [τὸ χαλεπόν] in setting forth [δηλῶσαι: showing, making manifest] how things seem by the present mode of passage [διέξοδος]" (48c). Thus, at this point there is a certain detaching of the discourse from the beginning to which nonetheless it now turns. Hence, along with the indecisiveness about the name and number of the beginning, there is a certain distancing of the discourse from it in advance. This detachment, this distancing, serves to indicate—in advance—that the beginning to which the discourse will now be, in some sense, addressed will not yield readily to being said. On the contrary, it will prove difficult, troublesome, perhaps even dangerous, to say—or to try to say—this beginning. It will turn out that Timaeus' withdrawal from saying the beginning corresponds precisely to the withdrawal of the beginning from being said, its withdrawal from (the) discourse.

But what is "the present mode of passage," this kind of discourse for which it would be difficult to set forth how things seem in the domain of beginning? Timaeus answers: "Keeping to what was declared at the beginning, the capability of likely discourse [τὴν τῶν εἰκότων λόγων δύναμιν], I will attempt, as earlier, to present from the beginning a discourse not less likely, indeed more so, concerning each thing and the sum-total of things" (48c-d). It is, then, in a likely discourse that Timaeus will speak of fire, air, water, and earth as they were before the generation of the heaven, even if it will be difficult, even in likely discourse, to speak of these beginnings, to say nothing of whatever might claim precedence even over them.[6] One thing that Timaeus will indeed venture to say is the difficulty, how it is that fire and the others elude discourse to such an extent that beyond a point one can only renounce the attempt to say them. If such renunciation is inevitable, if the withdrawal of the beginning or beginnings is finally to reduce likely discourse to mere stammering, then one cannot but wonder whether still another

---

6. At this point Timaeus speaks only of εἰκὼς λόγος, not of εἰκὼς μῦθος, whereas at the beginning of his first discourse he vacillated between the two expressions (see 29c, 29d, 30b). The question is whether the restriction that occurs at this point marks this portion of the dialogue as effecting the transition from invented μῦθος to true λόγος, the transition first mentioned by Critias and affirmed by Socratès (see 26c-e). If the restriction were taken to have such a textual function, one would still need to consider what comes to be marked when, having repeatedly referred to εἰκὼς λόγος (53d, 55d, 56a, 56b, 57d), Timaeus reintroduces εἰκὼς μῦθος in a very remarkable passage, in the second discourse, on play (59c).

kind of discourse might come into play, a third kind of discourse capable of becoming somehow a discourse on the third kind.

Timaeus declares: as before, so now, at the beginning of the discourse, we call on god the protector to bring us safe—in the sense of granting safe passage to port across difficult waters (διασώζειν),[7] thus passage across the depths, passage over the abyss—through a narration that is strange, out of the way, out of place, displaced—the word is ἄτοπος—as well as unusual or, literally, without ἦθος (ἀήθης), a narration without any accustomed place.

IMAGES OF THE Χώρα

Timaeus declares the new beginning, marks this other, difficult beginning: "Thus we begin the discourse anew" (48e). He begins by returning to the beginning, to the beginning of his first discourse, to the distinction with which that discourse began. Now it is to be a matter of compounding—or undoing (or both)—that distinction, which even the first discourse, as it began, left suspended, in question. Timaeus declares that now more distinctions must be made than before: whereas then we distinguished two kinds (εἴδη), now there is need to make manifest a third kind (τρίτον γένος). For the former discourse the two were sufficient: first, the paradigmatic εἶδος, laid down (set under) as intelligible (νοητόν) and perpetually selfsame, and, second, the imitation (μίμημα) of the paradigm, that which is visible and subject to generation. But now, says Timaeus, the λόγος seems to necessitate attempting to reveal an εἶδος that is difficult, troublesome, dangerous (the word is again χαλεπόν) as well as dark, dim, faint, obscure (ἀμυδρόν). Timaeus asks: What power (δύναμις) are we to suppose it to have by nature? He answers: "This, most of all, that it is the receptacle [ὑποδοχή], as it were, the nurse [τιθήνη] of all generation" (49a).

Thus, Timaeus sets at the beginning of his new discourse another counting, a counting of being, one might call it, in any case a counting that echoes the 1, 2, 3 . . . with which the dialogue begins, a counting that returns to—that repeats—that beginning. But now it is no longer, as in the first discourse, a counting in which a third is blended from the other two nor in which the resulting three are then blended into one. Now the third is other than the other two, and indeed one of the things that will prove difficult and obscure is precisely this otherness of the third; almost nothing will prove more difficult than saying the otherness of this obscure third. One might, for instance, say that it is other in that it is a *third kind of being*. Yet, strictly speaking, the name *being* (τὸ ὄν) has been reserved for

---

7. See Taylor, *Commentary on Plato's Timaeus,* 311.

the first kind; only it can be called *being,* whereas the second kind is becoming or the generated and the third kind is the receptacle of generation. Even to say that the third is a third kind is to broach difficulties and to risk obscurity, for a kind is, strictly speaking, an intelligible εἶδος (as, for instance, with the four kinds of living beings), whereas the third is distinguished from the intelligible εἴδη. If, nonetheless, one calls it a third kind, then the discourse will already have begun to get entangled to a degree that cannot but broach difficulty and expose the discourse to danger. It will already have begun to do something other than *just say* the third: for one will have to say also that it is a kind of kind beyond kind, a kind of kind outside of kind.

Yet the λόγος—Timaeus' εἰκὼς λόγος—has already begun to reveal the third kind, making it manifest through an image of it, of its power: it is the receptacle of all generation. Timaeus' λόγος has broached another image too, an image that is even more obtrusively an image, so much so that one could be tempted (yielding to a powerful tradition) to call it a metaphor: the third kind is, as it were, the nurse of all generation. Designating receptacle and nurse as *images* of the third kind has its justification in Timaeus' explicit characterization of the discourse as εἰκὼς λόγος, as a discourse oriented to and thus sharing in the character of images. In this connection the word *image* must, however, be rigorously constrained to the sense it comes to have in the dialogue. As a result a tension, irresolvable as such, is installed in the expression *image of the third kind,* for it will turn out that images are, as such, images of the first kind, not of the third kind. In any case, designating receptacle, nurse (as well as some others still to come) as images of the third kind is not to be construed as tranquil recourse to an unquestioned store of traditional rhetorical concepts.[8]

The word ὑποδοχή means not only *receptacle* but also *reception,* even a hospitable reception such as was proposed at the beginning of the dialogue, the hospitable reception now being accorded Socrates, the entertainment that Socrates, listening silently, is now receiving from his hosts. The word also means *support, aid, succor,* hence the connection with the image of the nurse, a kind of surrogate mother who holds, aids, and succors the newly born child. Much later in the dialogue Timaeus will, in precisely

---

8. In this connection Derrida calls attention to the trap that, in his judgment, few interpreters have escaped: "Almost all the interpreters of the *Timaeus* gamble here [*misent à cet endroit*] on the resources of rhetoric without asking about them. They speak tranquilly about metaphors, images, similes. They pose no questions about this tradition of rhetoric, which places at their disposal a reserve of concepts that are very useful but that are built upon this distinction between the sensible and the intelligible, which is precisely that to which the thought of the χώρα can no longer be accommodated" (Jacques Derrida, *Khôra* [Paris: Galilée, 1993], 21). It is precisely for this reason that the sense of image must be redetermined from the *Timaeus* itself and the word employed only in this sense, even at the cost (if it be an expenditure and not perhaps rather a return) of installing an irresolvable tension in all discourse on the images of the third kind.

this connection, conjoin the image of the nurse (τιθήνη) with that of the nurturer (τροφός) (88d). There is one other sense of ὑποδοχή that has special pertinence, a sense operative, for example, in a passage in the *Laws* in which the Athenian says: "If anyone knowingly receive any stolen article, he shall be liable to the same penalty as the thief; and for the crime of receiving [ὑποδοχή] an exile the penalty shall be death" (*Laws* 955b). The pertinent sense is that of harboring or sheltering something alien, and of doing so in a way that conceals.

Timaeus marks a transition: though what has been said is true, one needs to speak of it in a way that is brighter, more shining (ἐναργέστερον). It is of the third kind that Timaeus has just been speaking, and so it is now a question of how the third kind is to be spoken of in a brighter, more shining way. One strategy by which to begin doing so would be to speak of that which could light up the third kind and let it shine forth. But that which lights up everything—even, though in a unique way, the third kind—is *fire*. Thus, Timaeus turns to a discourse on fire and the others, by this route coming back to a discussion of that for the sake of which the entire second discourse has ostensibly been undertaken. To discuss these is, says Timaeus, necessary (ἀναγκαῖον), the discourse on what belongs to the order of necessity thus being itself necessitated.

But immediately he utters again—now twice—the word heard earlier when he forswore saying the beginning: χαλεπόν. The difficulty lies in saying which of these is to be called, for instance, water rather than fire. The difficulty lies in saying which is to be called which and in doing so in a saying that is trustworthy (πιστός) and stable, firm, sure (βέβαιος). Timaeus explains by referring to sight and to a kind of circle that can be observed in what we see of fire, air, water, and earth: we see what we now call water becoming by condensation stones and earth; we also see water dissolving into breath and air, and these, in turn, through combustion, becoming fire; in the other direction we see fire becoming air, air condensing into cloud and mist and then into water, and then again water becoming earth and stones.[9] Timaeus concludes: "Thus, in a circle they give generation to one another, as becomes manifest" (49c). It is precisely this circling of generation that constitutes the difficulty, that provokes the troublesome question: "Thus, since no one of these ever makes its appearance as the same, which of them can one affirm to be this, whatever it is, and not something else without incurring ridicule?" Timaeus answers: "There is none" (49c-d).

---

9. Taylor notes how common the schema of such cyclical transformation was in early Greek thought and observes, in particular, that at this point the language of the *Timaeus* echoes that of—or rather, attributed to—Anaximenes by the references to condensation and rarefaction and by the place given to air in the cycle (*Commentary on Plato's Timaeus,* 314f.). On the other hand, Cornford stresses the link with Heraclitus, taken as having "taught the complete transformation of every form of body into every other" (*Plato's Cosmology,* 178).

Having thus declared this interruption of a certain discourse on fire and the others, Timaeus then proposes another way of speaking of them. But having just begun to tell of this safest, most secure way, he literally interrupts his discourse[10] in order to declare, even more directly, that fire and the others elude discourse: each of them flees (φεύγει), not waiting to be called *that* (τόδε) or *this* (τοῦτο), nor any other name that would indict them for being fixed (μόνιμος).[11]

What, then, is that safest way of speaking of them? The passage in which—with the interruption just cited—he proceeds to describe it is one of the most disputed in the entire dialogue. According to what has come to be called the traditional interpretation, this safest way requires that one not call fire (or any one of the others) *this* but rather *suchlike* (in Bury's translation) or *what is such* (Gill's translation) or *what is of such and such a quality* (as Cornford translates, inserting the word *quality*, which is highly problematic, not to say simply inappropriate, in this context)—that is, not τοῦτο but τὸ τοιοῦτον.[12] Behind this type of translation is the following general interpretation: fire is not to be called *this*, because to do so would be to attribute to it a stability, a fixity, that it does not have; since it is always moving within the cycle of transformations, it does not wait to be called *this* (τοῦτο) or *that* (τόδε) but flees all discourse that would capture it with such words. One can say only that it is suchlike (τοιοῦτον)—that it is firelike—with such discourse merely inscribing it indefinitely, unfixedly, within a certain phase of the cycle of transformations.

But according to the other way of translating the passage, proposed by Cherniss, the safest way requires that one not say *this is fire, this is water,* etc., but rather say that *what on any occasion is such and such is fire,* and likewise for the others. Behind this translation stands an interpretation of the

---

10. The declaration interrupts the discourse at least in that it states in full generality what, both before and after it, is stated with regard to particular cases, fire, water, etc. If one accepts the interpretation of the passage defended by Lee, then one could refer to his schematizing of it to show that the general declaration actually interrupts a specific phase of the discourse, deferring the third term in the three-part schema and requiring, after the declaration, repetition of the first two terms. See Edward N. Lee, "On Plato's *Timaeus,* 49D4–E7," *American Journal of Philology* 88 (1967): 4–5.

11. This sentence has been variously translated depending on the overall interpretation of the passage, depending especially on which of the two different readings of the passage is accepted. Commentators have called attention especially to the fact that the sentence begins in the singular (φεύγει οὐχ ὑπομένον) and ends in the plural (μόνιμα ὡς ὄντα αὐτά). Cherniss suggests the following explanation (though not all have accepted it): "Apparently Plato, just because he has said that 'it,' the phenomenon, does not abide, immediately and without further explanation refers not to 'it' as a single thing but to 'them,' the multiple and transient phases of the phenomenal flux that cannot be identified as distinct objects" (Harold Cherniss, "A Much Misread Passage of the *Timaeus* (*Timaeus* 49C7–50B5)," *American Journal of Philology* 75 [1954]: 118f.; reprinted in Harold Cherniss, *Selected Papers,* ed. Leonardo Tarán [Leiden: E. J. Brill, 1977]).

12. Margel translates τὸ τοιοῦτον as *ce qui a tel aspect* (*Le Tombeau du Dieu Artisan,* 133).

passage as denying that anything distinct can be said of *this*, that is, of what Cherniss calls the phenomenal manifestation or the transient moments of flux. Names such as *fire* and *water*, which we naively and improperly apply to phenomena, properly denominate the *suchlike* or *what on any occasion is such and such* (τὸ τοιοῦτον), that is, the distinct and self-identical characteristics that recur in the phenomenal flux.

The debate between the respective advocates of these two interpretations has continued ever since Cherniss first proposed his translation in 1954, and it is by no means certain that it can be finally settled, at least on philological grounds.[13] Whichever interpretation is followed, the decisive

---

13. The debate began with Cherniss' paper of 1954, "A Much Misread Passage of the *Timaeus*," in which he proposed his translation of the passage and vigorously criticized virtually all previous translations of it into English, German, French, and Italian. Cherniss emphasizes how the passage proceeds to more expanded expressions for τὸ τοιοῦτον, calling it, at first, τὸ τοιοῦτον ἑκάστοτε and τὸ τοιοῦτον ἀεί, and, then, τὸ τοιοῦτον ἀεὶ περιφερόμενον ὅμοιον, and, finally, τὸ διὰ παντὸς τοιοῦτον. He undertakes to show that these elaborations support his translation and interpretation of the entire passage, as does the use of τὸ τοιοῦτον rather than simply τοιοῦτον. He formulates the general point of debate, as he sees it, in the following statement: "the fundamental mistake made by these and most interpreters, however, is their assumption that Plato must here be saying what name or kind of name the phenomenal 'phases,' 'moments,' or 'occurrences' should be called, whereas he has already said that these transient moments of flux cannot be called anything distinct from anything else" (122). Toward the end of his paper it becomes clearer that the recurrent, distinct, and self-identical characteristics denoted by such words as *fire* and *water* are to be rigorously distinguished from the phenomenal flux, the *this* (128–30).

Beginning with Cherniss' paper of 1957, "The Relation of the *Timaeus* to Plato's Later Dialogues" (*American Journal of Philology* 78 [1957], reprinted in Cherniss, *Selected Papers*), the debate has been complicated by the way it has been connected with other issues such as the dating of the *Timaeus* and its relation to the *Parmenides*, the *Theaetetus*, and the *Cratylus*. Unfortunately such discussions have almost invariably proceeded by reference to isolated passages extracted without any attention to the context, much less to the whole of the dialogue involved.

Cherniss' translation and interpretation were vigorously challenged by Norman Gulley in a paper published in 1960 ("The Interpretation of Plato, *Timaeus* 49D–E," *American Journal of Philology* 81 [1960]). Gulley gives his own translation of the passage, explaining it as follows: "Translated in this way, the argument of the passage is, briefly, that since the visible world is one of perpetual change, it is necessary to distinguish between a right and a wrong way of describing it. 'This' or 'that' (τόδε καὶ τοῦτο) is always wrong, since these terms suggest a reference to something substantial and permanent, whereas in fact the sensible world is a world of transient, yet recurrent, qualities or groups of qualities (subsequently called 'copies' or 'likenesses' of the eternal realities—50C, 51A), which are properly described as 'of such and such a kind' (τοιοῦτον). Thus the fact that the visible world is in continual flux does not entail that it is devoid of determinate and recognisable characteristics, but it does entail that there are no substantial and permanent 'things' in it" (54). Citing in full Cherniss' translation of the passage, Gulley marshals a variety of arguments against it. For example: (a) "His first difficulty is the clause 'the things which we point to with the use of the words "this" or "that," thinking that we are indicating something.' A very special emphasis is given here (as it is in the next sentence) to the terms 'this' or 'that' (τόδε καὶ τοῦτο), and the seemingly obvious implication of the clause is that, since the use of the terms 'this' or 'that' carries with it the assumption that a definite 'something' is thereby being indicated, it is wrong to apply these terms to what is *not* a definite 'something.' If this is Plato's point here, consistency seemingly demands that his point in the examples in the previous part of the sentence is that it is wrong

point in the entire passage is clearly the flight of fire and the others from discourse, whether, as in the traditional interpretation, that flight still allows a discourse that would inscribe them indefinitely within the cycle of transformations or whether, as in the other interpretation, the flight is so unconditional that the names one naively takes as designating what are thus called fire, water, etc. end up denominating something quite other than the phenomenal flux they were taken to name. In neither case is discourse capable of catching and holding these errant fugitives.

to apply the terms 'this' or 'that' to what is not a definite 'something,' to fire or to water. . . . Thus the sentence D4-E2 is saying that the terms 'this' or 'that' should not be applied to γιγνόμενα" (58). (b) "In fact, . . . Plato has previously made it clear that the 'elements' fire, water, air, and earth *are* constantly changing phenomena, and this in itself makes it implausible to read into what follows an injunction not to apply these terms (fire, water, etc.) to constantly changing phenomena . . ." (59). On the other hand, Gulley does grant that in one portion of the passage (E4-7) "there are ambiguities and difficulties, all of which Cherniss clearly brings out," though still he insists that "what precedes and what follows this sentence make clear that there is no warrant for trying to import into its meaning a distinction between 'this' and 'such' as references to different objects" (63).

In two papers published in the mid-1960s, Edward N. Lee supports Cherniss' interpretation and makes explicit some of its implications. In "On Plato's *Timaeus, 49D4-E7,*" he restates Cherniss' interpretation as follows: "in order to speak 'most securely' of the elements, we must not (as we now do) refer the term 'fire' (or whatever) to phenomenal stuff. Instead, that term should be referred to something else, to something that does not change, to which Plato here refers as τὸ τοιοῦτον ἑκάστοτε (etc.)" (3). Though Lee disagrees with Cherniss regarding some details (cf. 12-15), for the most part he defends him. In particular, he shows how E4-7, which Gulley admitted were ambiguous and difficult, can be made to fit into an overall schema in accord with Cherniss' interpretation, a schema generated by recurrence of the three-part form, μὴ X ἀλλὰ Y προσαγορεύειν Z (e.g., not *this* but *suchlike* is to be called *fire*) (4f.). He also defends Cherniss directly against Gulley's criticisms. For example: On Gulley's "reading of the basic schema, Plato is saying that phenomena can and should be referred to as 'suchlike' or 'of such-and-such a kind.' But how can this possibly square with what Plato himself says in the 'digression' at 49E2-4? Phenomena are 'fugitive.' They slip away from any designation that would convict them of being stable. . . . But if they are as fugitive as all that, how can they offer any foothold even to the designation τοιοῦτον?" (17). In a related paper, "On the Metaphysics of the Image in Plato's *Timaeus*" (*The Monist* 50 [1966]), Lee draws out the implication of Cherniss' distinction between the phenomenal flux (*this*) and the recurrent, self-identical characteristic (*suchlike*) denoted by such words as *fire* and *water:* what emerges is distinction between "four items: (a) the Form itself; (b) the recurring, invariant character we apprehend perceptually in phenomena of the same sort . . . ; (c) an individual occurrence *of* that recurrent character (an actual appearance of it in the Receptacle); (d) the Receptacle itself" (367).

Richard D. Mohr (*The Platonic Cosmology* [Leiden: E. J. Brill, 1985]) sides with Cherniss and Lee. Essentially he reproduces Lee's fourfold classification, though rather than referring to four items as such, he proposes to speak of the "double aspect" of the phenomena: "On the one hand, they are in flux; on the other hand, they are images of Ideas" (88).

It is difficult to be satisfied with the fourfold classification entailed by Cherniss' interpretation, since the entire discourse on fire, water, etc. is immediately preceded by a passage (48e) insisting on the distinction between *three* kinds, a distinction that will be repeated in several additional passages (e.g., 50c-d; 51e-52a) following closely upon the present passage. Mary Louise Gill, among others, points to this problem and undertakes to reinstate the traditional interpretation and translation, though in her judgment it remains uncertain whether the debate between the advocates of the two interpretations can be finally settled, at least on philological grounds ("Matter and Flux in Plato's *Timaeus,*" *Phronesis* 32 [1987]: 36).

But one interpretation renders Timaeus' discourse in this passage more dangerous, renders it such that it interrupts itself at the very moment that it prescribes the safest way. For in this passage there are two discourses in play, two levels of discourse. The first level is that of discourse about fire and the others. At this level, according to the traditional interpretation, one may utter in reference to fire (itself) such words as *this* and *suchlike.* According to Cherniss' interpretation, one would, at this level, utter the word *fire,* taking it to apply either to a phenomenon seen (or otherwise sensed)—to which one could at most point while uttering this word *this*—or to a recurrent, self-identical characteristic. Timaeus does not himself engage in this first-level discourse but rather engages in a discourse that would say which forms of first-level discourse are safest. Interpreting the passage in the traditional way, Timaeus' discourse is one that says the following: to that which is denoted by the word *fire,* one cannot appropriately apply the word *this* but only the word *suchlike.* If the passage is interpreted in the way proposed by Cherniss, Timaeus' discourse is one that says: the word *fire* designates the suchlike but it cannot be applied to (the) this. In order, on Cherniss' interpretation, for Timaeus' (second-level) discourse to be possible, the word *this* (or some other word, if the matter were reformulated, e.g., *phenomenal flux*) must function to designate that to which the word *fire* cannot be appropriately applied. To put it differently, it is—at the first level, taking Cherniss' interpretation—a matter of uttering a word *(fire)* and taking it (mistakenly) to apply to something that can in fact only be seen (moving in the cycle of transformations) but *not said,* something that can be, at most, silently pointed out. Then, in the second-level discourse, Timaeus says that the word uttered, the word *fire,* does not apply to that which Timaeus' discourse must somehow say (for example, calling it *this*), even though it is unsayable. That which Timaeus' discourse would say, that something is unsayable, can be said only if that something is, in Timaeus' discourse, said. What is said in Timaeus' discourse interrupts the very possibility of saying it. Or rather, if it is merely a matter of the safest and not of the only possible way of speaking of fire and the others, then in declaring that safest way, Timaeus' own discourse cannot but abandon that way. Such is the danger to which the discourse proves to be exposed. If, on the other hand, one construes it within the framework of the traditional interpretation, Timaeus' discourse is not interrupted by what is said but is constrained only to let the word *fire* erode into something like *firelike.* In this case his discourse must allow a certain slippage, a displacement, which is not without danger, for it does not itself simply coincide with that safest way that it would say. But it is not, as in the other case, interrupted.

I have traced these connections, not in order to support one or the other of the two interpretations offered for this passage, but in order to make explicit the doubleness of the discourse and the complexity thereby introduced into it. Irrespective of the interpretation, it can be said that the fire, air, water, and earth that are seen moving in the cycle of transformations flee from discourse. Since they are always becoming something else, they lack stability, selfsameness, and consequently they retreat from discourse. Indeed, the only way in which these fugitives exhibit—or rather, imitate—selfsameness is by their *circling around* from one to another.

Now it is apparent why, as the new discourse was about to begin, Timaeus forswore saying the beginning. For, insofar as it is a matter of fire, air, water, and earth as they were before the generation of the heaven, this beginning cannot be said. Timaeus has forsworn saying this beginning because it cannot be said, because fire and the others lack the stability that would allow them to be said, because they are fugitives from λόγος. Thus it is also that Timaeus, in that same connection, refused to extend to fire, air, water, and earth the name *element* (στοιχεῖον), which up to the time of Plato had nothing to do with such things, referring instead to syllables, that is, to the "elements" of discourse. It is precisely such coincidence of λόγος with fire, air, water, and earth that is now being denied: rather than being captured by λόγος and assimilated to it, fire and the others flee from it, retreat before it, elude it.

Now it is also apparent how, as Timaeus said (49a), the λόγος seems to necessitate attempting to reveal a third kind. One could say even that, for the break with the previous twofold, λόγος is the touchstone. When it touches—or attempts to touch—fire and the others, they take flight, making manifest their lack of selfsameness and determinacy. Indeed, they take flight in a way that is unthinkable within the framework of the twofold distinction, linked to ποίησις, between a paradigm and a product made to look like the paradigm. A couch, however imperfect it may be as compared with the utter selfsameness of its paradigm, does not go untouched by its name and does not turn—is not turning at every moment—into some quite different artifact. And however it may be with the stone of a temple, crumbling into grains of sand that in turn are dissolved and washed away by rainwater,[14] the temple will also typically undergo another, quite different kind of transformation, linked, not to the cycle of fire, air, water, and earth, but to the schema of ποίησις: it will be rebuilt, for instance, as a Christian sanctuary or perhaps as a storage depot for explosives, which, when accidentally detonated, will damage it severely, though not to the point of making it unrecognizable as still a temple, or rather, as the ruins of a temple, now to be preserved as such. Such recon-

---

14. This example brings especially to light the peculiar character of fire and the others as they were before the generation of the heaven, that is, when—in contrast to the very slowly transformed stone of the temple—they were not yet quite themselves. Once Timaeus' discourse arrives at the point where these are shaped into fire, air, water, and earth themselves, earth will be set outside the cycle of transformations (see 56d).

struction (and, though differently, destruction) is situated within the schema of ποίησις and its twofold distinction. One needs, then, to mark the difference between artifacts, which are fabricated and can be refabricated within the framework of the twofold distinction between a paradigm and things made in the image of the paradigm, *and* fire, air, water, and earth, as they are spoken of in the stammering discourse of the present passage.

It is imperative, then, not to generalize the discourse on (the flight of) fire and the others into a theory of visible things as such in which one would declare all such things incapable of any more than minimal denomination, including, not insignificantly, all those things of the cosmos that *have been named* in Timaeus' first discourse, operating, as it did, within the schema of ποίησις. Indeed, at the threshold of the chorology, Timaeus will say that each thing of this kind (the second kind) not only is like its paradigm but also *has the same name as the paradigm* (see 52a). Only fire, air, water, and earth, as they were before the generation of the heaven, as they were when they were not yet even quite themselves—only they are fugitives from λόγος. And it is precisely their flight that points to a third kind that would harbor them outside the twofold. One could say even that the very flight of fire and the others traces a way beyond the twofold, that these traces (as Timaeus will soon call them) mark a passage toward the receptacle in which they would be held, nurtured, sheltered.

Timaeus draws a certain contrast between the almost unspeakable fugitives and that which, previously called receptacle and nurse, he now refers to as that *in which* (ἐν ᾧ) each of them appears in being generated and *from which* (ἐκεῖθεν) again they perish. In a sense, the *in which* and *from which* of generation and perishing would be less resistant to λόγος than those fugitives that are generated in it and perish from it. For Timaeus says that it is in reference to that alone (μόνον ἐκεῖνο) that one can use the words *this* (τοῦτο) and *that* (τόδε) (49e–50a). Note that the discourse remains double: Timaeus avoids applying *this* or *that* (to the *in which* and *from which*) before saying, and in order to say, that these can be applied; he avoids such application (as I have not) by availing himself of the third form of the demonstrative pronoun at his disposal in Greek; but then, it would be necessary, strictly speaking, to turn back and, shifting the demonstratives, to confirm that ἐκεῖνο can also be said of it. Instead, Timaeus simply stresses that τοῦτο and τόδε are to be used only of the *in which* and *from which,* and not of any of those fugitives that are suchlike.[15]

---

15. How one translates and interprets the last part of the final sentence depends on whether one follows the traditional interpretation or Cherniss' interpretation of the earlier part of the passage (see note 13). In contrast to the traditional translation, which I have paraphrased, Cherniss translates the last part of the sentence as follows: "... it is safest to designate it [Cherniss identifies the antecedent as: ἐν ᾧ . . .] alone when we employ the word 'this' or 'that' but what is of any kind soever, hot or white or any of the contraries and all that consist of these, not in turn to call it any of these" ("A Much Misread Passage of the *Timaeus*," 347). Cherniss insists that the final occurrence of *it* also refers to the receptacle (357).

The *in which* and *from which* is, then, less resistant to discourse insofar as it can, unlike fire and the others, be called *this* and *that*. And yet, even if marking a certain, strange selfsameness on the part of what is thus called, these very designations also mark a withdrawal from εἰκὼς λόγος, from the discourse of images—these very designations of it as *this* and *that* (these most abstract names, everything—except the fire, air, water, and earth that are not yet quite themselves—being a *this* and a *that*) as well as, if to a lesser degree, the operative designations *in which* and *from which*. Indeed, the additional images that Timaeus is about to bring forth will themselves in some instances prove to be images of the third kind that also, as such, image the very withdrawal of the third kind from presentation in and through images.

The third kind will be addressed most directly when Timaeus comes to call it the χώρα. There, in the chorology, it will come closest to being said. As the discourse moves toward the chorology, there is a series of indicators that mark the increasing appropriateness of the discourse, that signal a certain tightening and sharpening of the discourse. One such indicator has already appeared: immediately after Timaeus introduces the third kind as receptacle and nurse, he voices the injunction that, though what has been said is true, one needs to speak of it in a way that is brighter (see 49a). Now, following the discussion of fire, air, water, and earth and its concluding differentiation between these and the third kind, another such indicator occurs: "Yet one must desire eagerly to speak of this again more clearly [σαφέστερον]" (50a). The deployment of εἰκὼς λόγος that then follows brings forth several additional images of the third kind.

Timaeus presents the image of gold that is modeled into all possible figures or shapes (σχήματα), each figure being immediately remodeled into another. Then he brings discourse to bear on this image: if someone were to point to one of the figures and ask what it *is*, the safest (ἀσφαλέσ-τατον) answer would be that it is gold; but as for the triangle and other figures formed from the gold, one should avoid speaking of them as being, since they are changing even while one is thus speaking. To the fleeting figures—as to fire and the others—one could safely apply only such names as *suchlike* (τὸ τοιοῦτον) (50a–b).[16]

What Timaeus presents is thus a kind of image of images, at least of such fleeting images as fire and the others can be said to be. What he presents is an image of images in a kind of artificial cycle of transformations. It is an image drawn from the sphere of τέχνη, and yet at the same time it is divergent from τέχνη; for an artisan does not make products of *all* sorts but molds the material in such a way that it becomes an image of the paradigm. The otherwise unceasing cycle of remakings—analogous to the cycle of fire,

---

16. The introduction here of the word τὸ τοιοῦτον not only links this discourse to the previous one on fire, water, etc., but raises regarding it the same disputed issues regarding translation and interpretation. For this passage, too, Cherniss offers and defends a translation quite different from the traditional one ("A Much Misread Passage of the *Timaeus*," 125).

air, water, and earth, indeed remodeling the course of τέχνη in the image of this cycle—would always be broken by the force that the paradigm exercises in τέχνη.

As all possible figures come to be modeled in the gold, so do fire, air, water, and earth come to be in the third kind and pass away from it. The gold is an image of that which receives all the fleeting images, an image of what Timaeus has called receptacle. Timaeus declares that this all-receiving nature is always to be called the same (50b), not in the sense of being called only by a single name, for already it has been called by several, but rather in the sense that it remains always the same throughout the reception of various figures, images, or traces. Timaeus says: never does it depart from its own power (δύναμις) (50b).[17]

And yet, it remains the same, not by retaining the same form, but by virtue of taking on no form whatsoever. Timaeus explains: "While it receives all things, nowhere and in no way does it take on any form [μορφή] like any of those things entering it. For it is laid down by nature as a matrix [ἐκμαγεῖον] for all things; being moved and shaped by those things that enter it, through them it appears [φαίνεται] different at different times" (50b-c). Timaeus thus adds another name, another image, of that which has already been called the third kind, the receptacle, a nurse, etc.: now it is called a matrix (ἐκμαγεῖον) in the sense of a mass of wax or other soft material on which the imprint of a seal can be made.[18] The image of molding or modeling, as with gold, is itself now remolded, remodeled, into another image drawn from τέχνη, that of impressing or stamping an impress or imprint on a matrix. Timaeus marks the shift, anticipating the discourse to come: "And those that enter and depart are imitations of those that always are [τῶν ὄντων ἀεὶ μιμήματα], being stamped from them in a way hard to declare and wondrous, which we shall consider hereafter" (50c). What happens, then, is that—or is as if—perpetual beings are—were—applied like a stamp to a matrix so as to leave in the matrix an impression similar to the stamp itself.

---

17. Ashbaugh takes gold as here illustrating what she calls the stability of the χώρα. She observes that the reason why gold is chosen for such illustration "appears in the discussion of metals (*Tim.* 59b-d). That section describes gold as a fusible variety of water that is quite dense because it is composed of fine, uniform particles that give the appearance of something shining *(stilbon)*. The offshoot of gold is *adamant (Tim.* 59b), a hard material likely to remind us of something stable because it endures through many changes" (Anne Freire Ashbaugh, *Plato's Theory of Explanation: A Study of the Cosmological Account in the "Timaeus"* [Albany: State University of New York Press, 1988], 121). Considerable caution (and no doubt some limiting qualifications) would be required if one were to sustain the reference to the *stability* of the χώρα; for, while indeed Timaeus says that it does not depart from its own power, he also will soon declare, for instance, that it is most difficult to catch (51a-b).

18. The same word is used in the passage in the *Theaetetus* where Socrates proposes the supposition that there is in the soul a block of wax (κήρινον ἐκμαγεῖον), memory being possible because perceptions and thoughts are imprinted on it (*Theaet.* 191c-d). See Taylor, *Commentary on Plato's Timaeus,* 321f.

Timaeus stresses that the third kind, this matrix, takes on no form, indeed has no form. For, in order to be capable of suitably receiving all forms, it must itself be devoid of form, as the base for a fragrant ointment must be as odorless as possible. One could say that in the matrix forms come and go; it comes to have, to receive, forms, and yet it does not have them itself, does not have them as proper to it itself. In other words, forms come to be *in* it without ever being *of* it.

But, though it itself has no form—and thus, as Timaeus will soon declare, is as such invisible—one cannot conclude that the third kind simply does not appear. On the contrary, it appears by way of those things that enter it, those things that it receives: "through them it appears different at different times." Immediately following the next indicator (proposing to speak "most correctly [ὀρθότατα]"), Timaeus speaks again of this appearing of the third kind: "That part of it that is made fiery [that has been inflamed: πεπυρωμένος] appears [shows itself, becomes manifest: φαίνεσθαι] as fire"—and likewise for the others (51b). One might suppose that as it thus appears—not as itself but as, for instance, fire—there would come also into operation a certain indexical function, a kind of pointing by way of discourse, an operation in which, by calling the third kind *this* or *that* (as indeed one can do appropriately), one would indicate that which appears (even though not as itself) through, for instance, the fiery part.

Just after his first mention of the appearing of the third kind, indeed right in the midst of his discussion of the τέχναι of modeling and stamping, Timaeus abruptly makes a transition from the order of ποίησις to that of procreation and birth. Again he counts the three kinds, but now in an order different from that previously followed: now he begins with the generated, then names that in which (ἐν ᾧ) it is generated, and then finally adds that from which (τὸ ὅθεν) the generated is copied and begotten (φύεται) (50c–d). The reference to begetting (hence to φύσις, which recurs frequently in this part of the dialogue) announces the transition that then ensues to the order of procreation and birth. The *from which,* which has just been described almost as though it were a stamp that comes to make its impression on a block of wax, is now likened to the father, the *in which* to the mother and the nature (φύσις) engendered between them to the offspring.[19] Curiously the artisan god, occasionally

---

19. Describing the χώρα as "the dark nocturnal space-matter of the universe" and as "chaos," Fink stresses its maternal nature: it is "the great mother, the *'earth'"* (Eugen Fink, *Zur Ontologischen Frühgeschichte von Raum-Zeit-Bewegung* [The Hague: Martinus Nijhoff, 1957], 187f.). Similar connections are to be found in the passage in the *Republic* in which Socrates describes the story to be told to the citizens of the city, the story according to which all were fashioned and reared under the earth and only then born from it, remaining therefore bound to the land: "When the job had been completely finished, then the earth, which is their mother, sent them up. And now, as though the land [χώρα] they are in were a mother and a nurturer [τροφός], they must plan for and defend it, if anyone attacks, and they must think of the other citizens as brothers and born of the earth" (*Rep.* 414d–e). Still another connection between the maternal or rather between women's way of life, on the one hand, and

called father in the first discourse, seems now to be completely absent.[20] The father is no longer the artisan god who looks to the paradigm but now is the paradigm itself.

Viewed in broader perspective, the move effected here is a transition from the order governed by the twofold distinction between paradigm and image (the order of production) to the order governed by the three-fold (the order of procreation and birth). The tension or even opposition between these two orders has been in play throughout much of the dia-logue up to this point, its discourse vacillating between the terms of τέχνη and those of ἔρως and φύσις. Already in Socrates' discourse, recapitulat-ing that of the *Republic,* the procreative and erotic proved to resist the ordering required of the technical city. Against this background it is evi-dent just how appropriate the emergence of the procreative order is in Timaeus' second discourse, where it is precisely a matter of addressing what falls outside the work of νοῦς and outside the supervision by which noetic sight governs ποίησις. On the other hand, Timaeus has ventured to express the threefold procreative order precisely by recourse to such modes of τέχνη as modeling and stamping. And even when finally he expresses this order as that of father, mother, and offspring, he reverts immediately to the technical images of modeling and stamping, though not without also slipping in another mode, the production of fragrant ointments. It is almost as if the likening of the threefold to father, mother, and offspring had been only a brief aberration, even an interruption. In the discourse there remains—but now even more openly—a hovering between the order of production and that of procreation and birth.

Timaeus insists once and for all on the differentiation: the mother and receptacle of all generation is not to be called earth, air, fire, or water. He continues in a way that gathers up all he has said about this third kind and that opens beyond to the chorology: "But if we call it an invisible εἶδος, formless, all-receiving, and, in a most perplexing way, partaking of the intelligible [μεταλαμβάνον δὲ ἀπορώτατά πη τοῦ νοητοῦ] and most difficult to catch, we will not be speaking falsely" (51a–b).

So difficult to catch that not even the net of kinds, of kinds of kinds, can effectively snare it, that which is nonetheless called the third kind is, says Timaeus, formless. It has itself none of those forms (shapes, determi-nations) that—in terms of the various images—can be received by it or stamped on it or that can impregnate it. Since it is *all*-receiving—not only a mother but, it seems, utterly promiscuous—it can itself have no form, no

---

the necessary, the errant, and the χώρα, on the other, is broached in the *Laws:* "Accustomed as they are to live a retired and private life, women will use every means to resist being led out into the light, and they will prove much too strong for the lawgiver" (*Laws* 781c).

20. This absence is confirmed at 53b.

determinations whatsoever. It can itself receive, be stamped or impregnated by, all those kinds called paradigms or intelligible εἴδη, but it is not *itself* determined by any of them, cannot itself have any of these determinations, cannot have them as determinations *of itself*.[21] The ramifications of this utter nondetermination are profound, or rather, abysmal. Suppose that for something to have meaning were defined as its being determined by such a determination. Suppose, further, that for a word to have meaning were defined as its expressing such a determining determination, its signifying the meaning of something. Then it would have to be said that the third kind has no meaning and that the name it is about to be called, the name χώρα, if it is a name, has no meaning. Both the χώρα and the word χώρα would be meaningless.[22] If, on the other hand, it should turn out that somehow, through some twist of λόγος, they have something like a meaning, it would have to be a kind of meaning beyond meaning, just as the third kind (to be said as/by χώρα) is a kind of kind beyond kind. Little wonder, then, that Timaeus has forsworn saying this beginning. Little wonder that the discourse has become χαλεπόν.

Being formless, the third kind is also invisible. Since it is not determined by any intelligible εἶδος, it has no look that, shining through it, could give it a visible aspect. On the other hand, its invisibility is what links it to the intelligible so that it is, as Timaeus says, "in a most perplexing way, partaking of the intelligible"—partaking of the intelligible, not by being determined by it as are generated things, but by being invisible, as are the intelligible εἴδη. Timaeus expresses the point succinctly by calling the third kind an *invisible* εἶδος. And yet, its invisibility cannot but be different. Whereas the invisibility of the intelligible is, in the end, just the other side of another visibility—that is, its invisibility to the senses is just the other side of its visibility to νοῦς—the invisibility of the third kind is a more insistent invisibility. And yet, if it were absolutely invisible, if it did not announce itself in any way whatsoever, then the discourse addressed

---

21. Referring to the numerous interpretations that since antiquity have sought to determine the sense of χώρα, Derrida writes: "They always consist in *giving form* to it by determining it, it which, however, can offer itself or promise itself only by escaping from all determination" (*Khôra*, 26f.).

22. Regarding what he calls "the thought of the khôra," Derrida writes: "It would no longer belong to the horizon of meaning [*sens*], nor to that of meaning as the meaning of being" (*Khôra*, 22f.). Presumably Derrida is alluding here to Heidegger and suggesting that the thought of the χώρα exceeds the horizon of Heidegger's thinking, at least of the inscription of that thinking that is governed by the question of the meaning of being. In Heidegger's own brief discussions of the χώρα, which conflate χώρα and τόπος and link Platonism to the transformation of the essence of place into space defined as extension, there is little to suggest any originary engagement with the Platonic discourse on the χώρα (see Martin Heidegger, *Einführung in die Metaphysik*, vol. 40 of *Gesamtausgabe* [Frankfurt a.M.: Vittorio Klostermann, 1983], 70f.; see also Heidegger, *Was Heisst Denken?* [Tübingen: Max Niemeyer, 1954], 174).

to it would be even more than most perplexing, even more than difficult, troublesome, dangerous. It would be utterly blind, completely unbound by anything beyond itself, and the chorology could not but simply fall back into itself. This is why it is of utmost consequence that, despite its invisibility, Timaeus does not deny it all appearing but grants that, in a part where it holds a trace, for instance, of fire, it appears as fire. Even if *as fire, it* nonetheless appears; it appears, even if never *as itself.*

Indeed, the spacing of the text is such here (51b) as to emphasize this appearing, the declaration of which is framed between two indicators. The first indicator is Timaeus' proposal to speak "most correctly." The second indicator is his proposal to present the discourse that most thoroughly distinguishes with respect to its theme. Between these two indicators stands Timaeus' declaration of the appearing of the third kind: "That part of it that is made fiery appears as fire"—and likewise for the others. Appearing as, for instance, fire, the third kind shows itself, becomes manifest, but never *as itself,* never without holding itself as such in concealment. Even in appearing, it remains most difficult to catch.

Timaeus' indication that the most thoroughly distinguishing discourse is now to be presented serves to mark the move to the threshold of the chorology. At this threshold Timaeus takes up again the twofold. That he does not simply and unconditionally assert the distinction between perpetual being and that which is generated but rather takes up the *question* of this distinction serves to confirm just how inconclusive, how questionable, the distinction remained when Timaeus introduced it at the beginning of his first discourse. But now he explicitly poses the question whether, in addition to the things we see, there is an intelligible εἶδος of each or whether what we take to be an εἶδος is nothing but discourse, mere λόγος. Yet even now he disclaims giving a definitive answer, one that would finally establish the distinction and, as it were, properly anchor everything. Instead, he casts a vote for a merely conditional, hypothetical declaration: if νοῦς and true opinion (δόξα ἀληθής) are two kinds, then so are the intelligible εἴδη and the things of sense. He then proceeds to specify the differences between νοῦς and true opinion, leaving the hypothetical premise untouched, letting it remain hypothetical, something laid down, indeed something laid down about what is laid down from λόγος, a hypothetical about the hypothetical as such. If there is to be an establishing of the distinction as such, the distinction between perpetual being and that which is generated, it will not occur prior to the chorology.

But at the threshold he merely delimits the first and the second kinds to the extent needed for the radical—or abysmal—differentiation to be ventured in the chorology.

First: "We must agree that one kind is the selfsame εἶδος, ungenerated and indestructible, neither receiving into itself any other from elsewhere nor itself passing anywhere else into another, invisible and in other ways nonsensible, noetic vision [intellection: νόησις] being assigned to look upon [ἐπισκοπεῖν] this" (51e–52a). Here Timaeus explicitly pairs the invisibility of the first kind with its visibility to noetic vision (νόησις); its invisibility is the other side of another visibility, of a visibility of another order, of the order of νοῦς. Timaeus also emphasizes the nonreceptivity of the first kind: such a selfsame εἶδος neither receives any other into itself nor itself passes into any other. It neither receives nor is received. Its utter nonreceptivity corresponds to its selfsameness: it is itself throughout itself, lacking all intrinsic connection to an other. It is simply one and the same, simply itself.

Second: "The second kind is that which has the same name as and is like the former [i.e., the first kind], sensible, generated [begotten/born: γεννητόν], ever carried about [tossed about, as at sea: πεφορημένον], being generated in some place [τόπος] and again perishing from it, apprehensible by opinion with sense" (52a). Timaeus' indication of the relation between the two kinds goes beyond anything said previously: things of the second kind, sensible things, have the same name and the same look as an intelligible εἶδος. A sensible thing is a duplicate of the corresponding εἶδος, a duplicate in a double sense, both in λόγος and for vision. It is as if the εἶδος had migrated, passing into another, even though Timaeus has insisted that an εἶδος—an intelligible εἶδος—can no more pass into another than it can receive another into itself. What Timaeus poses at the threshold—as he begins the counting in which the third kind will finally be called χώρα—is the question of the doubling of being. Or rather, in order to sound in it the note of errancy, let it be called the question of the *duplicity of being,* of duplicity in the double sense of doubling and of wandering, as in or into errancy.

CHOROLOGY

It is called a third kind, though in the sense of a kind of kind beyond kind. One would call it even a third kind of being, though only at the risk of letting the discourse drift beyond any hope of rigor: for even if, in addition to the first kind, the second kind could be said—by way of the duplicity of being—to have some slight share in being, there would seem to be only the most remote possibility of extending the word to the third kind, which is neither being nor a being, neither an intelligible being nor a sensible being. If it can be called a being at all, it can only be in a sense of being that exceeds being, in a sense of being that is beyond being (ἐπέκεινα τῆς οὐσίας).[23]

And yet, Timaeus has offered a series of images of it. It is pictured as all-receiving, as the receptacle of all generation, the *in which* and *from which* of all generation. Yet it not only receives but also harbors, shelters,

23. This expression, which in the *Republic* (509b) Socrates uses in speaking of τὸ

nurtures the fleeting newborn traces of fire, air, water, and earth. It not only nurtures and succors them like a nurse but bears, gives birth to, them (and so to all that arises from them): it is the mother. There are also images of it drawn from τέχνη. It is pictured in the image of gold being constantly remodeled, remolded, into every possible design; yet, over against this image, limiting the truth of the image, Timaeus declares the third kind to be invisible. It is portrayed also in the image of a matrix; yet, over against this image, limiting its truth too, the third kind is said to partake of the intelligible, to be like precisely that which would imprint its stamp on the matrix. It is, then, especially the technical images that prove manifestly limited. But then, if the third kind is, as Timaeus declares, completely formless, utterly amorphous, every image will be limited, assuming that it is the very nature of an image as such to present the form of that which it images but from which it is materially distinct. If the third kind lacks all determination, then one must wonder how there can be an image that has any bearing on it itself. In any case it will fall outside the horizon of meaning in a certain classical sense (even if precisely here in the Platonic text where one would locate the origin of this—and perhaps every—classical sense, even the sense of sense itself, a counterstress is already in force). Even what one might take to be its proper name, the name χώρα, will prove, in this classical sense, to be meaningless, and thus its very status as a word, if not as a proper name, will be disturbed. But then, if neither in an image nor in its proper name, how is the χώρα accessible at all? How is it that discourse about it, chorology, can lay at least some remote claim to truth? Two operations, at least, would seem to be involved: from the one side, an indexical operation, the kind of indicating carried out by the words *this* and *that,* and, from the other side, its peculiar appearing by way of, for instance, the fire that it holds and nurtures. Even of this appearing one could, it seems, catch only a glimpse, perhaps by spying a trace of fire in the interval in which, undergoing transformation, fire as such breaks down in a way that could release its momentary flash. How otherwise? Except perhaps in a dream.

As chorology Timaeus' discourse comes as near as it ever will to the

---

ἀγαθόν, is never used in reference to the χώρα. Yet there is every reason to ask, as does Derrida, about the possibility of extending the expression to the χώρα (see Jacques Derrida, "Tense," in *The Path of Archaic Thinking: Unfolding the Work of John Sallis,* ed. Kenneth Maly [Albany: State University of New York Press, 1995], 73f.). Let it suffice here merely to mention the enigmatic passage in Book 7 of the *Republic* in which Socrates tells of how the liberated prisoner, having escaped the cave, could finally turn his gaze upward: "Then finally I suppose he would be able to look upon the sun—not its appearances [its phantoms: φαντάσματα] in water or in some other base [ἕδρα], but the sun itself by itself in its own χώρα—and behold how it is" (*Rep.* 516b). I have discussed the passage, in the context of a discussion with Derrida, in "Daydream," *Revue Internationale de Philosophie* (1997).

beginning. In becoming chorology its palintropic engagement brings it into a region where it can most nearly, as enjoined, begin at the beginning, even if only in recommencing, in a second beginning. In this discourse Timaeus ventures to call by its proper name that which heretofore has only been counted or else addressed by the names of its images. Yet the differentiations that set it apart have such disruptive force that even the concept of proper name will in the end miss the mark and prove capable only of alluding to the sense—or nonsense—at issue here.

What about the word χώρα, if indeed in the *Timaeus* it functions as a word? The interruption of its meaning (in the classical sense) entails an enormous complication of the question of its translation. If, following Cornford and A. E. Taylor,[24] one proposed to translate χώρα as *space,* then one would have to set about immediately withdrawing from the word much that we cannot but hear in it. For clearly the χώρα is not the isotropic space of post-Cartesian physics. Nor is it even empty space, the void, as discussed in Greek atomism; for this is called τὸ κενόν and is in fact discussed as such later in the *Timaeus* (58b). It would hardly be otherwise if one were to translate χώρα as *place,* following Thomas Taylor, who in effect translated Chalcidius' translation of χώρα as *locus;*[25] for one would then have conflated the difference between χώρα and τόπος and would risk assimilating Plato's chorology to the topology of Aristotle's *Physics.*

Yet it is not only a matter of these translations being inadequate and in need of such extensive reservations that in the end they say next to nothing. In a sense they are not translations at all: for to the extent that the meaning of χώρα is interrupted, there can be no translation of it—not, at least, according to a certain classical concept of translation (the very one first formulated in the *Critias* [113a–b], thus having its origin precisely in this Platonic context). To propose a translation of χώρα would—according to this concept—be to say that both words, χώρα and its translation, have the same semantic correlate, the same meaning; translation would consist, then, in moving from one word to the other by way of this common meaning. Inasmuch as χώρα has no meaning—at least not in this classical sense—it is intrinsically untranslatable. It is such as to disrupt the very operation of translation, yielding to it perhaps even less than does a proper name, to which it is to this extent akin.

On the other hand, even in the *Timaeus* χώρα has certain semantic affinities based on its usage in other texts (where no such interruption

24. Cornford, *Plato's Cosmology,* 192. Taylor, *Commentary on Plato's Timaeus,* 343f.

25. Plato, *The Timaeus and the Critias or Atlanticus,* trans. Thomas Taylor, 171 (page citation is to the reprint edition). *Timaeus, A Calcidio Translatus Commentarioque Instructus* (London: The Warburg Institute, 1962), 50.

occurs) and of course on its connections within the Greek language as such. In this regard a kind of lateral translation or implication will remain operative, even if in a certain suspension, in the otherwise untranslatable occurrence of χώρα in the chorology. Thus, while leaving χώρα untranslated in the chorology, it will be granted that in other texts (and to a lesser degree in other parts of the *Timaeus*) there is justification for translating it, for instance, as place, as land, as country. It seems indisputable, for example, that it means something like place in a passage in the *Laws* where the Athenian, laying down regulations for commercial exchange, says that such exchange is to be made by a transfer of the article in the χώρα appointed for that purpose in the market (*Laws* 915d). One could still perhaps translate it as place, though certainly in a more exceptional sense, in two passages from other dialogues that refer to the χώρα of philosophy. The first, from the *Republic,* tells of the corruption of the best natures, how they are led to abandon philosophy, while other, unworthy men come to her; as a result, philosophy itself is corrupted, its χώρα having become empty (κενός) although full of fine names and pretentions (*Rep.* 495c). The second passage, from the *Sophist,* contrasts the sophist, who runs away into the darkness of nonbeing, with the philosopher, who is devoted to being but who is difficult to see because of the bright light of this χώρα (*Soph.* 254a). Here the place is, then, not only just that of the philosopher but also, as such, the place of the brightness of being, even (as the Stranger goes on to suggest) a godly place.

A number of affinities are evident in the *Laws,* where χώρα occurs with incomparable frequency and virtually always with senses that are decidedly prephilosophical or that at least remain certainly this side of the interruption that the *Timaeus* produces in the word. Sometimes χώρα is used in the sense of terrain or landscape and is described, for example, as rough (τραχεῖα) (*Laws* 695a) or as varied (παντοῖα) (*Laws* 833b); there is talk of adapting the sport of horse racing to the nature of the landscape (κατὰ φύσιν τῆς χώρας) (*Laws* 834c); and at the very beginning of the dialogue Clinias notes that the terrain of Crete is not level, not a plain (πεδιάς) (*Laws* 625c-d). One could say too, as it has, in fact, been translated: Crete is not a level country. There are passages in which χώρα designates country in the sense of farmland to be cultivated (θεραπεύειν), as a mother tends her children (*Laws* 740a; cf. 745d). But more often what is prominent when it is used in this general sense is its distinction from the πόλις: the country in distinction from the city. For example, there is reference to the country surrounding the city (*Laws* 704c) and to roads that run from the country into the city (*Laws* 763c); and there are several passages in which χώρα and πόλις are conjoined as two distinct regions, country and city (*Laws* 759b, 817a, 823e, 945d, 950d). More frequent are passages in which χώρα designates country in the sense of the entire territory, the entire political unit. Sometimes, when used in this sense, there is explicit reference to the πόλις as within the χώρα: the city is to be set as nearly as possible in the middle of the country (*Laws* 745b), and both the city and the entire country are to be divided into twelve parts (*Laws* 745c; cf. 745e, 758e, 760b–e, 761a, 763a, 969c). Quite frequently, it has this same sense in a more generalized mode, as in a passage in which the law is made to utter a chant proclaiming that whoever is caught robbing a temple, if he be a foreigner or a slave, will have a curse branded on his forehead and on his hands, will be scourged, and will then be cast out naked beyond the borders of the country (ἐκτὸς τῶν ὅρων τῆς χώρας) (*Laws* 854c–d; cf. 855a, 866c, 867e, 881b, 936a, 938c). Likewise in a passage that tells how a foreigner is to be received (ὑποδέχεσθαι) when he comes on public business from another country (ἐξ ἄλλης χώρας) (*Laws* 953b; cf. 930d, 953c–d). And in a passage that tells of those who, out of madness, do violence against the laws with the intent of overthrowing the constitution (πολιτεία) and who in the course of their deed commit murder and fail to purge their hands of the blood: such a person will depart into another country and place (εἰς ἄλλην χώραν καὶ τόπον) and remain as an exile for one year (*Laws* 864e). This passage is especially noteworthy because of its conjoining of χώρα and τόπος, a conjunction that, in the most problematic form, turns up at the heart of the chorology. But here it has no appearance of being problematic, no more than do the numerous other occurrences of χώρα in this generalized sense of country (*Laws* 662b, 705c, 706b, 707d, 708b, 737d, 752d, 830e, 847c, 871d, 874b, 920e, 949c; also *Rep.* 388a, *Pol.* 259a). Yet, even in this generalized sense, the word is in some instances sufficiently determinate that city and country are contained disjunctively within it: as in a passage telling how the Spartans banished excessive drinking from the land (ἐκ τῆς χώρας), so that drinking parties (συμπόσια) are to be seen neither in the cities (ἄστυ) nor in the country (ἀγρός) (*Laws* 637a).

The operation of the word χώρα in the discourses of the *Timaeus* and most notably in the chorology is not independent of the preunderstanding expressed in the translation of χώρα as place, land, and country. Indeed, a number of the connections broached and images evoked in the examples cited have implications for the chorology and its affiliated discourses, though of course only with various inversions and transformations, to say nothing of the highly problematized context in which these connections and images appear in the *Timaeus*. Not only is the χώρα interrogated as something like the place of the πόλις, but also it is linked to a certain bound or limit of the city, linked thus, in turn, to what is other than the city. And though the city is never mentioned in the chorology, though even the other discourses allied most closely with the chorology seem quite aloof from questions of politics, it is imperative to bear in mind that the larger context is explicitly political, that the entire extended series of discourses voiced by Timaeus is set between two discourses by Critias on the original Athens and is undertaken precisely for the sake of introducing the second, detailed—and, in the *Timaeus,* only projected—account that Critias is to give of ancient Athens: Critias' proposal says in effect that Timaeus' discourses are to provide the material, namely, the men generated by the discourse, or at least a number of exceptional ones (27a–b), which Critias is then to mold, through his discourse, into a city, into ancient Athens. Among the images evoked in the examples cited from the *Laws,* those of land, of mother, and of reception echo most distinctly what is said in Timaeus' second discourse. But the most distinct and far-reaching echo of all is that which sounds in the Stranger's discourse on the χώρα as the place of being, as the place of its shining, its brightness, for which only the philosopher, it seems, has eyes.

Even as it functions in the chorology, χώρα is linked decisively to what can be heard in the corresponding verb χωρέω, especially two of its senses. First, it means to make room for another, to give way or withdraw. Thus, a passage in one of the *Homeric Hymns* reads: "The earth gave way from beneath [γαῖα δ᾽ ἔνερθε χώρησεν]."[26] The relevant allusion is to the sense of withdrawing yet receiving, drawing something into itself in its very withdrawing. Χωρέω also means to go forward, to be in motion or in flux, as in the saying attributed to Heraclitus in the *Cratylus:* "Heraclitus says somewhere that everything moves [πάντα χωρεῖ] and nothing remains still, and, likening the things that are to the flow of a river, he says that you cannot step twice into the same river" (*Crat.* 402a). Saying the χώρα is not entirely unlike saying the flux.

Here is how the χώρα is said, the chorology, or rather a translation: "Moreover, a third kind is that of the χώρα, everlasting [ἀεί], not admitting destruction, granting an abode [ἕδρα] to all things having generation, itself to be apprehended with nonsense, by a sort of bastard reckoning [λογισμῷ τινὶ νόθῳ], hardly trustworthy; and looking toward which we dream and affirm that it is necessary [ἀναγκαῖον] that all that is be somewhere in some place [τόπος] and occupy some χώρα; and that that which is neither on earth nor anywhere in the heaven is nothing. As for all of these and others akin to them and concerning [their] wakeful and truly underlying nature, under the influence of this dreaming, we are unable to awaken, to distinguish [these], and to say the truth: that for an image, since not even that itself on the basis of which it comes to be generated belongs to the image but it is always brought forth as the phantom [φάντασμα] of something other—because of this it is appropriate for it to be generated in something other, clinging to being at least in a certain way, on pain of being nothing at all; whereas to the aid of that which *is* in the manner appropriate to being [τῷ δὲ ὄντως ὄντι] there comes the precise true

---

26. "To Demeter," 429f.

λόγος: that as long as one thing is something and another is something else, neither of the two will ever come to be in the other, so as to become, at once, one (and the same) and two" (52a–d).

Nothing could go more without saying than that this translation, even leaving χώρα untranslated, will not have been able to reconstitute the semantic configuration of the Greek text. At best it will only have avoided massively projecting back upon the Platonic text forms of discourse and conceptualities that that text in general first made possible.

The χώρα is said to be everlasting, perpetual, always (ἀεί), not admitting destruction, that is, ruin, corruption, passing-away (φθορά). This corresponds to its being rigorously distinguished from the generated: it is that *in which* that which is generated comes to be and *from which* that which is destroyed passes away, departs. It is presupposed by all generation and destruction and thus is not itself subject to generation and destruction. Thus, Timaeus says of it what he also said of the intelligible εἴδη, indeed from the point at the beginning of his first discourse where the distinction was first broached. In this way he now makes explicit another respect in which the third kind, as he said, in a most perplexing way partakes of the intelligible: both are everlasting, perpetual, always, admitting no destruction.

But, instead of calling it the *in which* and *from which* of generation, Timaeus now declares that the χώρα grants, furnishes, supplies (παρέχω) an *abode* to all things having generation, to all things inasmuch as they are generated. The word translated as *abode* is ἕδρα, which means *chair, seat* in more generalized senses and especially a seat or abode of the gods, hence also *altar* or *temple*. Although it is used later in the *Timaeus* to refer to the seat of an organ such as the liver (67b; see also 62a), in the present context the semantic link to temple would seem decisive: like a temple, the χώρα bespeaks an abode into which something higher is somehow (and even despite its elevation) to be received and held.[27]

Timaeus says that the χώρα is to be apprehended (reached, touched: ἅπτω), with nonsensation, by a sort of bastard reckoning, hardly trustworthy. The word translated as *trustworthy* is πιστόν; this is the same word that Timaeus used earlier when he declared regarding fire, air, water, and earth that one cannot say in a trustworthy manner which is which (49b), since, in the very moment when one would say what such a thing is, it is always already becoming another in the cycle of transformations. The χώρα is similarly elusive; it is, as Timaeus said, most difficult to catch. It eludes vision even more than do the fleeting traces of fire. It is invisible, indeed more insistently so than are the intelligible εἴδη. It does not appear *as itself* at all but only *as,* for instance, the fire that is held in and by it. As the likes of fire are held in the χώρα, they are mere fleeting traces (ἴχνος—

27. Χώρα and ἕδρα are also associated in the *Laws* (893c).

see 53b) of themselves, and such appearing in and as these traces hardly suffices to provide an *image* of the χώρα and thus a trustworthy basis for an εἰκὼς λόγος that would proceed from the appearing itself. Equally decisive is the lack of determinations: if the χώρα has no determinations whatsoever, then how can anything be said of it, since presumably to say something of it would be to ascribe a determination to it? Here, then, there can be only a *bastard* discourse, one whose legitimacy cannot be established. In Athenian usage a bastard (νόθος) was the child of a citizen father and an alien mother. As is the chorology: this bastard discourse is fathered by citizen Timaeus and is to be borne by the maternal χώρα in all its alien elusiveness, its alterity, its strangeness. But why does Timaeus say that this apprehension is with nonsensation (μετ' ἀναισθησίας)? Here there is no doubt an echo of what was said earlier about the intelligible, that it is apprehended without sense, that is, by νοῦς. But also, in the phrase "with nonsensation," there is expressed, more positively, the connection between such discourse and the peculiar appearing of the χώρα: what flashes up in this appearing are only the fleeting traces, which are not yet a matter of sensation, as the sense qualities as such come to be constituted only at the much later stage reached toward the end of the second discourse (61c–69a).

Timaeus says: looking toward the χώρα, we dream of it and affirm that it is necessary that all that is be in some place and occupy some χώρα. The reference to the necessary (ἀναγκαῖον) serves as a reminder that the entire second discourse has to do with necessity (ἀνάγκη). Presumably it is here in the chorology that Timaeus addresses the necessity that determines or underlies necessity as such. It is the necessity—even here already being folded into a dream—that all beings be in some place (τόπος) and that they occupy some χώρα. It is perhaps not entirely fortuitous that the word translated as *occupy*, κατέχον, has a double meaning: it can also mean *restraining* or *holding back*.[28] The beings that occupy the χώρα would, then, also be held back, withheld from it. As the figures are withheld from the gold in which they are molded.

But what about the dream? In the dream the χώρα appears as a place in which all that is must be. In this oneiric vision the χώρα—or rather its dream-image—hovers before us as a place so all-encompassing that whatever is set apart from it can only be nothing. But what is there in a dream? In the *Republic* Socrates tells Glaucon what there is in a dream; or rather, he asks Glaucon to confirm what he, Socrates, takes there to be in a dream. Socrates asks him: "Is the man who holds that there are beautiful things but does not hold that there is beauty itself and who, if someone leads him to the knowledge of it, is not able to follow—is he, in your opin-

---

28. "Crito had got up and gone away even before I did, because he could not restrain [κατέχειν] his tears" (*Phaedo* 117d). ". . . the troops on the warship in their turn could no longer restrain their laughter [γέλωτα κατέχειν] . . ." (*Laches* 184a).

ion, living in a dream or is he awake? Consider it. Doesn't dreaming, whether one is asleep or awake, consist in believing a likeness of something to be not a likeness but rather the thing itself to which it is like?" (*Rep.* 476c). Glaucon agrees that such a man is dreaming, and Socrates then goes on to contrast the dreamer with a man who believes that there is a beautiful itself and who is able to distinguish between it and the beautiful things that are likenesses of it. Glaucon agrees that the latter man is quite awake. What there is, then, in a dream is an image that goes unrecognized as an image, an image that in the dream is simply taken as the original. And in contrast to the dreamer there is the one who can distinguish between the image and its original, the one who is wakeful to the difference and who even in a vision of an image will set its original apart from it.

It is precisely such differences that go unrecognized as such in the dream of the χώρα. In the dream we affirm a double necessity as regards all beings: that they be in some τόπος and that they occupy some χώρα. Affirming these necessities as if they were one and the same, we are simply submitted in the dream to the image of a kind of place filled with all the things that are. What is decisive in the dream is the conflation of this image of the χώρα with the χώρα itself, that is, the failure, as always in a dream, to recognize the image as an image and to set the original, the χώρα itself, apart from it. Instead, the χώρα is simply conflated with the τόπος of all things. Here τόπος means, not just place in some vague, indeterminate sense, but rather something like a region in a sense inseparable from the fire, air, water, or earth that belongs intrinsically to the region; the upper region, for instance, is determined as that of fire and aether. Later Timaeus will say explicitly, referring to fire, air, water, and earth: "The greater part of each kind keeps apart in a region [τόπος] of its own because of the movement of the recipient" (57c).[29] Thus, the conflation of the χώρα with its image is a conflation of it with a kind of region of sensible things. In the dream we drift toward obliterating the difference between the χώρα and sensible things, even as there hovers before us the image of a kind of region of regions in which all things would have their place, this image of the χώρα remaining unrecognized in its difference from the χώρα itself.[30] But in the dream there is also an equally decisive conflation of the intelligible with the sensible: the dream vision is of a region in which all that is would be placed, whereas one who awakens from the dream will—as Timaeus goes on to say—recognize that the intelligible εἴδη are set apart, that they do not pass anywhere else into

29. Later Timaeus also refers to the shifting of bodies "up and down toward their own proper regions [τόποι]" (58b–c; cf. 63d). In the *Critias* τόπος clearly has the sense of region when Critias says: "Once upon a time the gods took over by lot the whole earth according to its τόποι" (*Crit.* 109b). Even in Aristotle such usage is still to be found: see *Progression of Animals,* 706b.

30. In the *Laws* (760c) one finds the phrase "τοὺς τῆς χώρας τόπους," which entails a differentiation between χώρα and τόπος.

another.[31] To awaken from the dream is to distinguish the three kinds conflated in the oneiric vision. It is to count them off in their distinctness: 1, 2, 3.

Timaeus tells of this awakening, says the truth that one would say if one were to awaken. This includes saying the precise true λόγος that would come to the aid of the first kind, to the aid of that which *is* in the manner appropriate to being: "as long as one thing is something and another is something else, neither of the two will ever come to be in the other, so as to become, at once, one (and the same) and two." To say it otherwise: whatever is distinctly one, that is, a selfsame intelligible εἶδος, will never come to be in another in such a way that, while remaining itself, remaining one, it also *is* the other and hence is two. The intelligible εἴδη undergo no reception, but each remains just itself, one, one with itself, selfsame. This utter selfsameness entails that, even though the intelligible εἶδος is what stamps (fathers, informs) the image, which thus shares its name and its "look," the intelligible εἶδος *cannot belong* to the image. This is why the image is a phantom in need of some means by which, though set apart from being, it can cling to being and avoid being nothing at all. The χώρα, in which the phantoms come and go, is that other that secures the image in whatever trace of being it has, so that, though remote from being, indeed set utterly apart from it, the image is still not nothing. The image can double the εἶδος without the latter belonging to it, without one becoming also two, hence not one, only because the image is borne by the χώρα, only because the χώρα nurtures the image, sheltering it in a kind of quasi-being, giving birth to it in granting it that being. Because it nurtures and shelters the image, the χώρα is anything but a mere mirror in which perpetual being would be reflected and the cosmos thus fabricated in the same way that all things could be made by the clever and wonderful man who took a mirror and carried it around everywhere (*Rep.* 596c–d). One could call it, rather, a ghost scene that, enshrouding precisely in letting appear, endows the fleeting specters with whatever trace of being they might enjoy.

Thus, it is the χώρα that makes possible the doubling of being in an image, the duplicity of being.[32]

But then, the very move that displaces or limits the twofold, namely,

31. "Plato says that these words resemble those of a man who is dreaming: there being is confounded with the *image of being.* For according to him the generated individuals, which one mistakes for true beings, can, it is true, exist only in a certain place; but true beings, the ideas, are no more in one place than in another, in one time than in another. They are, and that is all one can say of their existence" (Martin, *Études sur le Timée de Platon,* 2:176 n. LXI).

32. The relation between the duplicity of being and the χώρα is expressed negatively in the *Theaetetus* (180e): Melissus and Parmenides "maintain that everything is one and is stationary within itself, having no χώρα in which to move." See also *Parmenides,* 149a.

the introduction of the third kind, is at the same time what establishes the very possibility of the twofold, of the doubling of being in an image. Now it is evident why the first discourse had to leave the twofold suspended: the twofold *is itself suspended,* it remains impossible, as long as the operation of the third kind is lacking. One will always have to count on from two to three. And yet, as soon as the third kind is introduced, the twofold will have been limited, its exclusive dominion disturbed, displaced; and, in a sense of being beyond being, one will no longer be able to say that there are (*il y a*) only intelligible and sensible beings.

If one were to take metaphysics to be constituted precisely by the governance of the twofold, then the chorology could be said to bring both the founding of metaphysics and its displacement, both at once. Originating metaphysics would have been exposing it to the abyss, to the abysmal χώρα, which is both origin and abyss, both at the same time. Then one could say—with the requisite reservations—that the beginning of metaphysics will have been already the end of metaphysics.

One dreams of the χώρα. And one tells of it, Timaeus tells of it, in a bastard discourse, a third kind of discourse, one suited somehow to saying the third kind of being, a discourse engendered by intercourse with the alien, promiscuous—and yet ever virginal—mother.

One dreams *of* the χώρα. Even though in the dream one fails to distinguish properly the three kinds of being, even though one conflates these three kinds, still the χώρα is *disclosed* in the dream in which one dreams of it. The dream not only confounds but also discloses that of which one dreams, just as an image, even if not distinguished from its original, lets the original nonetheless show itself. One can awaken from the dream, even if, under the influence of this dreaming, one is *oneself* unable to awaken. One can awaken and can then draw the proper distinctions, as Timaeus demonstrates *in deed* by going on to say the truth that we would say on awakening. On awakening, the disclosure of the χώρα given in the dream can be developed by carrying out the distinctions that were not drawn within the dream. It is in this connection that one needs to attend to what, near the beginning of his third discourse, Timaeus says of the liver. One thing he says is that the liver replicates the χώρα within the human body. For this replica—though never for the χώρα itself—he uses the image of a mirror: the liver is made smooth and bright, and so "the powers of thoughts that proceed from νοῦς move in the liver as in a mirror that receives impressions and provides visible images" (71b). It is around the liver that a part of the soul "in the night passes its time moderately, being occupied in its slumbers with divination [μαντεία], since it does not partake of λόγος or discernment [φρόνησις]" (71d). Thus, in the lower parts of soul and body, there is this organ of divination, a gift of the god, given to man's foolishness. One is receptive to divination only when one's noetic power is fettered in sleep or distraught by disease or by divine inspiration. Timaeus says: "But it belongs to a man when in his right senses [ἔμφρων] to remember and ponder the things spoken of in dream or waking vision by the divining and inspired nature" (71e). As when, awakening from a dream of the χώρα, one ventures a bastard discourse on the χώρα. Or ventures to tell of the dream, of the awakening, and of the χώρα. As in chorology.

4

Traces of the Χώρα

FROM TRACES TO PRIMARY BODIES

As he approaches the chorology, Timaeus counts the three kinds three times. The first counting occurs near the beginning of the second discourse (48e): whereas previously two were distinguished, now a third kind must be declared. Adhering to the numbering schema established at the threshold and the beginning of the chorology, by which the first is the selfsame, intelligible εἶδος, the second the generated sensible, and the third the χώρα, the first counting may be represented thus:

1, 2—now 3

This counting expresses the framework of the first discourse (the twofold) and the transition from it.

The second counting comes just after the discussion of the fleeting fire, air, water, and earth circling in their cycle of transformations (which are not yet, in the strict sense, formations at all). The counting occurs in the discussion of the third kind as the receptacle of these fugitives, precisely at a point where Timaeus is in the midst of presenting the various images intended to portray its receptive character (50c–d): there is need to think of three kinds, that which is generated, that in which it is generated, and that from which it is copied and begotten. Adhering to the same numbering schema, this second counting may be represented thus:

2, 3, 1

This counting expresses the shift to the precosmic sensible, to the fugitive traces.

The third counting immediately follows the second (50d): it is fitting to liken the recipient to the mother, the *from which* to the father, and what is engendered between them to the offspring. In schematic representation:

$$3, 1, 2$$

This counting expresses the focus on the χώρα that comes into effect here and remains in force until the end of the chorology. It is not entirely fortuitous that this focus is established at precisely the moment when the χώρα is called the mother.

Then there is another counting of the three kinds at the point where the threshold of the chorology gives way to the chorology proper. Or rather, there is a reversion to the first—presumably proper—counting at this point where the χώρα is finally called by its proper name (52a–b): the first is the selfsame εἶδος, the second the generated sensible, and moreover a third kind is that of the χώρα. This is the counting in which the numbering schema is established:

$$1, 2, 3$$

But then, finally, just after the chorology, there is still another counting (52d): there is being, χώρα, and generation—that is:

$$1, 3, 2$$

This counting expresses schematically what the chorology has declared and in some respects shown: that the intelligible εἶδος and the χώρα are required for there to be a generated image, that is, a double of being outside being.

In carrying out this final counting of the three kinds, Timaeus is stating the account to which he gives—and says that he gives—his vote: it declares "being [ὄν] and χώρα and genesis to be [εἶναι], three in a threefold manner, before the generation of the heaven" (52d). Here there is a marked shift in the discourse, a transition from that most correct and most thoroughly distinguishing discourse required in the chorology, a kind of falling away from the demands of such a level of discourse. There are two indications of this falling away. The first is the designation of this account as ἐν κεφαλαίῳ, which indicates such a shift regardless of whether one takes the phrase merely as meaning *in summary* or as carrying still the reference to the head that was operative earlier. The second indication is provided by the very formulation of the account: each of the three kinds is said *to be* (εἶναι), even though one of them is called being (ὄν) and even though the chorology has declared that, in quite different ways, both the generated and the χώρα are remote from being.

On the other hand, the brief discourse (52d–53c) immediately following the chorology does venture certain extensions that in a sense move beyond the chorology. This discourse is no longer addressed just to the third kind, to the attempt to say the χώρα in an appropriate way. Rather, it is addressed also, indeed equally, to the second kind. The time is still that before the generation of the heavens, more precisely, a time when the primary bodies (fire, air, water, and earth) that constitute the second kind are *not yet themselves.* In this time when measure and order are lacking, this prenatal time of the cosmos, this time (before time) when, as Timaeus says, the god is absent, fire and the other three "have only a trace [ἴχνος] of themselves" (53b). Thus, the discourse is addressed to the χώρα and the traces. It pictures them together, portrays how the traces are *in* the χώρα.

In this discourse Timaeus refers again to the *appearing* of the χώρα. Reverting to a prechorological name, though one of the most telling, he speaks of how the nurse of generation "appears manifoldly to sight" (52d-e). Previous references have indicated that such appearing involves a certain distribution of the various traces: in the portion that, for instance, is fiery, it appears as fire. But now Timaeus speaks of the movement by which this distribution comes about. It is a complex movement, one that involves movements both of the χώρα and of the traces within the χώρα.

One could regard this discourse as responding at the most archaic depth to Socrates' desire for a discourse depicting a being, whether artificial or in repose, set in movement. The being to which Socrates referred was the city that he had just described, the citizens for which are to be supplied by Timaeus' discourse. Socrates' desire is what has set in movement the entire series of discourses that run throughout the *Timaeus* and continue in the *Critias.*

It is not without paradox that one can speak of the χώρα as itself in movement, as something—though not, of course, some thing—that moves. For the χώρα is not only utterly amorphous but also invisible, even insistently invisible, whereas the things that can be said, without further ado, to move are visible things, things that occupy some place and move to another, or at least that alter their position or state within a place. But how can the χώρα be in a place in which or from which to move? At most, and not with impunity, it might be said, as in the dream of the χώρα,[1] to be a kind of region of regions within which something else could move. Yet, in this regard it is imperative to remember that τόποι are not merely presupposed by movement but are determined by it: the upper region is the region to which fire by nature moves. It is precisely the determination of regions by the movements of the traces that Timaeus is describing here, even if it remains paradoxical, even within the dream, to speak of the χώρα as itself moving.

---

1. Reentry into the dream, at least a reengagement of a certain conflation of χώρα with τόπος, is marked by Timaeus' statement that each kind of trace occupied a different χώρα even before the universe was generated out of them (53a).

The movement of the χώρα results from a difference and imbalance of the powers (that is, of the traces) within it. Being unbalanced, the nurse sways unevenly, and it is shaken by the powers (as by an earthquake: σείεσθαι). But, in turn, the nurse shakes the powers; she moves them, making these fleeting traces fly off in various directions. Timaeus uses the image of winnowing to describe the result of this complex movement. The result is that the dissimilar are separated and the similar pushed together. Thus, even before the universe comes to be generated out of them, fire and the other three—still only as traces—are set apart from each other in—and so as to determine—different regions.

Now the god returns, the god who has put in no appearance since the beginning of the second discourse. Upon his return—or his arrival—the first thing he does, according to Timaeus, is to mark the traces of fire and the other three out into shapes by means of εἴδη and numbers. Thus it is that he shapes the traces into primary bodies, into fire, air, water, and earth as such, as themselves.[2] Since these are the very same bodies that the god took up—that Timaeus took for granted—when in the first discourse he set about making the cosmos, the account that Timaeus is about to give of the making of the primary bodies will bring the discourse to the point where it will have caught up with itself. Timaeus will have brought his discourse to bear on that for the sake of which he had to turn back in launching his second discourse. Now, with his discourse on the primary bodies, Timaeus will have come around to beginning at the beginning, even though he did not—and will not have done so—in the beginning. Or, more precisely, he will have come around to beginning *from* the beginning: for he has not been able to provide an εἰκὼς λόγος that would constitute the most correct and most thoroughly distinguishing discourse on the χώρα; unable to draw the χώρα into an εἰκὼς λόγος, Timaeus has had recourse to a bastard discourse in which the χώρα remains alien, from which it remains withdrawn. As with something of which one has dreamed in a dream from which one has now awakened.

Timaeus remarks, almost apologetically, that his account of how the god shaped the traces into the primary bodies will require an unusual kind of discourse, with which fortunately those listening have some acquaintance. One could call the discourse geometrical, were it not that it concerns the metric not only of the earth but also of fire, air, and water. But it will turn out that the earth's proper metric sets it somewhat apart from the other three.

---

2. Margel emphasizes that the traces, distributed to their proper regions, constitute the possibility of an organizing of the universe such as the god undertakes: "These traces . . . would constitute the *mimetic possibility* of an organization of the world. Without the possibility of these traces, without the possibility of effectively inscribing in each fugitive and dispersed apparition of the element the delimited (anterior-posterior) horizon of a specific form, the demiurge could never seize the elements in their stable contours separating them from one another" (*Le Tombeau du Dieu Artisan,* 143).

Timaeus details the various constructions carried out by the god. He begins with two kinds of triangles. One is the right isosceles, which has one single nature. The other is the right triangle with unequal sides, which, however, is unlimited (ἄπειρον); hence, from this unlimited variety, one must be chosen, and, says Timaeus, it is to be the most beautiful (τὸ κάλλιστον), if we intend to make a suitable beginning (εἰ μέλλομεν ἄρξ-εσθαι κατὰ τρόπον) (54a)—as is indeed to be made here at this point where account is finally being given of the beginning (the primary bodies) from which the god fabricates the cosmos. To prevent the unlimited from contaminating and virtually undoing in advance the shapes of all but one of the primary bodies, turning this would-be beginning back toward the more archaic, the god chooses, as the most beautiful right triangle with unequal sides, the one that, when conjoined with another like it, produces an equilateral triangle. Thus, beginning with the right isosceles triangle and the half-equilateral triangle, the god constructs from four of the former the square and from six of the latter a larger equilateral triangle. These figures are then used as faces to construct four of the five regular solids: from six squares the cube is formed, from six equilateral triangles the tetrahedron or regular pyramid, from eight equilateral triangles the octahedron, from twenty equilateral triangles the icosahedron.[3] Timaeus tells how the four solids are then assigned to the traces of fire (tetrahe-

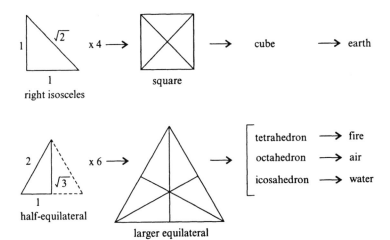

dron), air (octahedron), water (icosahedron), and earth (cube) so as to form the primary bodies, fire, air, water, and earth as such, as themselves.

There follows an extended discussion of the primary bodies, of their various kinds and of the transformations that can take place between

3. See Cornford, *Plato's Cosmology,* 211-19; also Heath, *History of Greek Mathematics,* 1:296f.

them through dissolution into their component triangles (which are so small as never to be seen [56b–c]) and reformation. Three points from this discussion are to be underlined. (1) Timaeus notes that there are various sizes of elementary triangles (57d) and that as a result there are different varieties of each of the kinds of primary bodies. In the case of air he mentions explicitly that there are varieties such as aether, mist, and others because of variation in the size of the triangles (58d). (2) He notes also that the primary bodies can themselves be compounded to form other things. For example, a certain kind of water, specifically, a kind of metal (since metals are kinds of water that are fusible), can be mixed with fine portions of earth to produce bronze (59b–c). (3) Three of the kinds of primary bodies (fire, air, water) can undergo transformation into one another, since they are composed of the same kind of elementary triangles. But because earth is composed of a different kind of triangle, it cannot change into any of the other three nor any of them into it. Timaeus is explicit: "Earth will never change into another form" (56d). He observes in this regard that earlier it appeared that all passed into one another, but he insists now that this appearance is not correct (54b–c). This observation and this insistence serve to call attention to the difference between these geometrically structured transformations and the fleeting, drifting, indeterminate circling of the traces in their circle of generation. In effect, Timaeus marks the difference between the primary bodies and the traces by insisting on this differentiation of earth from the other three, at the same time preparing for a later scene in which earth, in distinction from the other three, will play a distinctive role.

EPICHOROLOGY

Now that Timaeus' discourse has in a sense caught up with itself, the question is whether it reverts to the mode and structures that were operative before it broke off and opened the abyss toward which it was drawn by the traces of the χώρα. What, then, about the segment of discourse that ensues once the god has formed the traces into the primary bodies used by the god in fabricating the cosmos? Once the traces have thus been assimilated, once they are no longer traces, do there remain any traces of the χώρα? Is the χώρα in any way traced in the segment of discourse running from the account of the primary bodies to the little comedy with which the dialogue concludes?[4]

4. Taking the discussion of the primary bodies as the beginning in the specific sense mentioned above, there is then reason to regard all that follows it as in a certain sense a single discourse. This sense is indicated at the outset of the last major section of the second discourse, the section that follows the discussion of the primary bodies and is devoted to the sensible qualities (61c–69a). The indication lies in Timaeus' remark that the discussion of the sensible qualities is entangled with those of the flesh and of the mortal part of the soul, and conversely (61c). Since the latter constitutes the general theme of the third discourse, Timaeus is saying in effect that there is a kind of mutual envelopment operative between the last major section of the second discourse and the third discourse.

It is an old complaint, a complaint made by one of the earliest readers of the *Timaeus,* the complaint that having introduced the χώρα Plato then makes no use of it in the remainder of the dialogue. It is Aristotle's complaint, for instance, in the passage in *On Generation and Corruption* where he says: "And what is written in the Timaeus does not distinguish sufficiently. For it is not clearly said whether the all-receiving [τὸ πανδεχές] is separate from the elements. Nor does he make any use of it, after saying that it is a substratum [ὑποκείμενον] prior to the so-called elements, just as gold is the substratum of works made of gold" (329a). Whatever reservations one might voice about the appropriateness of such words as ὑποκειμενον, and however much one may insist that the *Timaeus* does mark clearly—as clearly as such intrinsically obscure matters allow—the differentiation between the receptacle and what Aristotle calls the elements (himself obliterating a decisive distinction), still the complaint is forthright, and it has continued to be put forth even by some recent commentators on the *Timaeus.*[5]

But what about the complaint? Is it sustained when one turns to the dialogue itself and reads with care and discernment?

In fact, there are several places in the *Timaeus* where statements of intent or reflections on the account under way would seem to indicate quite the contrary of what Aristotle says. For instance, at the beginning of Timaeus' second discourse, where he has just broken off and made a new beginning, he declares that the generation of the cosmos came about as a mixture, from the combination of intelligence (νοῦς) and necessity (ἀνάγκη). The discourse that follows makes it manifest that ἀνάγκη is a name for what comes to be called finally χώρα. And, as noted, if the passage is more carefully and discerningly translated, then it speaks, not just of combination (as if νοῦς and ἀνάγκη were simply united), but rather of a standing-together (σύστασις) in which there can also be hostility, conflict, as with two soldiers in close combat. Thus, the specific sense of the passage is such as to suggest that the necessary or choric moment will not be simply assimilated once the god returns, that this moment is not to disappear from the dialogue from that point on. Another instance is found just after the account of how the god assigned the figures of the regular solids to the traces. Reflecting on the account, noting that it is a likely discourse, Timaeus observes that indeed the god shaped the primary bodies in just the way described, at least—and this is the decisive indication—to the extent that ἀνάγκη permitted, to the extent that it gave way, withdrew (56c). There are other, fairly direct references to the χώρα in the epichorological discourse, as when, for instance, Timaeus says that the motion of the receptacle serves to keep the primary bodies apart in their respective regions (57c). To say nothing of the fact that

5. For example, by Edward N. Lee, "On the Metaphysics of the Image in Plato's *Timaeus,*" 349.

even in Timaeus' third discourse various names for the χώρα and the name χώρα itself are sounded.

There can be no question, then, but that the χώρα will remain to some extent in force after the god's return. At the very least it will limit what the artisan god can achieve in his cosmic fabrication; it will limit the productive operation of divine or noetic causes. And yet, unlike what is produced, unlike even production itself, the χώρα cannot become simply a *theme to be presented,* something to be presented, say, along with the operation of νοῦς. Why not? Precisely because the χώρα *cannot be presented.* It does not itself become present but only appears as something else, not as itself. It cannot be presented even in the sense of being the theme of a discourse that would determine it, for it withdraws from all determination and allows only a bastard discourse. The consequence is that the chorology *cannot be integrated* into the likely discourse that resumes following it[6] and continues to the end of the dialogue.

In a sense, then, Plato could not have made use of the χώρα in the rest of the dialogue. Yet this does not mean that the χώρα is not in force beneath the production of the various things the god will fabricate, but only that it is not in force as something present that could be represented, that is, imaged in a likeness in a likely discourse. How, then, is the χώρα in force? And how is it said in—or, in a sense, along with—the likely discourse that runs on to the end of the dialogue?

The word that names its way of being in force was introduced at the very beginning of the second discourse in Timaeus' description of the kind of cause that at that point has to be brought into consideration, not having been considered in the previous discourse. He calls it an *errant* kind of cause, *errant* (translating πλανωμένον) in the double sense of wandering and erring. How, then, is the χώρα in force? As errancy: as hindering, diverting, leading astray the work of νοῦς, as installing indeterminacy into what νοῦς would otherwise render determinate. And the χώρα is said in the epichorological discourse of the *Timaeus* by the way in which this discourse traces the errancy, that is, marks the traces of its operation in the very midst of the god's productions. The discourse marks the traces of the χώρα by marking the traces of its errant, indetermining operation.

In the epichorological portion of Timaeus' second discourse there are several such traces marked. Let me mention four.

The first occurs near the end of Timaeus' account of how the primary

---

6. Following the chorology, just after Timaeus has begun the discussion of the figures from which the god constructs the shapes to be imposed on the traces, Timaeus mentions a kind of discourse which combines likeliness with necessity (53d); this character of the discourse corresponds to its theme, the imposition of shapes (given as such to noetic vision) upon the traces (belonging to the realm of necessity). As the discourse moves away from the discussion of the necessary, Timaeus comes to speak simply of likely discourse (55d, 56a, 57d) or of correct likely discourse (56b).

bodies are produced by the assignment of the figures of the regular solids to the traces of fire, air, water, and earth. As noted, Timaeus explains also exactly how these figures are themselves constructed from two kinds of triangles, right isosceles triangles and triangles each of which consists of half an equilateral triangle. What is unusual in the account—and what marks the operation of errancy—is that, just at the point where it would seem that complete order had been constituted, Timaeus suddenly mentions that these two kinds of triangles occur in all different sizes (57d). Thus there proves to be an unlimited, indeterminately great variety of combinations. Inasmuch as this unlimitedness arises from the variation in the size of the triangles, it is linked to whatever topical or even extensional character may have come at this point to take the place of the withdrawn χώρα.

The second such trace takes the form of a curious gap that betrays the workings of errancy. In a sense it is an errancy that insinuates itself in the order oriented to νοῦς: there is a gap precisely in the construction of the regular solids, for, from the two kinds of triangles that provide the basis for the constructions, only four of the five regular solids can be constructed. From the two kinds of elementary triangles it is not possible to form the pentagonal faces from which could be constructed the fifth regular solid, the dodecahedron, which has as its faces twelve equal regular pentagons.[7] Timaeus calls attention to this gap, noting that there remains one other figure, the fifth, and remarking, without elaboration, that the god used it for decorating the universe,[8] though at this point there is as yet no universe, so that if the god does construct this solid, it will have to lie around unused until a much later time, indeed until the time when time itself comes (along with the heaven) to be generated. Yet, this gap in the construction of the regular solids points to another that consists in the noncorrespondence between the geometrical order (in which there are *five* regular solids) and the order of the traces (of which there are only *four*). This gap constitutes an intrinsic noncoincidence between the noetic and the necessary.

The third such trace occurs at the point where, as Timaeus is discussing the four kinds of primary bodies, there suddenly appears a kind of gap in the discourse, an indeterminacy, a certain silence within it. In speaking of air, he notes that there are different kinds of air, since the triangles that

---

7. Heath, *History of Greek Mathematics,* 1:296.

8. Since, of the five regular solids, the dodecahedron has the greatest volume and hence most nearly approaches a sphere, its assignment has a certain appropriateness. It may be, as certain commentators propose, that one is to imagine a flexible dodecahedron expanding into a spherical shape; a similar connection is suggested in *Phaedo* 110b (see Proclus, *In Platonis Timaeum Commentaria,* 3:141). As Cornford notes, the word διαζωγραφῶν is ambiguous: it may mean "painting it in various colors" or (as Cornford proposes) "making a pattern of animal figures thereon" (*Plato's Cosmology,* 218f.). Taylor proposes "broidering figures on it," suggesting that the figures or animals (ζῷα) meant are the constellations (*Commentary on Plato's Timaeus,* 377).

compose it can be different sizes. So, there is aether and mist and, he says, "other εἴδη [of air] without a name, produced because of the inequality of the triangles" (58d). But since, as he just mentioned, there are indefinitely many different sizes of triangles, he has now in effect introduced into the very eidetics of air an indeterminate proliferation. Proceeding to discuss water, he mentions the names of several kinds but then says regarding the various mixtures of various kinds of water: "most of the kinds thus generated are without names" (60a). The structure of the text is here most remarkable. Right between a passage in which he gives the names of some kinds of water and the passage in which he admits that many others have no names, Timaeus abruptly turns the discourse upon itself, calling it, not an εἰκὼς λόγος, but an εἰκὼς μῦθος and characterizing such storytelling as a pleasant, measured, and mindful play (παιδιά). Presumably the discourse here becomes, if it has not indeed already become, a matter of play, of playful stories, because of the indeterminacy, instability, wandering, and vacillation that belongs to things of the kind he is describing. He says even: let us give free rein to this play and go on with such stories. The question is: How far does this self-determination of the discourse as playful story extend? Does it extend only to the end of the discussion of the primary bodies? Or perhaps to the end of the second discourse? Or perhaps even to the end of the dialogue?

In any case it is difficult to determine whether the reappearance of the designation εἰκὼς μῦθος at this point in the dialogue signals anything beyond the playful and storylike character of a certain portion of the discourse to come. The one thing that seems clear in this regard is that the distinction between λόγος and μῦθος does not simply correspond to any of the basic distinctions that Timaeus draws between the kinds of being. It is not a matter of λόγος being appropriate for saying the intelligible εἴδη and μῦθος being suited to saying the χώρα. Neither does μῦθος enjoy any evident privilege as regards saying the generated sensible images; indeed it was precisely in reference to the latter that Timaeus first explained that what he would present would be an εἰκὼς λόγος (29b), even though, almost immediately and in the same connection, he spoke also of εἰκὼς μῦθος (29d). On the other hand, one could be tempted to consider whether, as with the μῦθος that appears in the *Republic* in the guise of κατάβασις, of the cave, and of the story of Er,[9] it is a matter of venturing to say with μῦθος the abysmal other than being. And yet, in the *Timaeus,* all the attempts to say the χώρα are punctuated by references to λόγος rather than μῦθος, as indeed one would expect on the basis of the original proposal, voiced by Critias and restated by Socrates, that they present a true λόγος rather than an invented μῦθος (26c–e). It is, then, only a question of whether, when it becomes a matter of tracing the χώρα, of marking

9. See *Being and Logos,* chap. 5.

the operation of errancy within the universe made by the god, a return of or to μῦθος becomes inevitable, even if of or to a μῦθος that seems only remotely akin to that with which the *Timaeus* began.

The fourth trace is marked in Timaeus' discussion of sensible affections. For in the course of this discussion, some things turn up that not only have no names but have no εἴδη, thus sensible things of a sort that are not even images of the intelligible. Timaeus mentions especially odors and declares that they "do not allow εἴδη" (66d). He calls them "half-kinds" (ἡμιγενές). Since they have no εἴδη, they cannot but lack names even more insistently than in the cases discussed earlier.

In Timaeus' third discourse also such traces of the χώρα are marked, this wandering, errant indetermination that haunts the works of the god and, perhaps even more, the works of the engendered gods to whom he delegates the task of making the other living beings, except for their immortal part. Nowhere is such a trace more unmistakably marked than in Timaeus' description of the making of the mortal part of the human soul. He says that the mortal soul has within it passions that are both fearful (δεινός) and necessary (ἀναγκαῖα). Then he tells how the mortal soul came about: "And blending these with undiscursive sensation and with all-endeavoring ἔρως, they compounded, in the manner of necessity, the mortal kind of soul" (69d). Thus are ἀνάγκη and its errancy (errancy itself) operative within the human soul from the very formation of its mortal part.

In Timaeus' discourse on the human body there are numerous indications as to how the χώρα is replicated within the body itself and through its double put in play there. It has been noted already how such replication is unmistakably indicated in the case of the liver: this organ is made dense and smooth and bright and sweet, yet containing bitterness; and so, as Timaeus says, "the power of thoughts that proceed from νοῦς move in the liver as in a mirror that receives impressions and provides visible images" (71b). A connection is also indicated to the spleen, to which is applied one of the words used just before the chorology to name the χώρα, namely, ἐκμαγεῖον. The function of the spleen is said to be to keep the liver bright and clean, as does the ἐκμαγεῖον that in preparation is laid beside a mirror. But now, though intimating the pertinent connection, the word does not signify *matrix* but rather *wiper* or *duster*.[10] Also, the lower belly, the abdomen, is explicitly called a receptacle (ὑποδοχή) for food and drink; its purpose is to prevent them from passing through too quickly, that is, to secure them in their flux. Timaeus observes that without this receptacle we would be plagued by insatiable appetite; and then, because of our gluttony, we would be rendered devoid of philosophy. So then, a playful story about how the belly—a double of the χώρα—makes philosophy possible.

---

10. On the meaning of ἐκμαγεῖον in this context, see Taylor, *Commentary on Plato's Timaeus,* 515.

One could add perhaps another kind of story, about how philosophy requires images, which the χώρα makes possible. But that would be another story!

Even the word χώρα is found in Timaeus' discussion of the origin of disease—appropriately so, since the description pictures disease as like a reversion to that state of imbalance and shaking that was said to prevail when, before the arrival of the god, the χώρα was filled with the traces of fire, air, water, and earth. Referring to these four, but now as the primary bodies from which the human body is composed, Timaeus says: "When, contrary to nature, there occurs an excess or deficiency of these or a change in the χώρα from the proper to an other, then the body loses its selfsameness and there results disease [νόσος] and unlimitedness [ἄπειρον]" (82a). When Timaeus goes on to speak of the treatment of disease, specifically of the restoration of symmetry between soul and body, he declares that this involves imitating "the nurse of the universe" (88d); that is, recalling the earlier role of the image of the nurse, it involves imitating the χώρα. This is to be accomplished by never allowing the body to be at rest, by continually producing internal vibrations keeping it in movement, duplicating the state of the χώρα filled with traces being winnowed out.

In Timaeus' third discourse there are numerous touches of comedy. As in the picture of someone making himself like the χώρα and its traces in order to treat his illness, especially in the case of a man, considering the maternal nature of the χώρα. Several of the comic touches have indeed to do with sex, with the difference and relation between the sexes.

As, for instance, the little comedy of fingernails. Timaeus says: "For those who constructed us knew that out of men women would someday spring, and all other animals, and that many of these creatures would need for many purposes the help of nails [ὄνυξ];[11] hence they impressed upon men at their very birth the rudimentary structure of nails" (76d-e). The story is that from men are born women and then animals! And men are burdened with nails because they will be needed by animals. Perhaps also by women.

But what is most remarkable in this regard is the way in which the third discourse and hence the *Timaeus* as a whole draws to an end. Just short of the end the discourse appears to reach a kind of climax, to culminate in an ascent. Timaeus comes to speak only of the divine part of the soul (housed in the head) and of our looking to the harmonies and revolutions of the cosmos in order to make the revolutions in our head, disturbed by and at birth, like those of the cosmos. The ascent is nothing short of a reversion to the sphere of Timaeus' first discourse; both in tone

---

11. The word ὄνυξ covers not only nails but also the animal counterparts, claws and hooves.

and in content, it sounds very much like the injunction issued at the end of the first discourse, just before that discourse was interrupted for the sake of the turn back toward the χώρα. In this ascent, as previously, it is a matter of mimesis and of the structures within which mimesis operates; it is a matter of an imitation that looks to a paradigm in order to make something (now one's divine part) like the paradigm. Most remarkably, it is at precisely this point that a kind of comedy breaks out, a kind of sex comedy, which comes thus to interrupt the ascent, just as previously, in the first discourse, the ascent was interrupted by the necessity of turning to the χώρα and just as in the story of the eidetic city the ascent is interrupted by the force of ἔρως.

Timaeus of course is speaking: "And the marrow that we call seed, inasmuch as it is animate and has been granted an outlet, has endowed the part where its outlet lies with a love for generating by implanting therein a lively desire for emission. Wherefore in men the nature of the genital organs is disobedient and self-willed, like a creature that is deaf to λόγος, and it attempts to dominate all because of its frenzied desires. And in women again, owing to the same causes, whenever the womb or uterus, as it is called—which is an indwelling creature, desirous of child-bearing—remains without fruit long beyond the due season, it is vexed and becomes errant; and by straying all ways through the body and blocking up the passages of the breath and preventing respiration, it casts the body into the utmost distress and causes, moreover, all kinds of maladies; until the desire and love [ἡ ἐπιθυμία καὶ ὁ ἔρως] of the two sexes unite them" (91b-c). Thus, at the very moment of ascent—or in the moment of its interruption—there comes a comic transition from male to female, to the prospective mother, whose womb can become errant, wandering (πλανώμενον). Timaeus tells of how the plowland of the womb gets sown with living beings, who are nourished there and then in birth are brought to the light of day. Timaeus appears to draw a conclusion: "In this way women and all that is female have come to be" (91d). But he has not shown how women specifically come to be, how there comes to be anything female, how sexual differentiation originates, but has rather just taken it for granted, as ludicrously as in the comic transition from male to female genital organs. One wonders whether sexual differentiation is any less elusive than the differentiation between those beings that Timaeus has likened to father and mother: on the one side, being itself, the intelligible εἴδη, on the other side, that kind of being beyond being that in its most nearly proper name is called χώρα.

Then comes a comic transformation of the way up, the ascent, the flight. For, as soon as the woman has given birth and Timaeus has drawn his ludicrous conclusion, he continues: "Now, as for the race of birds, they are derived by transformation, growing feathers in place of hair from men [males: ἀνήρ] who are harmless but light-minded" (91d).[12] Little wonder that the discourse is abruptly dragged down to earth, telling of those animals that—derived from men ignorant of philosophy and of the nature of the heaven—have dragged their front limbs and head down to earth. Downward the discourse continues to plunge at a rapid pace, to animals with elongated heads, to those so foolish that they require the support of many feet, on to those that inhabit the depths of the water, the dialogue coming to its conclusion in this descensional bestiary.

So then, not only playful stories but comic ones, comedies that interrupt the high-minded ascent of those who would fix their gaze upward or suspend themselves in the clouds. Comedies that release the play of ἔρως and that draw us back toward the abyss. It is with such comedy that the *Timaeus,* this most abysmal of dialogues, comes fittingly to an end.

THE POLITICAL FRAME

But what about the city? After all, it was for the sake of a political discourse that Timaeus undertook his extended cosmology. More precisely, the Timaean cosmology follows two incomplete political discourses, Socrates' recapitulation of yesterday's discourse and Critias' outline of the discourse he will present in detail later. The Timaean cosmology would carry out the preparation for that political discourse that Critias has promised; it would effect the transition from the promise of a political discourse to that discourse itself. What, then, about this framing of the cosmology? What about this political frame in which it is set? What is the relation between a cosmology that in its most archaic phase becomes chorology and a discourse on the city, a politology that would turn back from the eidetic city to the original Athens as which the Socratic city comes to life in its vital movement against another city? What does the χώρα have to do with the city?

It is also a question of the relation between Socrates and Hermocrates and of their role in the *Timaeus.* Both have listened in silence to Timaeus' long discourse as it ventured to say, and then to trace, the χώρα. Both have been to this extent receptive, imitating in their comportment something like the χώρα, the receptacle, both taking part, as guest and host, respectively, in the reception that constitutes the event or deed (ἔργον) of the dialogue. Socrates' silence provides a necessary counterpart to Timaeus' speech, representing the very silence that cannot but constitute the interstices of a speech that ventures bastard discourse on the χώρα. Yet surely the silence of Hermocrates is different. Surely it does not belong in any such way to discourse on the χώρα—at least, not unless Her-

---

12. David Krell calls special attention to this passage in his provocative essay "Female Parts in *Timaeus,*" *Arion,* n.s., 2/3 (1975): 418.

mocrates can hear in that discourse an echo of something very different. For Hermocrates is a man of war and of the city, one whose brilliant speech was to be engaged in dealing with the invasion by which Athens would expand by subjugating Syracuse, by taking over the land of this other city. As one who will become renowned for his military intelligence, for his cleverness and resourcefulness in devising stratagems by which to guarantee military success, but also for the oratorical skill, even the statesmanship, by which to persuade his countrymen to follow his lead, Hermocrates listens to the Timaean cosmology as one who represents the city at war. The question is whether, in listening to the chorology and to all that prepares for and follows it, Hermocrates can have heard echoing from it something about the city at war. The question is whether from the chorology there is a kind of reflection out upon the political discourses that frame the Timaean cosmology.

Among the various clues, one of the most conspicuous occurs in the course of the descensional bestiary with which the *Timaeus* comes to its conclusion. Speaking of the wild animals that go on foot, Timaeus outlines their descent, which is from nonphilosophical men but (in another order of descent) toward the *earth*: they have dragged their front limbs and head down to the *earth*, planting all four feet there, because of their kinship with the *earth*, because they are of the same kind as it. Furthermore, those foolish ones that require the support of many feet are dragged down still more to the *earth*, to say nothing of those no longer in need of feet whose entire body is stretched out upon the *earth*, those that crawl along the ground.

Does reference to the earth provide, then, a way of dealing with the question of the political frame of the *Timaeus*? How is it, in particular, that reference to the earth belongs to political discourse?

The answer, most succinctly, is: *necessarily*—taking necessity to have the sense it has in the *Timaeus*. Discourse on the city will at some point or other be compelled, of necessity, to make reference to the earth; at some point or other it will have to tell of the place on earth where the city is—or is to be—established and to tell how the constitution (πολιτεία) of the city both determines and is determined by this location.

This turn to the earth is manifest in the *Republic*. The necessity that compels it comes into play from the moment that Socrates sets out, in Book 2, to watch a city coming to be in λόγος in hopes of also seeing justice and injustice coming to be in it, or rather, from the moment he proposes to Adeimantus that, as he says, they "make a city in λόγος from the beginning" (*Rep.* 369c). Already in the beginning, something like a reference to the earth comes into play. Socrates explains how it happens that the city comes to be: since no one of us is self-sufficient, but, having many needs, we call upon others in order to satisfy these needs, many come to be gathered into one dwelling place (οἴκησις); to this place where people live together (συνοικία) we give the name *city* (πόλις). Thus, from the beginning of Socrates' discourse on the city, from the beginning of the city itself as he watches it—or rather, makes it—come to be, the city involves not just an assembly of men, not just a community of associates (κοινωνοί), but their assembly at a common dwelling place. The city is precisely this place where they live together.

In determining this place to which many are gathered, this place where they live together, needs will be decisive; Socrates ventures even to suggest that what really makes the city are our needs (χρεία), our dependence on certain things necessary for us, on certain necessities. In particular, our principal needs for food, shelter, and clothing determine what Socrates calls the most necessary city (ἡ ἀναγκαιοτάτη πόλις), the city of utmost necessity, the city in which would be satisfied just those needs imposed upon us with necessity, by necessity, those needs that must of necessity be satisfied. This city would have to consist, first, of a farmer, that is, a γεωργός, literally, one whose work (ἔργον) consists in plowing the earth (γῆ), in tilling the soil; then, second, of an οἰκοδόμος, literally, one who builds (δέμω) dwellings (οἰκία) in this dwelling place (οἴκησις), this place where people dwell together (συνοικία). Thus, the first two citizens gathered into the city bear in their very occupations reference to the city as a place of dwelling on the earth, a place where dwellings will be needed and where men will live from the earth, by cultivating it, by tilling the soil. Only after having mentioned these two does Socrates then mention those who provide for the need to cover the body. In contrast to the determinacy with which the first two citizens were introduced, the number of these therapists of the body is indefinite: a weaver and a cobbler and some others. The total number needed for this city of utmost necessity is thus also indefinite: Socrates says that it would consist of four or five men (ἄνδρες: men as opposed to women—note that up to this point there is no mention of women, of procreation, or of children). Adeimantus' answer is appropriately indefinite: so it would seem (φαίνεται) (*Rep.* 369c-e).

Socrates proceeds to establish that, since men's various natures are different, it is better that each practice the τέχνη for which he is by nature best suited. But the immediate result is that the city must then be expanded: for the farmer will not make his own plow if it is to be a good one, or his hoe, or other agricultural implements, nor will the others make the implements they need for their respective τέχναι. Hence, there must also be gathered into the city carpenters, smiths, and other artisans (δημιουργοί), as well as shepherds and other herdsmen to supply the animals and animal products needed by the others. Thus, the very small dwelling place (πολίχνιον), if it is to have all these, will turn out, as Adeimantus insists, to be not a small city (*Rep.* 369e-370d).

At this point the reference to terrestrial place becomes more explicit than ever: Socrates declares that it will be almost impossible to establish the city in a *region* (or place: τόπος) where it will not need imports. This need, in turn, results in still further expansion of the city: it must include merchants to carry on foreign trade, more farmers and artisans to produce the goods to be traded, and all those involved in maritime work. Even beyond these, Socrates adds finally the shopkeepers and wage-earning laborers.

With the city seemingly complete, Socrates turns to a description of the way of life led by the men of such a city. He tells of how they will make bread and wine and of how, reclining on simple rustic mats, they will feast with their children, drinking their wine and, while being pleasantly together, singing hymns to the gods, and not producing children beyond their means, lest they fall into poverty or war (*Rep.* 370d–372c).

This passage is remarkable. Here Socrates mentions children for the first time, as well as the production of children, even though—remarkably—there is still no reference to women. Even the production of children is mentioned almost as if it were an afterthought, and the requirement or fact of these arcadian artisans' not producing too many children is tacked on almost as if it were the easiest thing of all, as if ἔρως could, almost without effort, be regulated in accord with their means, their property (οὐσία). Nonetheless, Socrates does mention—for the first time—the consequences that excess in this regard could have: falling into poverty or into war. It will soon become evident how thoroughly the further development of the city turns on this disjunctive connection: that if one exceeds one's means (again: property, substance, what is one's own—οὐσία), one will have to go to war in order to avoid falling into poverty, that is, in order to increase one's property.

But what is most remarkable is the way in which Glaucon, provoked by this arcadian scene, intervenes at this point, voicing demands the consequences of which Socrates immediately draws out. Interrupting Socrates' dialogue with Adeimantus, Glaucon asks whether there are to be no relishes or delicacies (ὄψον means meat or anything eaten with bread to give it flavor, hence, sauce, seasoning, delicacies, rich fare). Socrates enumerates some of the finer foods the arcadian artisans will enjoy (olives, cheese, onions, figs, etc.), but, in the scorn that Glaucon then casts upon this city, it becomes manifest that even such bounteous gifts of the earth fall short of what he—and that is to say, among other things, the Athenians of the time—would demand. For the city that Socrates and Adeimantus have made in λόγος Glaucon calls a city of pigs. Responding to Socrates' request, he begins detailing some of the things lacking in this city (couches, tables, sweets), but Socrates promptly generalizes: it is not merely the genesis of the city as such that is to be considered but the genesis of the luxurious city, that is, of a city in which one would live comfortably and enjoy all manner of delicacies and refinements (*Rep.* 372c–e).

The first consequence is foreseeable: it will be necessary to enlarge the city again in order to cater to all these additional needs. Now it will be necessary to add hunters, painters, musicians, poets, cooks, doctors, and makers of women's adornment; thus, here finally, in the reference to those having to do with women's adornment (περὶ τὸν γυναικεῖον κόσμον), or, as one could also translate, with the female world, here finally, if still indirectly, there is mention of women in the city, but only at the stage where it is a matter of adorning the simple arcadian city by introducing such things as women's adornment.

But there is another consequence, a reassertion, though different, of reference to the earth. Socrates notes that the luxurious city will require not only additional artisans but also additional land or country. Therefore, he continues, we will have to take some of our neighbor's land; and, in turn, our neighbor will need to take some of ours, if he too goes beyond the limit of necessary needs. The word translated here as *land* or *country* is χώρα (*Rep.* 373d).

The need generated by the swarm of unnecessary needs, the necessity of taking some of the neighbor's land, requires, then, *going to war*. In turn, it becomes necessary to enlarge the city by an entire army. Socrates mentions, for the first time, the guardians (φύλακες), among whom he will soon distinguish between mere auxiliaries or soldiers and the rulers. Indeed, the double quality that quickly proves to be imperative for the guardians—that these human watchdogs must be both spirited and philosophic (θυμοειδὴς and φιλόσοφος)—opens upon the entire remainder of the *Republic.* One could say, therefore, that virtually everything—and certainly the further course of the *Republic*—is launched by the reference to the earth, to terrestrial place, to the need that arises to acquire additional land by going to war against one's neighbor. In a sense it is only at this point that the discourse becomes genuinely political, in distinction from the story of the arcadian arisans, who, it seems, would have need neither of rulers nor of the laws and other means by which rulers govern a city. In any case, the introduction of the guardians—necessary in order to take some of the neighbor's land—and, in particular, the identification of their double quality open onto the decisive disjoining—and paradoxical conjoining—of philosophy and politics that runs through the central Books of the *Republic* and that brings it about that the philosophic city has finally, at the end of Book 9, to be declared "a paradigm laid up in heaven," one that is "nowhere on earth" (*Rep.* 592b). Thus, although reference to the earth is operative in the earliest stages by which the city is built in λόγος, the course of the *Republic* (including the story to be promulgated about humans being earthborn) produces a kind of reversal such that what finally proves to be lacking is precisely this being-on-the-earth, this having a terrestrial location. What the city proves to be is only "a paradigm laid up in heaven," a city that is only the idea of a city, not a city that could simply as such be somewhere on earth. It is a city that has still, as Socrates demands when he recapitulates this discourse in the *Timaeus,* to be set in motion, to be brought to life, to be depicted going to war against another city. In order to take some of the land of that other city. In order, even in a state of excess that it could in deed never exchange for arcadian simplicity—in order to secure itself in a place, in order to be somewhere on earth.

Critias' discourse in the *Timaeus* presents in outline the city going to war, presents it as archaic Athens going to war against Atlantis. What proves distinctive about this city (what especially distinguishes it from the Socratic city) is that it is—or was—somewhere, in a singular terrestrial place. It has been noted how various indications are given that this *being precisely where it is* is distinctive for this city, for example, Critias' explicit declaration that in founding the city the goddess was careful to choose a fruitful place (τόπος), one with a temperate climate, one that would bring forth the wisest men, that would produce men who, like Athena herself, would be lovers of war and of wisdom.

Thus, even if only an outline, Critias' discourse serves to establish the connection of the city to terrestrial place, to the earth. On the other hand, Timaeus' discourse sets up a certain semantic affiliation between earth and χώρα. In his first discourse Timaeus describes the earth as "our nurturer [τροφός]" (40b). Then in his third discourse he refers to what is indisputably the χώρα and calls it both by a name given it earlier, nurse (τιθήνη), and by exactly the same name given to the earth, nurturer (τροφός) (88d). From this coincidence of names (even strengthened by the way in which *nurturer* proved to be one of the most telling names of the χώρα) one cannot conclude that the χώρα and the earth are somehow the same; for Timaeus insists vigorously on the difference between the χώρα and the fire, air, water, and earth that it receives, holds, and nurtures. Nonetheless there is a certain semantic affiliation between χώρα and earth, one that operates more openly as, more remote from the chorology, χώρα regains those senses that are, of necessity, reduced in and around the chorology, such senses as land, country, terrain, and place.

This affiliation, together with the referral of the city to terrestrial place, broaches an analogy. This analogy would relate the χώρα and the earth to the respective oppositions that are shown to require, yet to be limited by, them. Thus it would read:

χώρα : intelligible/sensible :: earth : paradigm of city/image (actual city)

But if indeed the *Timaeus* broaches the semantic affiliation on which this analogy is built, it is the *Critias* that bears out and confirms the decisiveness of the referral of the city to the earth. For it turns out that this fragment of a dialogue, marked explicitly as the sequel to the *Timaeus,* is about almost nothing else but the earth. Precisely here where the living city is to be described, what comes into play is a kind of Platonic geology.

A few indications need to be given.

Critias begins his discourse by proposing to describe first the original Athenians and then their enemy; he will speak of the power (δύναμις) and the constitution (πολιτεία) of each city. But in fact Critias begins with the gods: "Once upon a time," he begins, "the gods were taking over by lot the whole earth according to its regions [τόποι]" (*Crit.* 109b). Thus the very first move ventured in the discourse is a reference to the earth and to its regions, to terrestrial places. He continues: "So by just allotments they received each one his own, and they settled their countries [χῶραι]." In particular, he goes on, "Hephaestus and Athena took for their joint portion this land [χώρα] of ours as being naturally suited and adapted for excellence and discernment [ἀρετὴ καὶ φρόνησις], and in this land they put good men as belonging to the earth itself [αὐτόχθονας] and conveyed to their intellects [νοῦς] the order of the πολιτεία" (109b–d). Note here especially how the instituting of the πολιτεία is conjoined to men's being set on the earth as beings of the earth.

Critias proceeds to describe the land where Athena and Hephaestus had founded their city. He says that in the excellence of its earth it surpassed all others. As evidence of this, Critias mentions that even what is now left of Athenian soil rivals that of others in its productive capacity, even though, jutting out into deep sea, its soil has been washing away throughout the nine thousand years since its founding, leaving now only the body or corpse of the land (σῶμα τῆς χώρας). But in the beginning there were high arable hills and plains full of rich soil. In the mountains there were forests with lofty trees rather than the bare slopes seen today. The plentiful rains sent by Zeus were held by the deep earth rather than running off into the sea. Thus—says Critias—the farmers (γεωργοί) enjoyed excellent land and an abundance of water. Even when Critias turns to consider the city (ἄστυ: city as distinguished from the surrounding country), what he stresses is the richness of the earth that originally composed the acropolis (*Crit.* 110e–112b).

Nor does the emphasis change when Critias turns to a consideration of the city that in the beginning warred against the Athenians, namely, Atlantis. Again Critias begins with the gods' portioning of the earth, and, observing that Poseidon received the island of Atlantis as his allotment, Critias notes that the city where Poseidon assembled the children he begot by a mortal woman was set on a plain that was the fairest of all and highly fertile. On a mountain near this plain had lived a man called Evenor, who, says Critias, had sprung from the earth itself. But when the earthborn Evenor and his wife died, leaving their daughter Cleito, Poseidon was struck with desire for her and fathered those who would become the rulers of the city. Arranging the terrain in concentric circular bands alternately of water and of land, he provided for his progeny—set on the inner island— by bringing up from beneath the earth two springs of water and by producing from the earth all kinds of food in plenty. Poseidon fathered five pairs of sons and set them to rule over the various regions (τόποι) of the country (χώρα). Even in this regard Critias slyly mentions that one of the sons, the younger of the third pair, was named 'Αυτόχθονα, which means: of the earth itself. Even when he comes to describing the palace that the Atlantans constructed, aided always by Poseidon, he does not fail to mention a grove sacred to Poseidon, one that contained trees of all kinds and that were of marvelous beauty and height, as he says, "because of the excellence of the earth [ὑπὸ ἀρετῆς τῆς γῆς]" (*Crit.* 117b).

If one is attentive to the city's being-on-the-earth and to the semantic affinity between earth and χώρα, if one ventures to draw out the implications of the analogy built on these connections, then one will have begun to regard the *Timaeus* in its political frame. One will have begun to consider how the question of a terrestrially placed city could require a chorology and how it might be that such a one as Hermocrates could hear echoing even from the chorology something politically decisive. It would be a matter of persevering with the thought that the χώρα enables and limits sensible images of the intelligible as the earth enables and limits terrestrial images of that city that is "only a paradigm laid up in heaven."

5

Reinscriptions

FORGERY

Would anything ever have escaped the tracings of the χώρα? Would its errancy ever have ceased to bring about the indetermining operation that inexorably unsettles from below, as it were, everything that would be established in full integrity from above? Would anything ever have been spared the almost invisible—and thereby most dangerous—fissures that it seems to trace everywhere while itself remaining utterly and persistently out of sight? Precisely because it operates always under cover, by stealth, there would seem to be no defense to prevent its overtaking all things.

Can even the intelligible remain aloof from the operation of the χώρα? Can the exclusion of this operation from the intelligible be guaranteed once and for all and even beyond the defense erected by the Platonic text? Or is its shadow not already cast across that establishment, even if still almost indiscernibly? Is that shadow not already engaged precisely in the establishment? For the very integrity of each intelligible εἶδος is constituted by an absolute negation of reception, of reception in either direction: an intelligible εἶδος can neither receive nor be received into any other being. And yet, is it possible for negation to be absolute in every respect and thus to absolve totally what it sets apart, to absolve it completely from that which is negated? Or must negation not also determine, that is, set apart only by also setting into relation? Is the negation of reception nothing but pure singular integrity? Or is the negation of a certain spacing not itself another spacing? One would call this another *kind* of spacing, were it not the very integrity of kinds that is put in question by the determinacy of negation. Is it not in view of such an other spacing that the question of the community (κοινωνία) of kinds can be broached (see *Soph.* 251a–252e)? And would it be completely out of the question to wonder whether

Socrates is alluding to such a spacing of the intelligible when, in Book 7 of the *Republic*, he tells how the escaped prisoner comes finally to look upon "the sun itself by itself in its own χώρα" (*Rep.* 516b)?[1]

Yet, if a certain defense tends to limit—perhaps even must limit—the vertical reach of its tracings, there is little to limit its horizontal extension, to prevent it from installing even in the lineage of philosophy itself the indetermining operation of what could be called, literally, its nonsense. For instance, in the reception and reinscription of texts, an operation that belongs to and in an essential way punctuates that lineage, the workings of errancy will not have been lacking. Hence, for this reason, and not only because it is a question of reception, the question of the Postplatonic reception and reinscription of the *Timaeus* and especially of the chorology is not simply extrinsic to all that is in question in the chorology itself.

It is not certain who invented the story, perhaps not even entirely certain that it was simply invented, for instance, by someone such as Aristoxenus who was maliciously intent on discrediting Plato.[2] In any case it is a story of which there are several variant versions, all bearing on Plato's authorship of the *Timaeus*. Iamblicus is perhaps most discreet. In his *Life of Pythagoras* he tells the story in the course of a discussion of the careful secrecy by which the Pythagoreans preserved the mystery of their writings. He observes that for a long time no Pythagorean writings appeared publicly and that it was only with Philolaus that the secrecy was betrayed: "Philolaus first published those three celebrated books that, at the request of Plato, Dion of Syracuse is said to have bought for a hundred minae."[3] Diogenes Laertius also writes of this purchase. Referring to "Philolaus of Croton, a Pythagorean," he continues: "It was from him that Plato, in a letter, told Dion to buy the Pythagorean books." But Diogenes Laertius' version of the story goes on to make it explicit that it was a matter not only of reading the Pythagorean books but of reinscribing at least one of them, one that Philolaus, it seems, had actually composed. In Diogenes Laertius' version: "Hermippus says that according to one writer the philosopher Plato went to Sicily, to the court of Dionysius, bought this book from Philolaus' relatives for forty Alexandrian minae, and from it copied out [μεταγεγραφέναι] the *Timaeus*." Diogenes Laertius adds still another variant: "Others say that Plato acquired the books by securing from Dionysius the release from prison of a young man who had been one of Philolaus' pupils."[4] In whatever way he acquired the book, whether by having someone else buy it or by simply buying it himself or by securing Philolaus' pupil's freedom in exchange for it, the point on which Diogenes

---

1. See above, chap. 3, n. 24.
2. See G. S. Kirk and J. E. Raven, *The Presocratic Philosophers* (Cambridge: Cambridge University Press, 1962), 308.
3. Diels-Kranz, Die Fragmente der Vorsokratiker (Dublin/Zurich: Weidmann, 1968), 14.17.
4. Ibid., 44.A1.

Laertius seems most intent is that Plato used the book as the basis for the *Timaeus*. Construed in its most insidious form, the rumor was that Plato was guilty of plagiarism, that the *Timaeus* was a forgery.

It is likely that such rumors, or at least the suspicions that they created about the *Timaeus,* contributed significantly to the reception granted to a work entitled *On the Nature of the Cosmos and the Soul* (Περὶ φύσιος κόσμω καὶ ψυχᾶς); the work bore the signature of Timaeus of Locri and was accepted as genuine by most Neoplatonic commentators, including Proclus.[5] This work purported to be the original discourse of Timaeus, from which Plato had composed the *Timaeus* merely by elaborating the discourse and adding to it the introductory speeches. It was as if the appearance of the work by Timaeus of Locri had realized some obscure longing to recover the origin of—an origin for—the *Timaeus.* It was as if what the chorology discreetly says of itself could be extended to the entire dialogue and this bastard discourse regarded as the offspring engendered when one of Athens' most celebrated citizens came in contact with the obscure foreign source.

But it is a forgery, this work in which the name *Timaeus of Locri* is inscribed as the alleged author. No doubt it was precisely because it was a forgery that its author (who cannot be identified) inscribed the name *Timaeus of Locri* at the very beginning of the work, so that what one reads, first of all, is: "Timaeus of Locri spoke as follows."[6] The work was composed so as to appear to be that of a fifth-century B.C. writer. But its use of the Doric dialect (in which one from Locri, in southern Italy, would have written) is not consistent, and, most obtrusively, there are numerous elements in the work that are indisputably Postplatonic. The work is not attested before the second century A.D., and it is widely regarded as having been composed either in the first century B.C. or the first century A.D. Its affinities with Middle Platonic thought are evident, and it may indeed have originated in Alexandria.[7]

Though it was to have been the original on which Plato based the *Timaeus,* it is in fact only a remote image derived from the Platonic text, a faint reinscription of the dialogue. Taken from the *Timaeus,* it gives virtually nothing itself but only dogmatizes, simplifies, and flattens out the Platonic discourse. Between the *Timaeus* itself and the forged text, in the transition from the original to this errant image, there seems to be nothing but loss.

One thing that is lost is the dialogue form and all the possibilities such form offers, for instance, for leaving matters open, for letting them remain

---

5. See Proclus, *In Platonis Timaeum Commentaria,* 1:1.

6. Timaios of Locri, *On the Nature of the World and the Soul,* text, translation, and notes by Thomas H. Tobin (Chico, Calif.: Scholars Press, 1985), 32f. (marginal page number: 93a). Subsequent references to the work itself will be indicated by *TL* followed by the marginal page number.

7. See Tobin's Introduction in ibid., 1–28.

in a certain suspension; these possibilities and others are subtly transferred even when a portion of a dialogue assumes the form of monologue.
Hence, the contrast is enormous between the stylistic resources of the Platonic discourses of Timaeus and those of the flat declarations put forth in
the forged work.

Also lost are the discourses that precede Timaeus', those by Socrates
and by Critias; in the forged work there is no trace whatsoever of these
other discourses, nor, therefore, any integration of a Socratic moment
into the context of the discourse. Lost, too, is the opening scene of the
Timaeus, and thus all that is signaled in word and deed both in that scene
and in the discussions that frame and punctuate the Socratic and the Cri-
tian discourses. All reference to the *Republic* is missing; in fact the forgery
excludes the entire political frame of the *Timaeus.* Reference to Athena is
gone, corresponding to a suppression of mythical elements that the forgery effects throughout. Above all, the dramatic character integral to the
Timaeus is lost altogether, its character as enacting a reception, as enacting in its very setting precisely what the discourse comes to address in and
around the chorology. There is a loss, too, of all the caution and reserve
that the discourse of the *Timaeus* exercises upon itself. What the forged
work says of the cosmos and the soul is declared with a straightforward-
ness that excludes even the slightest hint of a need to wonder whether the
discourse truly touches upon—whether it is such as could truly touch
upon—things themselves. Not that the forged work fails to reinscribe the
division that corresponds to that between the three kinds: it proclaims that
there are three ways in which things come to be comprehended or declared
(γνωρίζεσθαι), one way corresponding to each of the three—hence, by
νοῦς through knowledge, by sense perception and opinion, and by bastard reckoning. One of the few contributions offered by the forged work is
its explanation of the need for bastard reckoning, an explanation that only
serves once and for all to demonstrate how thoroughly the forgery closes
off the question of the third kind. For the work explains that the third
kind must be known by bastard reckoning "because it can never be known
directly but only by analogy" (*TL* 94b). Yet what is perhaps most remarkable is that once these three ways have been proclaimed the text never
returns to them, never takes its own measure by reference to them, never
expresses reservation about itself by reference to them—in short, never
interrupts for a moment its dogmatic tone.

The extreme simplification and flattening-out that the forgery effects
on the discourse is demonstrated perhaps most strikingly if one compares
the passage that forms the conclusion of Timaeus' first discourse with the
corresponding passage in the forged work. This is the passage on the
greatest good of vision: in the Platonic text Timaeus describes how vision,
by allowing us to behold the noetic revolutions in the heaven, makes it
possible for us to imitate within ourselves those celestial revolutions, to

imitate within our own souls the order beheld in the starry heaven above (47a–c). But in the corresponding passage in the forged work, one reads simply: "As for types of sense perception, the god has fastened sight to us for the contemplation of the heaven and the acquisition of knowledge." The mimetic reflection of the visible heaven back into the soul is lost entirely. As is also that of music: regarding the good of hearing, all that is ventured is that "he produced hearing for the apprehension of words and melodies" and that "one who is deaf from birth will later be unable to utter words" (*TL* 100c).

There would be loss enough if the forged work only dogmatized, simplified, and flattened out the discourse of the *Timaeus,* or, more precisely, its presentation of the discourse of Timaeus. But there is indeed an even more severe loss. One might consider it simply a matter of distortion, were it not such as to conceal and exclude completely that which it distorts. What is submitted to this excluding distortion is precisely the chorology and much of the discourse surrounding it. At the core of the distorting operation is a distortion of the χώρα itself, its distortion into matter (ὕλη). Without the slightest sign of caution or reservation, the forged work identifies matter with the various images that the *Timaeus* offers of the χώρα: "Matter, however, is a matrix and mother [ἐκμαγεῖον καὶ ματέρα]," as well as "nurse [τιθάναν]." Reaffirming the author in the clumsiest of ways, the forged work underwrites the distortion: "He said that this matter was everlasting, but not immovable, in itself patternless and shapeless, but receptive of every pattern." And then, as if to seal the distortion: "Matter is called τόπος and χώρα" (*TL* 94a–b).[8]

This distortion is accompanied by another, by a distortion of the very form of the *Timaeus,* a shifting around of various portions in such a way that the forged work comes to have the simple form of division into two parts, the first dealing with the cosmos, the second dealing with human beings and other mortal creatures. Most decisive among these shifts is that by which the initial portion of Timaeus' second discourse (leading up to and including the chorology) is moved to the beginning of the work and what remains of that portion is combined with the account of the works of νοῦς. The difference between Timaeus' first discourse and his second, the discontinuity marked by the interruption and new beginning, is abolished through this distortion of the form of the text. This leveling of difference does not so much expel the chorology as, rather, require that its expulsion be already in effect, that it be already withdrawn into oblivion. It is this loss that clears the way for such bland and dogmatic proclamations as that with which—after its false declaration of authorship—the forged work begins: "There are two causes of all things: νοῦς . . . and ἀνάγκη . . ." (*TL* 93a).

8. The work goes on eventually to identify ὕλη with ὑποκείμενον (*TL* 97e).

REDUCTION

Yet it was not in this forged work that the distorting identification of the χώρα with ὕλη originated. The identification was in fact common in Middle Platonism. For instance, in *On the Generation of the Soul in the Timaeus* Plutarch insists that corporeal being (ἡ σώματος οὐσία) is none other than what Plato called the all-receiving nature, the abode (ἕδρα), and the nurse (τιθήνη) of all generated things (5, 1014c–d). Thus, Plutarch links the material (ὑλικόν) to the χώρα (6, 1014e). And finally, reiterating the three kinds counted in Timaeus' second discourse, Plutarch continues: "It is matter [ὕλη] that he calls χώρα, as he sometimes calls it abode [ἕδρα] and receptacle [ὑποδοχή]" (24, 1024c).

By the time of Plotinus the identification can be taken for granted, indeed to such an extent that a treatise on matter can begin: "What is called matter [ὕλη] is said to be some sort of substratum [ὑποκείμενον] and receptacle of forms [ὑποδοχή εἰδῶν]; this account is common to all those who have arrived at a conception of a nature of this kind" (II.4.1). Some measure of just how far this distorting identification has removed Neoplatonic thought from the chorology can be taken by reference to certain of Plotinus' discourses on matter. For all their philosophical and poetic force and even though—perhaps even because—one still hears faint echoes of things once said of the χώρα, one realizes that such discourses as the following belong to a world quite remote from that of the *Timaeus:* "Matter, then, is incorporeal. . . . It is a ghostly image of bulk . . . ; it is invisible in itself and escapes any attempt to see it and occurs when one is not looking, but even if you look closely you cannot see it. . . . Whatever announcement it makes, therefore, is a lie . . . ; its apparent being is not being, but a sort of fleeting frivolity [παίγνιον]; hence the things that seem to come to be in it are frivolities, nothing but phantoms [εἴδωλα] in a phantom, like something in a mirror which really exists in one place but is reflected in another; it seems to be filled, and holds nothing; it is all seeming" (III.6.7).[9]

It is not insignificant that in stating what had become the common account Plotinus identifies matter not only as the receptacle but also as

---

9. Against the background of this distorting assimilation of the χώρα to matter, it is curious, to say the least, that under the title "Une Mère de Glace" Irigaray cites Plotinus on ὕλη as if the cited passages were about the χώρα. In this context she hardly cites Plato at all, and when she does it is screened through Plotinus and presupposes the identification of the χώρα with ὕλη. For example, she writes: "Matter (we read) is 'the receptacle and nurse of all generation'" (Luce Irigaray, *Speculum of the Other Woman*, trans. Gillian C. Gill [Ithaca: Cornell University Press, 1985], 173). But this is obviously not what we read in the *Timaeus* nor in any other text by Plato, who uses the word ὕλη only occasionally and then only in the sense of a building material such as wood.

substratum, using precisely the word (ὑποκείμενον) by which Aristotle defines matter.[10] One could say even that that to which the receptacle, hence, the χώρα, comes to be assimilated is determined by the two terms ὕλη and ὑποκείμενον, that it is ὕλη as ὑποκείμενον. If, then, one would address this assimilation at the site where its resources originated, one must turn to Aristotle.

Indeed the assimilation itself is already in force in Aristotle's text. One finds it, for instance, in the passage cited earlier from *On Generation and Corruption* where Aristotle voices the complaint that Plato, having defined the receptacle, then makes no use of it subsequently. The definition that Aristotle declares Plato to have given is linked to the image of the gold that is constantly remodeled, an image that Aristotle tends to privilege, no doubt because it most readily suggests that the receptacle is a substratum for all things. For, according to Aristotle, this is what Plato declared the receptacle to be: "a substratum [ὑποκείμενον] prior to the so-called elements, just as gold is the substratum of works made of gold." Though in this context Aristotle refers to one other image of the χώρα, that of nurse (τιθήνη), he forgoes drawing on the content of that image and, instead, moves immediately to identify the receptacle with "primary matter" (329a).

Yet the passage that is, at once, both most decisive and most puzzling occurs in Book 4 of the *Physics:* "This is why Plato says in the *Timaeus* that matter and the χώρα are the same; for the receptive and the χώρα are one and the same. Although the manner in which he speaks about the receptive in the *Timaeus* differs from that in the so-called unwritten teachings, nevertheless he declares that place [τόπος] and the χώρα are the same" (209b).

One cannot but be struck by the lack of correspondence between this passage and the text of the *Timaeus.* The passage declares three identifications: that of the receptive (μεταληπτικόν) with the χώρα, that of matter (ὕλη) with the χώρα, and that of place (τόπος) with the χώρα. Only the first of these identifications has any basis in the text of the *Timaeus,* and then only if one disregards any difference that might distinguish μεταληπτικόν from the Platonic words δεχόμενον and ὑποδοχή.

For the identification of ὕλη with the χώρα, there is no basis in the *Timaeus.* Plato never uses the word ὕλη in Aristotle's sense, a sense that, one suspects, comes to be constituted and delimited only in and through the work of Aristotle. When Plato does, on a few occasions, use the word,

10. "For I say that matter [ὕλη] is the primary substratum [τὸ πρῶτον ὑποκείμενον] of each thing, from which, as something inherent but not as an attribute, something else is generated" (Aristotle, *Physics* 192a).

it has the common, everyday sense of building material such as wood, earth, or stone.[11] Following Aristotle's own strategy in *On Generation and Corruption,* one could refer to the image of the constantly remodeled gold as providing support for the identification. But reference to this image could be decisive only if one privileged it over most of the others, disregarding, for instance, the image of the nurse, which represents the relation between the χώρα and the sensible in a way quite irreducible to that between matter and the things formed from it. What is perhaps even more decisive is that all these are *images* of the χώρα, images declared in an εἰκὼς λόγος, which is to be distinguished from the bastardly discourse in which one would venture to say the χώρα. As soon as one begins to grant the multiplicity of images of the χώρα and to differentiate also between the discourse on these images and the bastardly discourse on the χώρα (that is, between the εἰκὼς λόγος and the chorology), it will be manifest that the χώρα cannot, on the basis of the *Timaeus,* be identified with ὕλη. Despite the image of the constantly remodeled gold, the χώρα is not reducible to that from which things are made, nor, specifically, to the primary substratum underlying the simplest things, which Aristotle—contrary to the *Timaeus*—calls elements. Given the decisiveness and even the manifestness of the difference between χώρα and ὕλη, one cannot but suspect that their identification serves to transpose into the economy of Aristotle's thought a moment of the Timaean discourse that otherwise would simply be lost or else would disrupt that economy. But the effect of this transposition is a reduction of the χώρα, a reductive reinscription of the chorology and the other discourses around it. Even if Aristotle stops short of integrating the χώρα into an eidetic economy, into an economy of meaning of the sort that it resists abysmally in the *Timaeus,* his reduction of the χώρα to ὕλη does serve to situate it at the limit of the eidetic and to that extent to assimilate it to the eidetic economy.

As to the identification of τόπος with the χώρα, one has only to refer to the chorology to show how it is unfounded; but what is remarkable in this regard is that the chorology, while maintaining the difference between τόπος and χώρα, shows how the identification, though illegitimate, is nonetheless motivated. For the chorology tells of how we dream of the χώρα and of how in that dream we conflate τόπος and the χώρα, between which, upon our awakening, it would be imperative to distinguish. It is as if Aristotelian physics remains absorbed in the dream, reducing the χώρα

---

11. "But Aristotle's term for matter (ὕλη) is not used even once by Plato in that sense. To Plato it had only the more common meaning of wood, earth, or specific type of stuff" (George S. Claghorn, *Aristotle's Criticism of Plato's "Timaeus"* [The Hague: Martinus Nijhoff, 1954], 6). See also Cornford, *Plato's Cosmology,* 181. Note Plato's use of ὕλη in the *Timaeus* (69a) in a sense that suggests pieces of wood that have been prepared for the carpenter to fasten together.

to τόπος, dreaming of the χώρα as a place that would have a place within the economy of that physics, that metaphysics.[12]

APPROPRIATION

Remote it is indeed from the χώρα. Constrained, too, if one can say that to bind something to the imagination is to constrain it. And yet, in the one text without which the entire movement of German Idealism would be unthinkable, Kant writes: "Now it is clear that there must be a third thing [*ein Drittes*], which is homogeneous, on the one hand, with the category and, on the other hand, with the appearance and which makes the application of the former to the latter possible."[13] If, in a way that is not entirely foreign to Kant, one takes the categories as expressing the forms or articulations of being as these are thought by the understanding or intellect, then it will be evident that they correspond, within the context of modern (Postcartesian) philosophy, to what in the *Timaeus* was called the first kind. And then it will be equally manifest that, since appearances correspond to the second kind, this declaration regarding the necessity of a third kind corresponds to the declaration made at the outset of Timaeus' second discourse and, most rigorously, in the passage across the threshold of the chorology. The third must be homogeneous with the first, that is, in a most perplexing way, partaking of the intelligible. As Kant says: "This mediating representation must be pure (devoid of everything empirical), and yet, while it must, on the one hand, be intellectual, it must"—as homogeneous with the appearance—"be, on the other hand, sensible."[14] It is homogeneous with the appearance and falls to this extent on the side of the sensible precisely because all sensible appearance occurs in it—that is, it is receptive of all without itself being determined by any of those things it receives. Moreover, the third is what makes possible the application of the category to the appearance, of the intelligible to the sensible, allowing sensible appearances, determined as objects, to cling to being at least in a cer-

---

12. In his interpretation of Aristotle, Heidegger insists that the distinction between the allegedly general character of metaphysics (of what came to be called metaphysics) and the apparently regional character of physics breaks down, indeed to such an extent that "metaphysics is 'physics' in a quite essential sense—i.e., a knowledge of φύσις (ἐπιστήμη φυσική)." On this basis Heidegger concludes that Aristotelian physics plays a fundamental role in the history of Western philosophy, that is, of metaphysics: "The Aristotelian 'Physics' is the concealed—and hence never sufficiently thought through—basic book [*Grundbuch*] of Western philosophy." On the other hand, the reduction of the χώρα that is effected by Aristotelian physics offers a basis for putting in question the interpretation of Aristotle's thought as belonging to "the era of the completion [*Vollendung*] of Greek philosophy," or at least for reopening the question as to the sense of that completion. See Martin Heidegger, "Vom Wesen und Begriff der Φύσις: Aristoteles, Physik B, 1," in *Wegmarken*, vol. 9 of *Gesamtausgabe* (Frankfurt a.M.: Vittorio Klostermann, 1976), 241f.
13. Kant, *Kritik der reinen Vernunft*, A138/B177.
14. Ibid.

tain way, enabling the duplicity of being. Thus is it made possible for appearances to be determined by the categories, that is, the possibility of a priori synthetic knowledge is vindicated.

Kant concludes his discourse on the necessity of the third by naming it: "Such a representation is the *transcendental schema.*"[15]

As such a third, the transcendental schema interrupts the twofold structure of the *Critique of Pure Reason,* a structure manifest in the division of the Transcendental Doctrine of Elements into Transcendental Aesthetic and Transcendental Logic. This twofold structure rests on the division of human knowledge into the two stems, sensibility and understanding. But if there must be a third and if the third is irreducible, then, in enabling the twofold (the application of category to appearance), it will have interrupted it and destabilized the very structure of a critique of reason.

Kant writes that transcendental schematism is "an art concealed in the depths of the human soul, whose true modes of activity nature is hardly likely ever to allow us to discover and to have open to our gaze."[16] One could say, as Timaeus says of the third kind, that it is most difficult to catch.

Thus, even though remote from the Timaean discourse, even though constrained within the exigencies of modern thought, transcendental schematism is a reinscription of the chorology.

Yet it is not Kant but Schelling who most decisively reinscribes the *Timaeus* and its chorology. In Schelling's case, unlike Kant's, the reinscription is determined by return to and from the text of the *Timaeus.* Schelling's recently published Plato studies[17] attest to this return to the Platonic text and serve to underline the singular decisiveness that this text had for Schelling's thought. These very early studies, primarily of the *Timaeus,* make it possible to amplify the brief indications given in Schelling's works and, in particular, to mark certain points in those works where reinscription of the *Timaeus* is carried out. By filling out the reinscription along lines traced by the early Plato studies, one can transpose mere general indications into the textual specificity corresponding to Schelling's reinscription of the *Timaeus* in the text of modern philosophy, his reinscription of the dialogue into a text that while belonging to modern philosophy also renders it radically questionable, perhaps for the first time. In this way a certain measure can be taken of the decisiveness of the *Timaeus* for Schelling's thought.

---

15. Ibid.

16. Ibid., A141/B180–81.

17. Most notably, F. W. J. Schelling, *"Timaeus." (1794),* ed. Hartmut Buchner (Stuttgart-Bad Cannstatt: Frommann-Holzboog, 1994). Further references are indicated in the text by *T* followed by page number. Additional material belonging to Schelling's early Plato studies appears as two appendices in Michael Franz, *Schellings Tübinger Platon-Studien* (Göttingen: Vanderhoeck & Ruprecht, 1996). Franz notes that these texts are only preliminary transcriptions and do not constitute a historical-critical edition.

At what point does the reinscription occur? At what point in Schelling's work? At what point in the movement that came to be called German Idealism?

Indications are there from the beginning, from before the beginning: for instance, in the recently published notebook dating from August 1792, two years before Schelling's first published work. Composed while Schelling was still a student in Tübingen, the notebook is entitled *Vorstellungsarten der alten Welt über Verschiedene Gegenstände gesammelt aus Homer, Plato u.a.*[18] At the very beginning of the text, Schelling cites in Greek a passage from the *Timaeus,* from the end of the second discourse (68e-69a). The passage can be rendered: "Therefore there is need to distinguish two kinds of causes, the necessary [τὸ ἀναγκαῖον] and the divine [τὸ θεῖον], and in all things to seek after the divine for the sake of gaining a life of happiness, so far as our nature [φύσις] admits thereof." This passage reiterates the opening passage of the second discourse, a passage that Schelling will cite in another notebook two years later: "For this cosmos in its origin was generated as a compound, from the combination [σύστασις] of ἀνάγκη and νοῦς" (48a).

But what is the point of the reinscription? Why, how, where is it carried out?

The question of the *why* will compound itself almost immediately, indeed, in a way that can perhaps be described only as abysmal. For the point of the reinscription is to set the ground apart, to set apart that to which every question that asks *why* is directed. Setting ground apart cannot but render more problematic every such question of ground and, above all, the question that asks about the ground of the setting apart of ground.

But *how* is the reinscription carried out? With what kind of stylus will Schelling have rewritten the ancient text *within* the text of modern philosophy? What about the eye that will have caught a glimpse of the blank space closed off within that densely figured text? How will the hand have been deployed to wield the pen within that space—or rather, to set its point dancing so as to reinscribe as lightly as possible what was said—and not said—in the pertinent discourse of the *Timaeus?*

Where, then, is the reinscription carried out? Where in Schelling's work?

Perhaps almost everywhere. For what Schelling rewrites within the text of modern philosophy is a discourse on nature, on nature in its capacity to withdraw, on secluded nature. It is well-known that the question of nature is precisely what precipitated Schelling's break with Fichte's *Wissenschaftslehre,* which reduces nature to a mere not-I posited by the I, that is, reduces it to a mere object brought forth by the transcendental imagination. That in this reduction only the merest residue remains as a kind of

18. Franz, *Schellings Tübinger Platon-Studien,* Appendix I (pp. 252-71).

surd (the *Anstoss*) serves to mark for Schelling the limit, the incompleteness, of the *Wissenschaftslehre*. What is thus called for is a philosophy of nature that would complement transcendental philosophy (or—in a sense that becomes increasingly compelling—would displace it) and thus compensate for the absence of nature from transcendental philosophy.

Schelling's criticism of transcendental philosophy becomes more comprehensive and more radical in his work of 1809, *Philosophical Investigations of the Essence of Human Freedom:* "All modern European philosophy since it began with Descartes has this common defect, that nature does not exist for it and that it lacks a living ground [*dass die Natur für sie nicht vorhanden ist, und dass es ihr am lebendigen Grunde fehlt*]."[19] In this work Schelling ventures to recover such a living ground, to differentiate secluded nature from the self-positing subject to which otherwise—and indeed throughout modern philosophy—it is assimilated. It is precisely in the course of this differentiating recovery of ground that Schelling comes openly—perhaps most openly—to reinscribe the *Timaeus*.

Yet the reinscription comes, not at the highest point of the investigation, but rather at its deepest point, where it is most fundamental. At this point Schelling draws the most fundamental of distinctions, setting the living ground apart from the being whose existence it would ground. The distinction is fundamental in a twofold sense: it is the foundation of all the other principal determinations to be developed in the investigation (for example, that of the distinction between good and evil), and it effects the very setting of the fundament, setting it apart from the being whose existence it would ground. Most succinctly, it differentiates between ground and existence (*Grund, Existenz*). Even in the case of God the distinction remains in force, forestalling any reduction of the grounding relation in God to the virtual identity entailed in the determination of God as *causa sui*. Even though the ground of God's existence is inseparable from God, it is necessary to differentiate between God insofar as he exists and the ground of his existence. In this connection Schelling refers to the ground of God's existence as "the nature in God" (*PU* 358), thus indicating unmistakably that even in the sphere of the divine what is at issue is the seclusion of nature. It is in this same connection that Schelling delimits nature as such, nature as ground, nature as secluded beyond the limit: "Nature in general is everything that lies beyond the absolute being of absolute identity" (*PU* 358). Secluded nature Schelling also calls *die anfängliche Natur,* distinguishing it—though only relatively—from ordered nature. The distinction is only relative because *die anfängliche Natur* is also the unruly (*das Regellose*) that precedes the establishment of rule,

---

19. Schelling, *Philosophische Untersuchungen über das Wesen der menschlichen Freiheit und die damit zusammenhängenden Gegenstände*, in *Sämtliche Werke* (Stuttgart and Augsburg: J. G. Cotta'scher Verlag, 1860), I/7: 356. Further references to the *Philosophische Untersuchungen (PU)* are given in the text according to the pagination of this edition.

order, form, and that even in ordered nature still persists as capable of breaking through again. Secluded nature is originary (*ursprünglich*) not only in the sense that it precedes order and form (creation consisting, then, in bringing the unruly to order) but also in the sense that it remains as the irreducible ground always capable of breaking through the order brought by creation. In Schelling's words: "This is the incomprehensible basis of reality in things, the irreducible remainder, that which with the greatest exertion cannot be resolved in the understanding but remains eternally in the ground" (*PU* 359f.). The unruly ground Schelling also calls *longing* (Sehnsucht)—"the longing felt by the eternal One to give birth to itself" (*PU* 359). He also calls it simply *darkness* (Dunkel), broaching with this name a discourse of birth, since "all birth is from darkness into light." That discourse continues: "Man is formed in his mother's womb, and from the darkness of non-understanding (from feeling, longing, the glorious mother of knowledge) lucid thoughts first grow" (*PU* 360).

It is at this point that Schelling inserts a decisive indication referring this entire development back to the *Timaeus* and broaching in effect a reinscription. The originary longing, says Schelling, is to be represented as moving "like an undulating, surging sea, similar to Plato's matter" (*PU* 360). In its movement, originary longing, that is, the darkness from which understanding is born, that is, the secluded ground, that is, *die anfängliche Natur,* is similar to Plato's matter.

What is to be understood by Plato's matter? There can be little doubt but that Schelling is reproducing the identification that goes back to Aristotle; the decisive question, on the other hand, will be whether Schelling also reproduces the reduction that, from Aristotle on, has seldom if ever ceased to operate. In any case the early Plato studies make it abundantly clear that Schelling is referring to the χώρα. The connection is evident if one recalls, for instance, the account, immediately following the chorology, of the movement of the χώρα and of the traces of fire, air, water, and earth held by it: "But because of being filled with powers that are neither equal nor balanced, in no part of itself is it balanced, but sways unevenly everywhere and is shaken by these [powers] and shakes them in turn as it moves" (52d–e). Just such a scene is what Schelling reinscribes as the unruly ground, the irreducible remainder, secluded nature. Schelling's reference to birth and the mother further corroborate—and, in turn, are put in perspective by—the identification of Platonic matter with the χώρα.

Among Schelling's early Plato studies, the most notable text is his commentary on the *Timaeus.* This text is found in a notebook entitled *Über den Geist der Platonischen Philosophie* and follows a series of short texts entitled collectively *Form der Platonischen Philosophie.* The *Timaeus*-essay is a coherent, self-contained text. It divides into two parts, which are roughly equal in length. The first part presents an interpretation of

Timaeus 28a–47c—that is, of Timaeus' first discourse. The second part is devoted to *Timaeus* 47c–53c—that is, to the initial portion of Timaeus' second discourse, up through the passage that immediately follows the chorology. The second part of the *Timaeus*-essay includes also a discussion of the *Philebus,* especially of the forms of ἄπειρον and πέρας. Although it is not itself explicitly dated, the *Timaeus*-essay can be dated 1794, between the months of January-February and May-June. Thus it comes at the very beginning of Schelling's career and, specifically, just before his first major published work, *Über die Möglichkeit einer Form der Philosophie überhaupt.* One notes that the Fichtean terminology of Schelling's first publications is conspicuously absent from the *Timaeus*-essay.[20] This suggests already a certain reversal of the usual view: rather than coming only after his appropriation of the *Wissenschaftslehre* (and precisely as critique of Fichte), Schelling's engagement with the question of nature— even of secluded nature—actually preceded that engagement.

Three points stand out in the first part of the essay, though without at all exhausting its content.

(1) Almost at the beginning Schelling identifies a "main principle" (*"Hauptsatz"*) by quoting the passage (27d–28a) in which Timaeus distinguishes between τὸ ὄν and τὸ γιγνόμενον, that is, between *being,* which is ungenerated and which is apprehended by νόησις with λόγος, and *becoming* (that which is generated), which never is and which is apprehended by δόξα with αἴσθησις. Schelling comments: "Thus here Plato himself explains ὄν as something that is the object of pure understanding [*das Gegenstand des reinen Verstandes*]" (*T* 23). In turn, Schelling identifies τὸ γιγνόμενον as: "the empirical, that which has arisen through experience." Hence, one recognizes from the outset that Schelling is interpreting Plato's text by means of *Kantian concepts:* he takes *being,* hence, the intelligible εἴδη, as concepts of pure understanding, or, he adds, as ideas of pure reason.

(2) Schelling cites and briefly discusses *Timaeus* 30c–d, the passage in which Timaeus characterizes the cosmos as a living being (ζῷον) and asks about the paradigm in the image of which the demiurgos made it. He then identifies the paradigm as the νοητὸν ζῷον, the living being apprehended by νόησις. Schelling proceeds then to the point that is to be stressed: "The key to the explanation of the entire Platonic philosophy is the remark that everywhere he carries the subjective over to the objective [*überträgt* can also mean here: transfers, transposes, translates]. From this arose for Plato the principle (present, however, long before him) that the visible world is nothing but an image of the invisible" (*T* 31). Close attention to this passage and its context makes it clear that the pertinent carrying over of the subjective to the objective is not at all a matter of subjectivation, as

---

20. See Buchner's Editorischer Bericht in *T* 3–21.

though the subject cast something upon preexistent objects or viewed them only through its own subjective lens. Rather, what is at issue here—and what allows Schelling to make the connection with the Platonic principle—is *objectivation*. The passage is addressed to the way in which what is subjectively given to our empirical receptivity gets constituted as something objective, as something that is no longer merely relative to our sensibility. For Plato this objectivation takes place through the referral of the visible to the invisible; it occurs precisely insofar as the visible (the subjective) comes to be taken as an image—as a mere image: *Nachbild*—of the invisible (the objective). Yet the Kantian terms in which Schelling casts this referral are evident: even to characterize it in terms of the opposition subjective/objective is already to broach a Kantian formulation. The connection becomes still more manifest when Schelling goes on to write: "Insofar as the whole of nature as it appears to us is not only a product of our empirical receptivity but properly a work of our power of representation [*Vorstellungsvermögen*], to this extent the represented world belongs to a higher power than mere sensibility and nature is presented as a type of higher world, which expresses the pure laws of this world" (*T* 31). Regarding the principle that the visible is an image of the invisible, Schelling adds: "But no philosophy would ever arrive at this principle if it [viz., the principle] did not have its philosophical ground in us" (*T* 31). In other words, the referral from visible to invisible is to be found already operative in the subject, in the relation between sensibility and understanding—indeed not only operative but *grounded* in the subject, in the relation between its receptivity and its powers of representation. Only because the principle is in us can philosophy ever have discovered it.

(3) Schelling again confirms the Kantian parameters of his interpretation when he writes that Plato "must therefore have assumed ideas . . . only insofar as they are dependent, directly or indirectly, on the pure form of understanding" (*T* 32). Does this mean, then, that the Platonic ideas are simply identified with the pure concepts of the human understanding? One cannot but wonder how such an identification could ever be reconciled with the *Timaeus*, much less derived from it. In fact, Schelling's interpretation stops short of posing such an identification. Instead, Schelling regards ideas as, first of all, concepts in the *divine* understanding: "In general in the entire investigation of the Platonic theory of ideas, one must keep it always in mind that Plato speaks of them always as ideas of a divine understanding, which would become possible in human understanding only through an intellectual communion of man with the origin of all beings [*nur durch intellektuelle Gemeinschaft des Menschen mit dem Ursprunge aller Wesen*]" (*T* 37). The sense of correspondence with the *Timaeus* itself is readily apparent: in the account given by Timaeus in the dialogue, it is the god who has the eidetic paradigm in view and who fash-

ions the cosmos in accord with it. On the other hand, this shift does not entail for Schelling that the ideas are to be taken as *existing* in a higher world. The referral of ideas back to the understanding (even if divine) is what is decisive, and it is the decisiveness of this referral that allows Schelling to forestall all that would arise if recourse were had to simply positing the existence of the ideas. Schelling is explicit about the difficulties that would arise, that is, about the reduction of sense that could not, then, be evaded: "As soon as the concept of existence is applied to something supersensible, whether to an idea or to objects insofar as they exist outside their idea, it loses all physical significance [*Bedeutung*] and retains merely logical significance. . . . The concept of existence, applied to the idea of God, is an abyss for human reason [*ein Abgrund für die menschliche Vernunft*]" (*T* 44).

In the second part of the *Timaeus*-essay there are again three points to be stressed. These points are not exhaustive and, in particular, do not touch on Schelling's extended discussion of the *Philebus,* an apparent digression, aimed, it seems, at recovering a Platonic language in which to express the Kantian categories, or rather in which the categories were already, in the Platonic text, profoundly expressed.

(1) Schelling begins by making the transition that Plato's text makes and itself marks, the transition to Timaeus' second discourse: "Now Plato proceeds to the necessity . . . that was effective in the coming-to-be of the world" (*T* 50). Schelling identifies the main principle that comes thus into play, citing—in Greek, as always—the passage with which Timaeus' second discourse in effect begins: "For this cosmos in its origin was generated as a compound, from the combination of ἀνάγκη [in Schelling's translation: *Notwendigkeit*] and νοῦς" [*Timaeus* 48a, cited in *T* 50]. Granted the investigation of the role of νοῦς that the first discourse has carried out (doubled by commentary in the first part of the *Timaeus*-essay), Schelling notes that it is to ἀνάγκη that Plato's text and his own commentary must turn.

(2) Schelling observes that everything comes to hinge on introducing a third kind alongside the paradigm and the image, which, Schelling notes, presupposes the third kind. Schelling quotes the passage in which Timaeus calls the third kind "the receptacle [ὑποδοχή], as it were, the nurse, of all generation" (*Timaeus* 49a, cited in *T* 53). But what Schelling himself especially calls it—indeed in this very context—is *enduring substance,* a substance (*Substanz*) that enduringly (*beharrlich*) underlies all change of appearances, as the gold mentioned in the *Timaeus* underlies the change of figures modeled in it yet without itself being identical with any of these figures. But since the receptacle itself is receptive of *all* forms, since it is "the substratum of all the various forms" (*T* 54), it can have no determinate form whatsoever; it can receive determinate form only through imitation of the intelligible originals. In Schelling's words, "Thus the substance itself (which

has existed unalterably from eternity, δι' αναγκης)[21] was the substratum of all the various forms that arose through imitation of the original, pure, intelligible forms" (*T* 54). Yet, as itself formless, this substratum must also be itself invisible: "Insofar as it is the final empirical substratum of all the forms that are brought forth through the creation of the world, [it] cannot become visible, because nothing but these forms (imitations, images, of the pure forms of the understanding) can become visible to us" (*T* 56–58). Schelling appropriately cites in this context one of the most decisive passages from this portion of the *Timaeus:* "But if we call it an invisible εἶδος, formless, all-receiving, and, in a most perplexing way, partaking of the intelligible and most difficult to catch, we will not be speaking falsely" (*Timaeus* 51a–b).

(3) Schelling calls the receptacle not only the enduring substance or substratum but also *matter* (Materie),[22] confirming with this appellation that "Plato's matter," as he will call it in 1809 when he likens originary longing to it, is none other than the Timaean receptacle, the χώρα. Such matter is not something that one could ever come across as such in the visible world; it is in this sense not a material substance at all. Rather, this "nature [φύσις] that receives all bodies" (*Timaeus* 50b) is a matter prior to all generation of things, a pregenetic nature that makes possible the genesis of the visible world, a proto-matter "before the generation of the heaven" (*Timaeus* 48b).[23] In this connection Schelling insists—no less than does, though in different terms, the Timaeus of Plato's dialogue—on the difference between the all-receptive matter and the elements that come to appear in it; this difference is what precludes regarding the cosmos as simply composed of air, earth, fire, and water. Yet the difference is not utter separation, not even utter distinctness: the *Timaeus* openly declares that the invisible recipient—the all-receiving matter, in Schelling's terms—which never appears as itself, can come to appear (even though not *as itself*) only by way of the appearing of an element held by it, as when, for instance, it appears as fiery. Schelling says of matter: it appears to us "only under a form that is not its form" (*T* 58).

Krings' commentary appended to Schelling's *Timaeus*-essay offers several significant indications of just how thoroughly Schelling's interpretation of the *Timaeus,* and especially of the chorology and the discourses around it, remains in play in the series of writings on the philosophy of nature that Schelling produced during the late 1790s.[24] One of the most

---

21. In Schelling's citations from the Greek text, all accent marks are lacking.

22. The identification is also found in Hegel: "Thus the principle is that which is without form but is receptive of all form, that which we call 'matter,' 'passive matter'" (*Vorlesungen* [Hamburg: Felix Meiner, 1996], 8:46).

23. See the commentary appended to the text of Schelling's *Timaeus*-essay: Hermann Krings, "Genesis und Materie—Zur Bedeutung der 'Timaeus'-Handschrift für Schellings Naturphilosophie," esp. 131–35.

24. Ibid., 127, 143–45.

striking of these indications is that given regarding that work in which by its very title Schelling refers back to the *Timaeus*. Though indeed *Von der Weltseele* (1798) devotes much of its attention to contemporary investigations of nature, with only scant allusions to the world-soul (or other themes) of Plato's *Timaeus,* there are passages that are quite remarkable in this regard. For example, in the Preface Schelling discusses the conception of an originary *Naturprinzip,* which would be prior to the distinction between organic and inorganic; this *Naturprinzip,* which can be called the world-soul, would indeed precede all natural appearances in the sense of being the activity and productivity underlying these appearances. Schelling writes that it "can be nothing determinate or particular. For this very reason," he continues, "language has no proper designation for it; and the most ancient philosophy [*die älteste Philosophie*] (to which, after it has completed its cycle, our philosophy gradually turns back) has handed it down to us only in poetic representations."[25] Krings insists that what Schelling calls here "the most ancient philosophy" is none other than Plato's; even if this identification remains perhaps less than certain, there is much to suggest that the poetic representation mentioned is the εἰκὼς λόγος of the *Timaeus* and that this nature that is neither determinate nor particular is the receptacle. Another passage near the end of the work serves to reinforce this suggestion. The language of the passage is virtually that of the *Timaeus,* indeed of the second discourse, of that very portion of it to which the second part of Schelling's *Timaeus*-essay is devoted: "For this reason, this principle, although receptive of all forms, is itself originally formless (ἄμορφον) and never presentable [*darstellbar*] as determinate matter."[26]

However, with the inception of Schelling's philosophy of identity (as announced in the 1801 work *Darstellung meines Systems der Philosophie*) there is manifestly a shift in the stance taken toward the *Timaeus.* Krings suggests that the shift is such as to distance Schelling's thought decisively from the *Timaeus,*[27] indeed so decisively as to preclude any expectation of reinscription. Schelling's statement in the Introduction to *Ideen zu einer Philosophie der Natur* would, then, be definitive. Referring to the opposition between spirit and matter, Schelling writes: "The greatest thinkers of antiquity did not dare go beyond this opposition. Plato still set matter in opposition to God."[28] But the very sense of the philosophy of identity involves its going beyond this opposition: "Nature is to be visible spirit, spirit invisible nature." Thus, the philosophy of identity would establish "the absolute identity of the spirit within us and the nature outside us."[29]

25. Schelling, *Von der Weltseele,* in *Sämtliche Werke,* I/2: 347.
26. Ibid., 621.
27. Krings, "Genesis und Materie," 145–48.
28. Schelling, *Ideen zu einer Philosophie der Natur,* in *Sämtliche Werke,* I/2: 20.
29. Ibid., 56.

The question is whether the move beyond the opposition simply terminates in absolute identity or whether it reopens the opposition within and yet beyond absolute identity, posing a nature that "lies beyond the absolute being of absolute identity" (*PU* 358), a secluded nature that is both in God yet also the ground of God's existence. Prior to the 1809 work on freedom, one finds, to be sure, a surprisingly critical tone: in *Philosophie und Religion* (1804) Schelling contrasts the concepts of the *Timaeus* with "the elevated moral spirit of the more genuine Platonic works such as the *Phaedo* and the *Republic*."[30] Indeed, he goes so far as to entertain serious doubts whether Plato is even the author of the *Timaeus*.[31]

But in the 1809 work on freedom this critical tone is muted and the earlier doubts replaced by mere reservations and hopes that the darkness surrounding this part of Platonic doctrine will soon be dispelled.[32] Schelling identifies the doctrine to which he is referring: it is "the interpretation of Platonic matter according to which it is a being [*Wesen*] originally resisting God and therefore in itself evil." Then, over against such a mere dualism of good and evil, Schelling refers to another "sense in which it could be said of the irrational principle that it resists the understanding, or unity and order, without therefore assuming it to be an *evil* principle" (*PU* 374). His mention of "previous considerations" confirms that the reference is to the distinction between ground and existence, which Schelling in fact goes on to recall in its bearing on God: "But God himself requires a ground in order that he can be; however, it is not outside him, but within him. And God has a *nature* within himself, which, though belonging to him, still is different from him" (*PU* 375). Schelling poses even the prospect of another interpretation of Plato: "In this manner, too, we might well explain the Platonic saying that evil comes *from the old nature*. For all evil strives to return to chaos, i.e., to that state in which the initial center [*das anfängliche Centrum*] was not yet subordinated to light; it is an upsurging of the centers of yet unintelligent longing [*der noch verstandlosen Sehnsucht*]" (*PU* 374). Such an interpretation would align the Timaean distinction between νοῦς and ἀνάγκη, not with a mere dualism of good and evil, but with the distinction between God himself and the

---

30. Schelling, *Philosophie und Religion*, in *Sämtliche Werke*, I/6: 36.

31. Krings notes that the authenticity of the *Timaeus* was not contested by the philology of the time. He concludes that Schelling's doubts about Plato's authorship of the dialogue were based on philosophical rather than philological grounds, specifically, on his doubts whether such dualism as can be found in the *Timaeus* could have been taught by Plato (Krings, "Genesis und Materie," 149).

32. Remarking that as long as this is not accomplished "a definite judgment . . . is indeed impossible," Schelling goes on in a footnote to express his hope that "the quick-minded Böckh" will soon produce the needed elucidation (*PU* 374). Krings mentions a note that Böckh added to his text in a collected edition of 1866: in the note Böckh says that Schelling "took back his doubt" about the authenticity of the *Timaeus* (Krings, "Genesis und Materie," 150).

nature that is within God yet different from him. It would also align this entire discussion with the earlier one that likens originary longing (moving "like an undulating, surging sea") to "Plato's matter" (*PU* 360).

Thus situated beyond the simple dualistic interpretation of the *Timaeus,* Schelling's work on freedom would indeed reinscribe the Timaean distinction between νοῦς and ἀνάγκη, reinscribe it as the fundamental distinction between existence and ground.[33] And yet, at what Schelling designates as "the highest point of the entire investigation" (*PU* 406), there emerges the question of a "beyond" even of this distinction. But if there is to be a move even beyond the distinction between existence and ground, even beyond the difference separating absolute identity from the nature that lies beyond the absolute being of absolute identity, then everything will depend on the sense and intent of this move. The question is whether the move simply dissolves the opposition into an antecedent unity or whether it is a move toward thinking this opposition more rigorously.

Schelling is explicit about the consequence of not thinking the opposition in a way that situates it beyond mere dualism: "But this system, if it actually is thought to be the doctrine of two absolutely different and mutually independent principles, is but a system of the self-laceration and despair of reason" (*PU* 354). It is the prospect of this consequence that drives thinking on beyond the mere duality of ground and existence, that drives thinking on to what would be antecedent to the opposition: "There must be a *Wesen before* all ground and before all existence, thus before any duality at all; how can we call this anything but the original ground [*Urgrund*], or rather the unground [*Ungrund*]?" Schelling insists, however, that this unground is not the identity of the opposites, not absolute identity, but rather absolute indifference (*die absolute Indifferenz*). One passage, hardly adequate to convey the complexity of this context, will nonetheless suffice to indicate its direction: "Instead of annulling the differentiation, as was supposed, the unground much rather posits and confirms it" (*PU* 407). Thus, the move beyond the opposition of ground and existence is not such as to dissolve the opposition into an antecedent unity. The move beyond to absolute indifference does not, then, dissolve the opposition opened up in the *Timaeus* between νοῦς and ἀνάγκη, the opposition that Schelling reinscribes as that of existence and ground.

---

33. The following passage also attests, if more obliquely, to the reinscription: "As concerns the plurality of possible worlds, infinite possibility certainly seems to be offered by matter [*Stoff*], which is in itself unruly [*ein an sich Regelloses*] (such as the original movement of the ground in our explanation), that is still unformed but receptive to all forms" (*PU* 398). The passage is to be read against the background of Schelling's identification, in the *Timaeus*-essay, of the receptacle with matter, though in this passage he uses *Stoff* rather than *Materie.* Note also that the question of a plurality of worlds is explicitly taken up in the *Timaeus* (31a–b).

Rather, the move is an initiative toward thinking this opposition in a way that forestalls its recoiling destructively on that thinking, its recoiling in such a way as to produce the self-laceration and despair of reason.

There are several points that are striking with respect to Schelling's *Timaeus*-essay, some because of their directive presence, others because of their absence. Four may be singled out.

First, there is Schelling's remarkable effort to avoid a simple ontic interpretation of the Platonic εἴδη, an interpretation that would take them to exist in an alleged higher world. Even though today one would resist the assimilation to Kantian concepts, it is important—and perhaps instructive—to note that the referral of the εἴδη (as ideas) to the under-standing (as constituting conditions of possibility) is precisely what allows Schelling to avoid an ontic interpretation.

Second, there is Schelling's recognition of the radical dimension—or better, the pre-cosmic, pre-genetic dimension—opened up through the chorology and the discourses around it. This dimension proves indeed so radical, in Schelling's reinscription of it, as to threaten reason as such with self-laceration and despair and thus to require of it a perhaps entirely unprecedented initiative.

Yet, third, it is striking that in his remarks on the third kind Schelling insistently reinscribes its name as *substance, substratum,* and especially *matter.* On the other hand, there is only the slightest mention of the name given it in what I have called, on the basis of that name, the chorology. To be sure, Schelling does cite a passage in which, counting the three kinds, Timaeus calls the third kind by the name χώρα. But Schelling's sole perti-nent comment serves in effect to forestall the disruptiveness that this name might otherwise exercise on the reinscription. The comment in fact refers to other, related words such as τόπος and ἕδρα, and only indirectly to χώρα: "These explanations are too definite for one to be able to under-stand what is involved in them as *space* [Raum], as, so far as I know, most interpreters have done" (*T* 74). Thus, Schelling does not even come to the point of asking how, in thinking the third kind, one is *to think together* the two otherwise disparate senses expressed, on the one hand, by such words as *substance, substratum,* and *matter* and, on the other hand, by various designations related to *space.* Even less does he set about undoing, for instance, Chalcidius' rendering of χώρα as *locus,* in the direction of trans-lating χώρα back into Plato's Greek.

Finally, it is extraordinarily striking that the very thinker who declared art the organon of philosophy and who regarded poetry as that from which philosophy arose and to which finally it would return could, even in this very early text, have paid such scant attention to the artistry and poetry of the *Timaeus.* No attention is given to the dramatic and dialogi-cal form of the text nor to the reflections that the discourse exercises upon itself, as in the determination of its character as εἰκὼς λόγος. Indeed,

Schelling's commentary skips entirely over the opening scene, the discourse by Socrates on the city, and the story that Critias tells about ancient Athens, thus omitting the entire political discourse by which Timaeus' cosmology is framed. One can only wonder how Schelling's interpretation of the dialogue—and his later reinscription of it—might have been transformed, had he taken to heart what only a few years later would be declared by Schleiermacher, that in the Platonic dialogues "if anywhere, form and content are inseparable and every proposition is to be rightly understood only in its place and in the connections and delimitations that Plato has assigned to it."[34]

But what about the beyond of the Schellingean reinscription, this powerful appropriation that to an unprecedented degree lets what was called χώρα come again to a manifestness befitting its seclusion? What about the beyond of this reinscription that ventured to reconstitute something like the chorology in the midst—indeed at the very center—of modern thought and that seriously faltered perhaps only in not shaping its discourse to the retreat of the χώρα, that is, in not openly declaring itself a bastardly discourse? Whatever may lie beyond this reinscription, one could hardly imagine the way toward it not leading back through a dream of an original chorology, not the dream told of within the chorology, but a dream of a chorology told by one whose discourse would truly befit the χώρα, one capable of speaking in such a way as to begin at the natural beginning. Is it perhaps to such a one that the *Timaeus* alludes at the beginning? Is it such a one that, at the beginning, Socrates counts by not counting, this fourth who is doubly absent and whose part will have been filled, insofar as possible, by Timaeus and the others?

34. Friedrich Schleiermacher, "Einleitung," in *Das Platonbild: Zehn Beiträge zum Platonverständnis*, ed. Konrad Gaiser (Hildesheim: Georg Olms, 1969), 10.

English Index

Albinus, 75
Anaximenes, 100n
Aristocles, 10
Aristotle, 2, 8n, 75n38, 115, 152-153, 154n12, 158
Aristoxenus, 147
Ashbaugh, Anne Freire, 108n17
Atticus, 59n16
Augustine, 79n47

Baracchi, Claudia, 28n
beauty (*see* καλόν), 48, 53, 57, 59, 129
being (*see* οὐσία), 9, 47, 66, 67, 126, 134; and generation, 55, 159; and the third kind, 65, 68, 74, 98, 99
Bloom, Alan, 19n
Brague, Rémi, 59n17, 78, 79n48, 81-82, 95n
Brann, Eva, 22n20, 23
Burnet, John, 10
Bury, R. G., 101

causality (*see* αἰτίον), 50, 90
Chalcidius, 2, 3, 47n; translation of χώρα, 115, 166
Cherniss, Harold, 101-102, 104, 106n, 107n
chorology (*see* χώρα), 1, 3-5, 10, 11, 56, 96, 106, 107, 112-127
Cicero, 47n
Claghorn, George S., 153n
Cleitophon, 10
comedy, 24-29, 40, 62, 89, 130, 136-138
Cornford, Francis, 11, 22n20, 23, 41n, 66, 72n, 78n43, 81n, 92n2, 100n, 101, 115, 133n8
cosmos (*see* κόσμος), 2-4, 10, 15, 27, 30, 69; the soul of cosmos, 9, 58-74; and movement, 80-81
Crantor, 2, 65, 67, 71n, 75

Dercylidas, 10
Derrida, Jacques, 99n, 111nn21,22, 114n
Descartes, René, 157
Diogenes Laertius, 147
discourse (*see* λόγος): and nature, 6; and myth, 39, 44, 85; and intellect, 47-48; and the soul, 74-76; its kinds, 54-55; its elements, 94, 105; its fugitives, 35, 101-107, 125; likely discourse, 55-57, 97, 132; bastard discourse, 124, 128, 132, 138, 153, 167

doubling: of signature, 1; of discourse, 105-106; the duplication of being, 69, 70, 126; the duplicity of being, 113, 122
drama, 1, 149; dramatic date of dialogue, 11, 21-23
dream, 5, 10; of the χώρα, 118-124, 127

earth, 85, 130, 139-145
Empedocles, 11, 62
erotic, the (*see* ἔρως), 38, 40, 58, 62, 86, 110; relation between sexes, 18-21, 25-27, 88, 136; its technical ordering, 20, 24-31, 52, 63
errancy (*see* πλανητά/πλανάω), 91-93, 132-135; of discourse, 63-65
Euclid, 61

Fichte, J. G., 156, 159
Ficino, Marsilio, 2
Fink, Eugen, 109n
form, 108, 110

Gadamer, Hans Georg, 3n2
generation (*see* γιγνόμενον), 9, 37, 41, 112, 113, 119; and opinion, 48, 54; and being, 48, 159
German Idealism, 2, 154, 156
Gill, Mary Louise, 101, 103n
Gulley, Norman, 102n

Heidegger, Martin, 14n10, 51n4, 51n6, 154n12
Heraclitus, 100n, 118
Hesiod, 53, 85-86
Hyland, Drew A., 24n26
hypothesis, 7, 48

Iamblichus, 10, 59n16, 147
ideas (forms), 48, 161
image/imagination, 1, 38, 51, 57, 74, 92, 99, 120-122, 136, 153; and εἶδος, 38, 51; and discourse, 55, 89, 107; of eternity, 77-82; transcendental interpretation of, 156, 159-162
intellect/intellection (*see* νοῦς): and discourse, 47-49; and εἶδος, 98, 99, 125, 137; and the intelligible paradigm, 84, 91, 111, 113; and necessity, 93, 131, 150, 156, 161, 164, 165; and the sensible, 10,

Greek Index

Italicized references indicate those passages in which the meaning of the term is determined philosophically.

John Sallis is Liberal Arts Professor of Philosophy at Pennsylvania State University. His previous books include *Phenomenology and the Return to Beginnings; Being and Logos: Reading the Plationic Dialogues; The Gathering of Reason; Delimitations: Phenomenology and the End of Metaphysics; Spacings—Of Reason and Imagination; Echoes: After Heidegger; Crossings: Nietzsche and the Space of Tragedy; Double Truth; Stone;* and *Shades—Of Painting at the Limit.* He is an editor of numerous books, including, most recently, *Retracing the Platonic Text* and *Interrogating the Tradition: Hermeneutics and the History of Philosophy,* and is the founding editor of *Research in Phenomenology.*

LaVergne, TN USA
13 November 2009
164014LV00002B/5/P